IMAGES
of America

BLOOMFIELD REVISITED

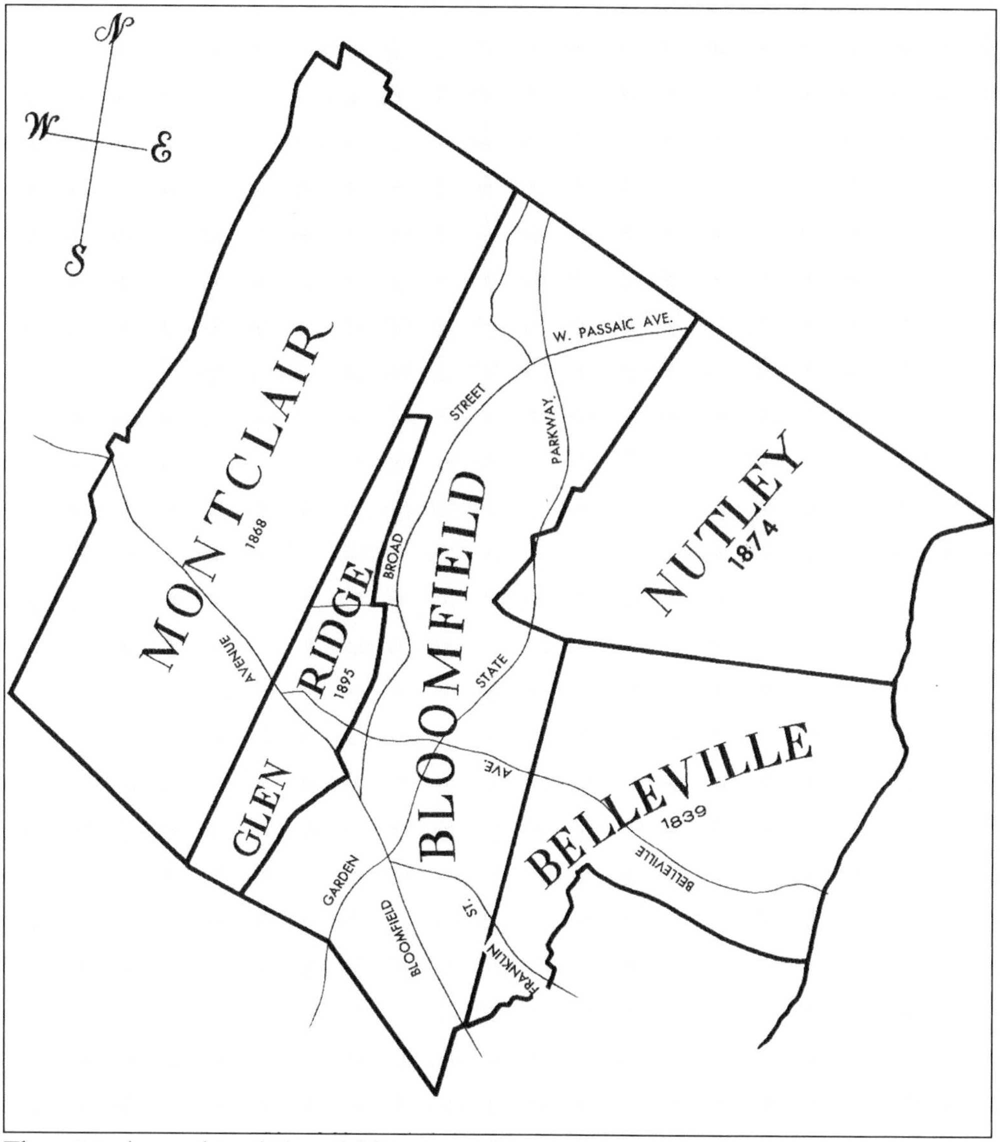

The original township of Bloomfield was quite large, comprising 20 square miles that extended from the Passaic River on the east to the top of what the first settlers of Newark called First Mountain. This map shows the township in 1812. It also shows the various towns that have since become independent.

On the cover: The Morris Canal was begun in 1825 and opened in 1831 from Phillipsburg to Newark, then extended in 1836 to Jersey City. Visitors to Bloomfield in 1832 described the canal as beautiful with views of farms, trees, and wildflowers along the banks. Since the canal was idle on Sunday, it was used for recreation by the towns through which it passed. (Courtesy of the Historical Society of Bloomfield.)

IMAGES
of America

BLOOMFIELD REVISITED

Frederick Branch and Jean Kuras

ARCADIA
PUBLISHING

ISBN 978-0-7385-4541-7

Published by Arcadia Publishing
Charleston, South Carolina

Printed in the United States of America

Library of Congress Catalog Card Number: 2006923344

For all general information contact Arcadia Publishing at:
Telephone 843-853-2070
Fax 843-853-0044
E-mail sales@arcadiapublishing.com
For customer service and orders:
Toll-Free 1-888-313-2665

Visit us on the Internet at www.arcadiapublishing.com

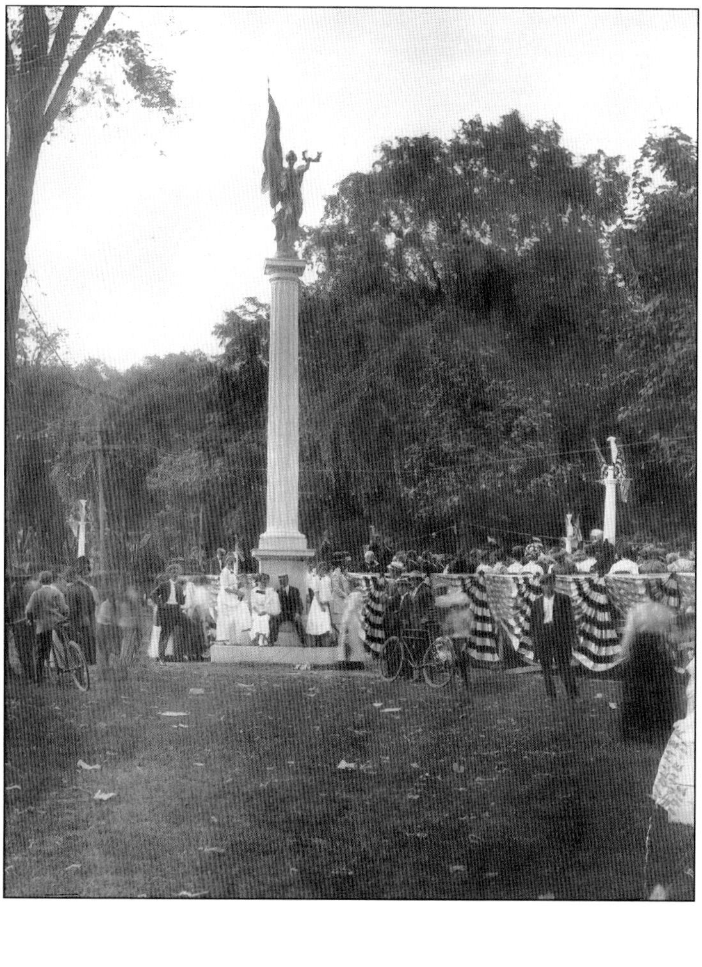

One of the highlights of Bloomfield's 100th anniversary celebration in June 1912 was the unveiling of the Soldiers and Sailors Monument, which stands today at the end of the green as a memorial to those who served courageously in the nation's wars. Sally James Farnham, a student of Frederick Remington, designed the memorial. The cost was defrayed by subscription among schoolchildren, who raised $5,000.

Contents

ACKNOWLEDGMENTS

Bloomfield Revisited was a huge undertaking for us. Our personal lives could not be put on hold and writing such a book takes hours of research in the library, on microfilm, and studying archival maps. We have searched through file cabinets, folders, shelves, and scrapbooks of the museum of the historical society to gather a marvelous collection of photographs. The book could not have been completed had we not gotten such satisfaction and, indeed, pleasure from the project and invaluable assistance from many people.

The late curator emeritus Lucy Sant Ambrogio's efforts of cataloging the museum's acquisitions helped tremendously. Hardly a work session went by when Sallie Black's book was not used, an "Aha!" punctuating our success in tracking down some little known fact. Sallie and Lucy, in whichever heavenly museum you are, we both thank you.

John Sitnik of the Glen Ridge Library, a gentleman in every sense of the word and an outstanding professional librarian, gave inestimable help with the photographs we used from that library's collection. We also appreciate the generosity of Kim Reilly of Oakeside.

We are indebted to Mary Shoffner, John Gibson, and Ray Neveil who looked through their own collections to generously lend us some wonderful pictures, and we acknowledge the kind permission of the New Jersey Historical Society for the use of its images.

We further thank the staff of the Bloomfield Library. Long days and nights were made more pleasant by their courteous and friendly assistance.

INTRODUCTION

The founding of Newark begins with the founding of the colony of Newark. In May 1666, a group of ships carrying about 30 Puritan families from Connecticut made their way up the clear waters of the Pesayak River (Passaic River) seeking a new home where they could freely practice their religion. The righteous Puritans were nearing the end of a pilgrimage to a promised land in the vast wilderness. Knowledge of the landscape was vague. Little was known about it except that it was, according to a report by Capt. Robert Treat, a land of rich fields and woodlands with plentiful streams.

In 1679, just 13 years later, English landowners cleared the land to the west. They began settling in the region along the Second and Third Rivers and the Native American trails that ran from the Passaic River to the top of Orange Mountain. The Crane, Baldwin, Davis, Dodd, Morris, and Ward families were among the first of these settlers.

At first, probably because of the threat of Native American attack, these people did not build houses on their land, but preferred to live in the safety of the village of Newark. While we do not know if there was a house built before 1695, landlords did make use of woodlands and grazing lands, driving their cattle along routes that are still marked by modern roads to their plantations in the northwest.

At about the same time, Dutch settlers purchased a large tract of land from the Lenni-Lenape Indians, adjoining the Newark settlement on the north. Originally called Aquackanonck, it was identified at Stone House Plains as early as 1696 and was named Brookdale in 1873.

In 1702, a sawmill was established on the Morris Plantation at Bay Avenue and Morris Place. Samuel Ward's wool mill began operation in 1725 and George Harris's mill shortly thereafter. Copper was mined in Watsesson and Chestnut Hill (now Glen Ridge) by 1735. With a mill to saw wood, a mill to card and weave wool, and an abundance of fieldstone to be quarried, the construction of houses began. Anthony Olive built a house in 1712, David Dodd's appeared in 1719, and Abraham Van Giesen's was built the same year on the Third River. Jasper Crane farmed at the headwaters of the Second River, and others followed him onto Watsesson Plain. About a dozen more houses, which have since been destroyed, were built before the American Revolution.

In the autumn of 1796, the community made preparations for the groundbreaking for a new house of worship on land donated by the Davis family. The congregation of the Presbyterian Society chose Bloomfield as the parish name and carved "Bloomfield, 1796" into the white marble tablet, which remains in place over the church's main door today.

The area northwest of Newark remained attached to the expanding town, but by 1812, the new township felt strong enough to assert its independence. The New Jersey legislature passed an act separating the township of Bloomfield from Newark. It was incorporated under the name "Inhabitants of the Township of Bloomfield in the County of Essex." The town embraced the area from the Passaic River to the Watchung Mountains and from Passaic County to Newark, a total of 20.5 square miles. Today it has an area of only 5.4 square miles due to the separation of several new communities.

In 1839, Belleville was set off, taking 2,466 of the population and leaving Bloomfield with 2,523 people, according to the 1840 census. West Bloomfield, or Cranetown, separated and formed Montclair in order to float bonds to finance the extension of the railroad to which the rest of Bloomfield was opposed. In 1871, Woodside, now North Newark, and the Forest Hill section of Newark also separated. In 1874, Franklin, now Nutley, became independent from Belleville. A squabble over paved roads was the official reason for losing Glen Ridge in 1895, but relations had been strained for some time and the division was inevitable.

The industrial growth of Bloomfield was given a huge boost with the opening of the Morris Canal in 1825. Until then, the transportation of raw materials and finished goods from the early mills struggled over muddy roads and was a serious problem. The canal, however, provided a faster and easier way to bring coal from Pennsylvania and iron ore from northern New Jersey. New factories sprang up along its route, which ran from the Clifton border, through the Brookdale section, and then south to the aqueduct near Newark Avenue. There the canal turned east on its way to Newark and eventually Jersey City.

From the Civil War on, growth and changes in Bloomfield correlated with those throughout the nation. Large numbers of immigrants settled in town. The community became more diverse as new houses of worship were formed and additional social and cultural organizations developed. New lines of business, commerce, and industry engaged citizens in the changing conditions and a challenging future.

In 1912, when Bloomfield celebrated its centennial, Bloomfield's 45 industries showed their products in an industrial exhibit at Berkeley School. More than 1,000 of the town's men and women served in World War I. In 1920, the town's population reached 22,019. Ten years later, the town could boast of 85 manufacturers with products ranging from organs and lightbulbs to safety pins and silk stockings.

In 1962, when Bloomfield held its sesquicentennial celebration, it had grown to over 50,000 residents. Its growth was due in part to residential development, such as replacing farms in the north, converting single-family houses to multiple dwellings in the older section, and constructing new apartment complexes. Growth was further stimulated by the construction of highways and access to convenient transportation. The town benefited from the enterprising efforts of heavy industry, light industry, retail establishments, and professional and commercial services.

Transportation, education, and geographic location have helped transform Bloomfield from a village in the midst of a farming township to a city of nearly 48,000 people. The early village stores, the saw, grain, and paper mills, and the cotton, woolen, and hat factories were the forerunners of Westinghouse, General Electric, Schering, and other large industries once active in town. Today institutions of government and education and a network of social, fraternal, and cultural organizations support dynamic changes. The wheel of time has carried the town forward to become a vital suburban community.

This second book about Bloomfield renders a kaleidoscope of people, neighborhoods, commercial activity, and events. The moving panorama gives readers a sense of what has gone by: the war years, the development of the Garden State Parkway, and the changing neighborhoods. Attention is turned to many people, some remembered only by a small circle of family and friends, others recognized throughout the community. These are the images of a town and its families, who led their lives eager to fulfill the promise of opportunity that America offered to everyone.

One

Pride of the Town

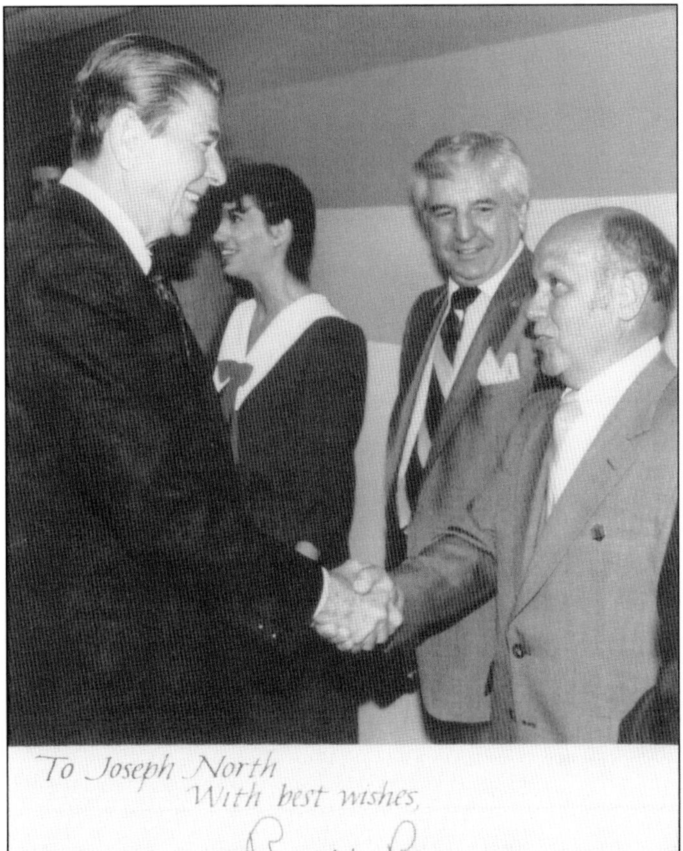

June 13, 1985, was the historic occasion when Pres. Ronald Reagan was welcomed into Bloomfield's municipal building by (from left to right) councilwoman Louise Palagano, councilman Jim Gasparini, and township administrator Joseph North. North later commented that "President Reagan had the wonderful ability to make each of us in the receiving line feel that our greeting was important to him." Mayor John Kinder and Gov. Tom Kean accompanied the president.

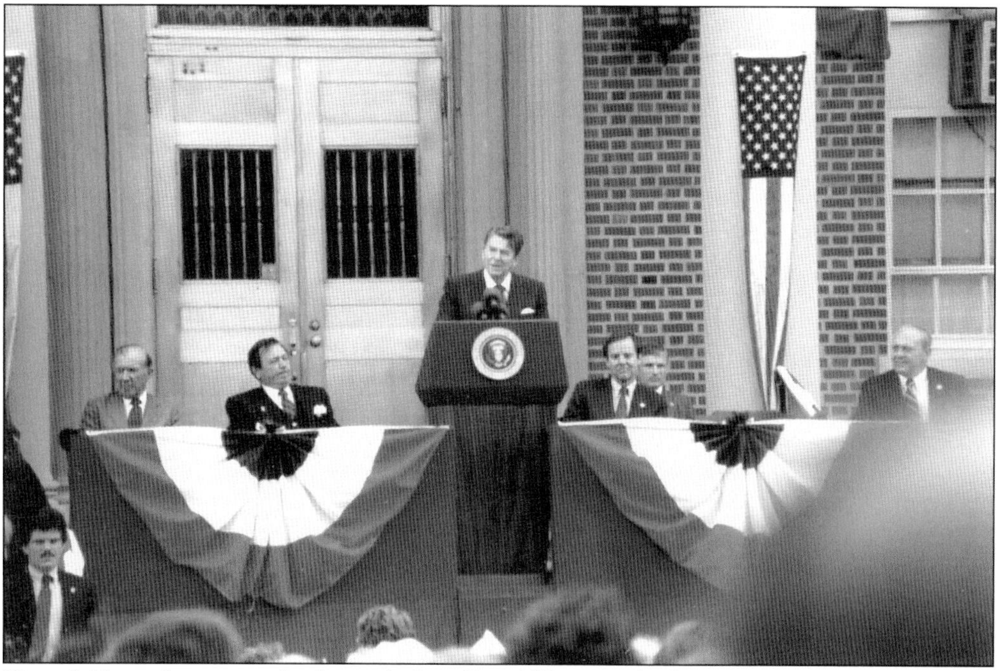

Bloomfield was chosen as a whistle-stop by Pres. Ronald Reagan after he received the recommendation from Gov. Tom Kean. Bloomfielders bustled about making proper preparations. The bronze doors of the municipal building were polished, the sidewalks scrubbed, and bunting, banners, and flags were in place. President Reagan's speech on the steps of town hall was heard by 12,000 townspeople. Mayor John Kinder (on the president's right) and Gov. Tom Kean flank the president.

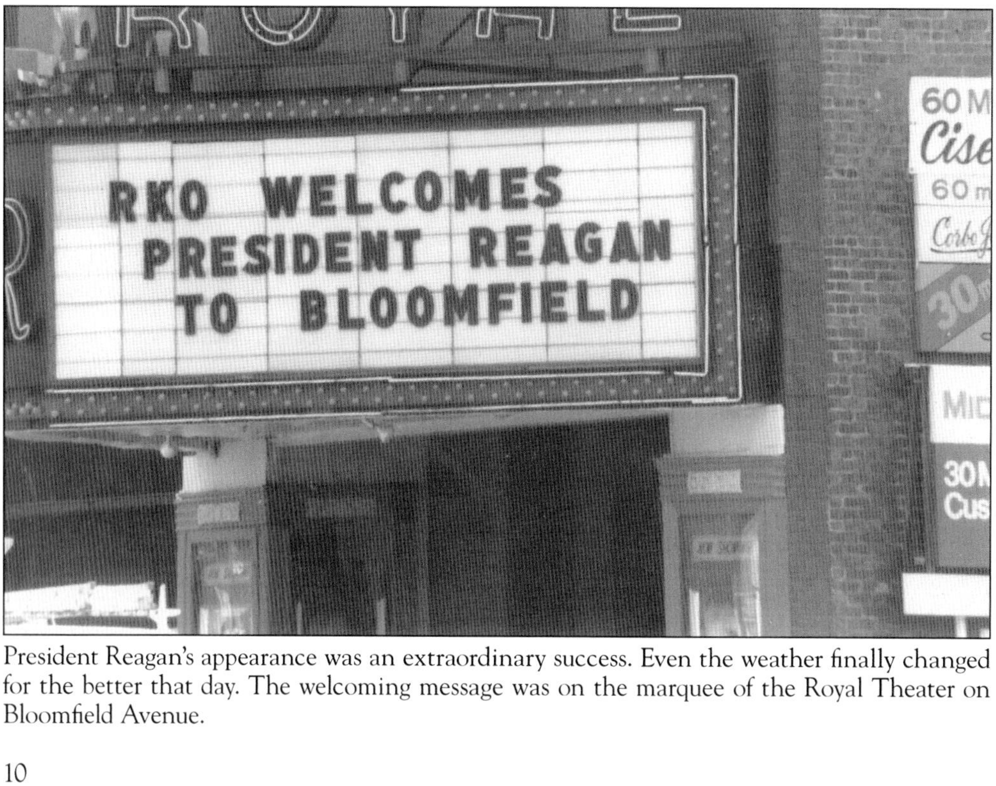

President Reagan's appearance was an extraordinary success. Even the weather finally changed for the better that day. The welcoming message was on the marquee of the Royal Theater on Bloomfield Avenue.

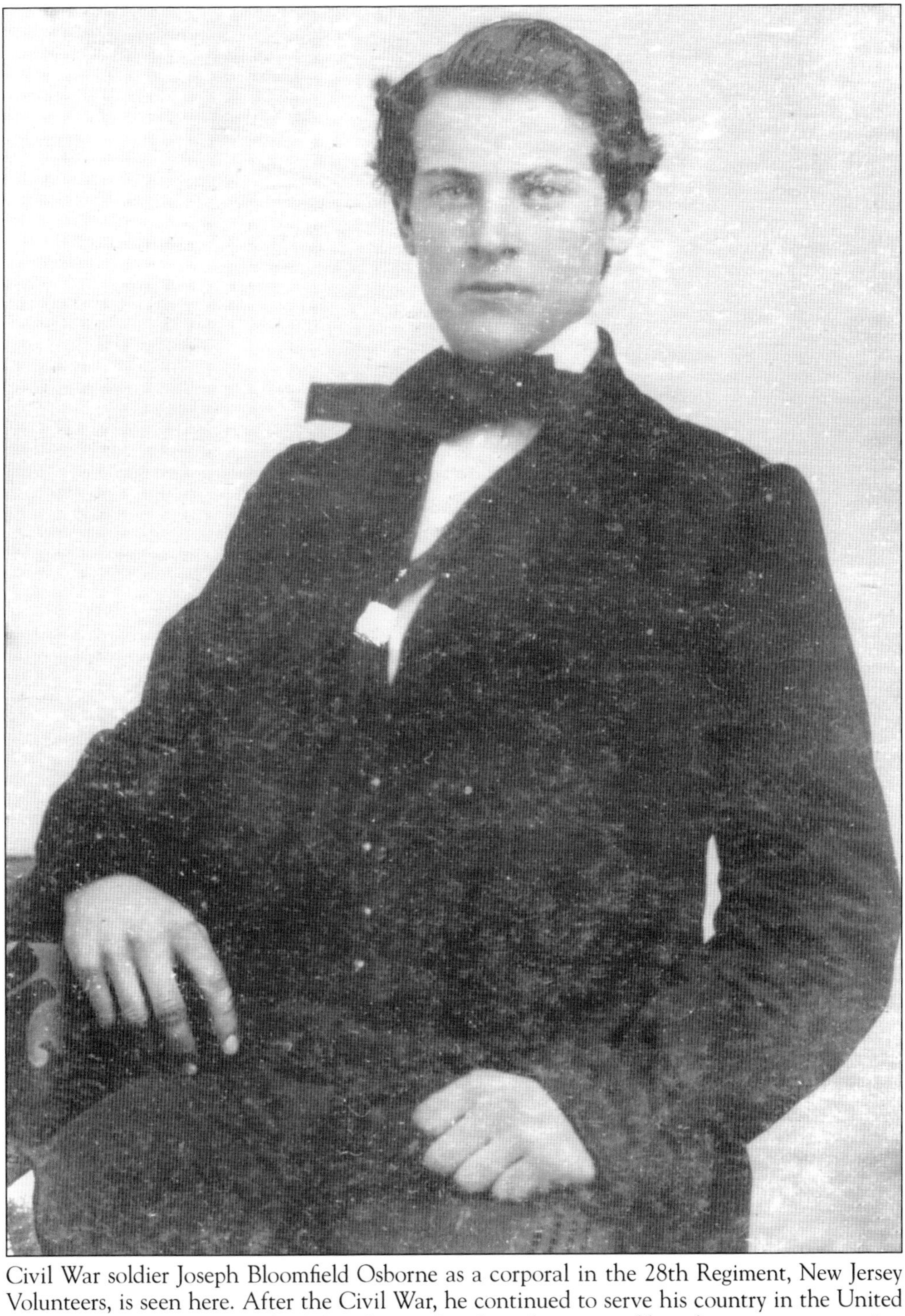

Civil War soldier Joseph Bloomfield Osborne as a corporal in the 28th Regiment, New Jersey Volunteers, is seen here. After the Civil War, he continued to serve his country in the United States Navy. He was married to Marie Louise Landau, who survived him for many years, passing away in 1934 at the age of 91. Their son, Harry Osborne, was town treasurer for many years and vice president of the old Bloomfield National Bank.

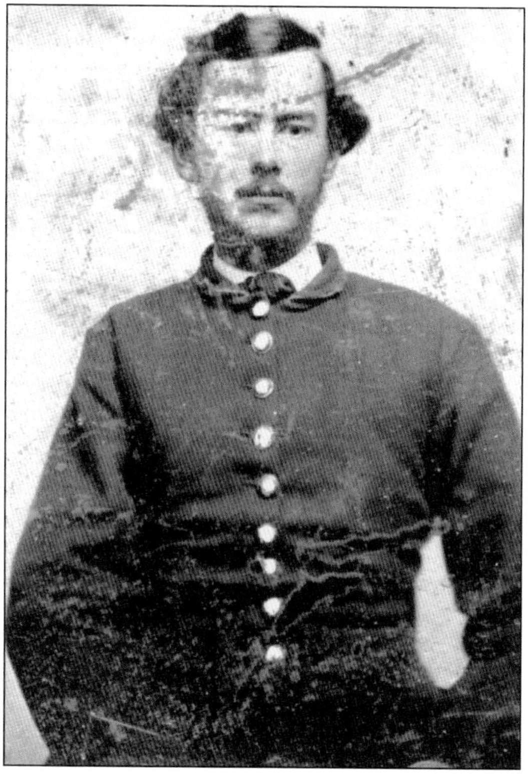

The young men who left their homes to take part in the Civil War were enrolled primarily in the 26th New Jersey Volunteer Infantry mustered in at Newark. A member of the Hagen family (left) wears the Union blue. The Hagen family lived on Spruce Street and worked as weavers. John C. Bancroft (below) of Beach Street was another of the boys in blue.

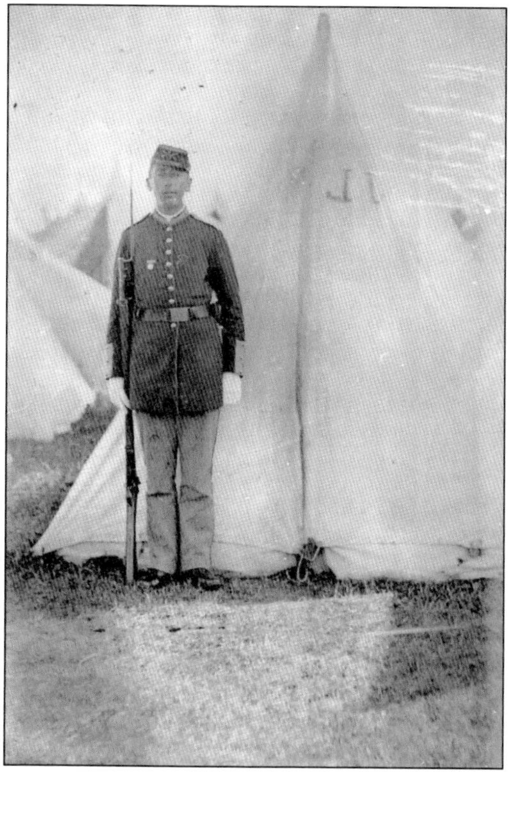

William Colfax was the grandson of Robert Colfax, who was a captain during the American Revolution. Robert Colfax went on to serve as a privateer until he was captured and held on an infamous British prison ship moored in New York Harbor. In 1869, William Colfax established a business at Broad Street and Belleville Avenue selling groceries, hay and feed, dry goods, and oilcloth.

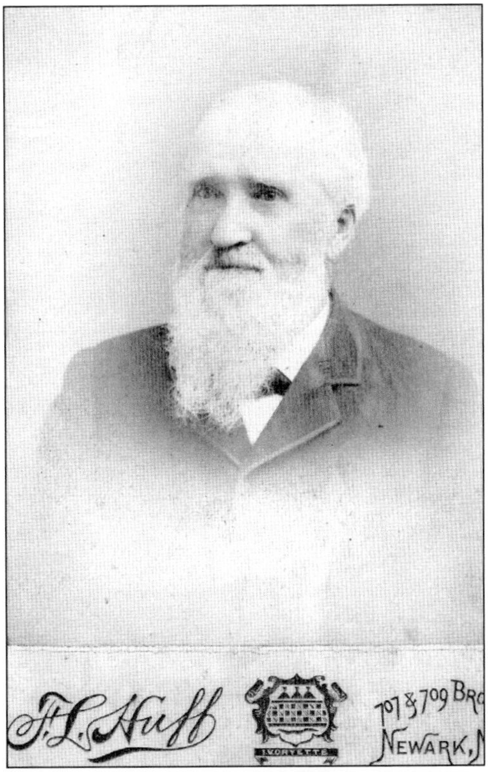

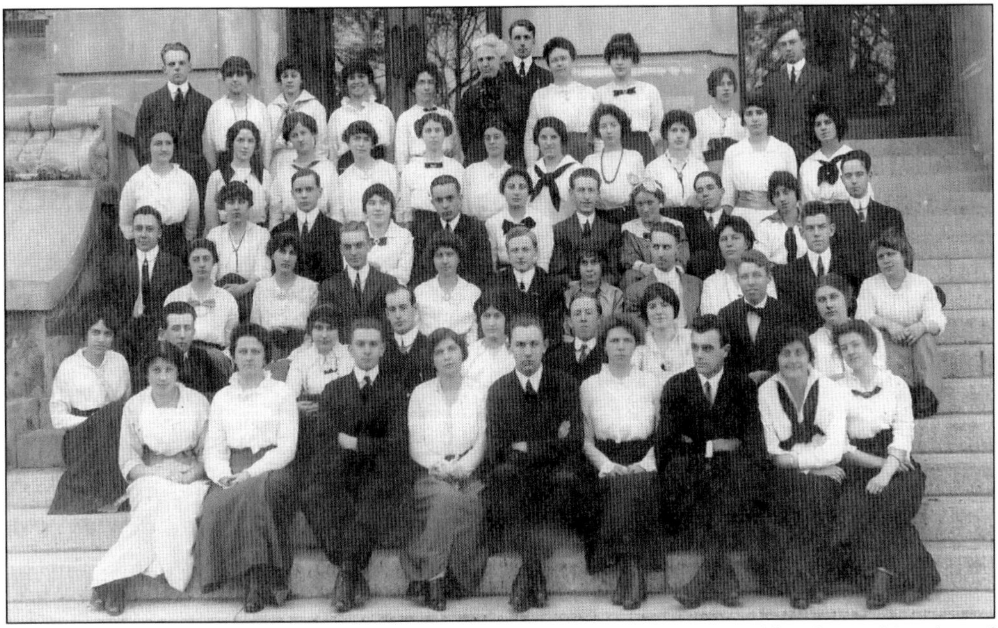

Elizabeth Heywood Wyman (sixth row, fourth from right) was the granddaughter of Sarah and Warren Baldwin. Her grandfather served in the legislature and was credited with a major part in carrying through the legislation that authorized a public school system in New Jersey. Wyman attended Barnard College, where she and three classmates founded Alpha Omicron Sorority in 1897. After graduation, she joined the teaching staff of Bloomfield High School.

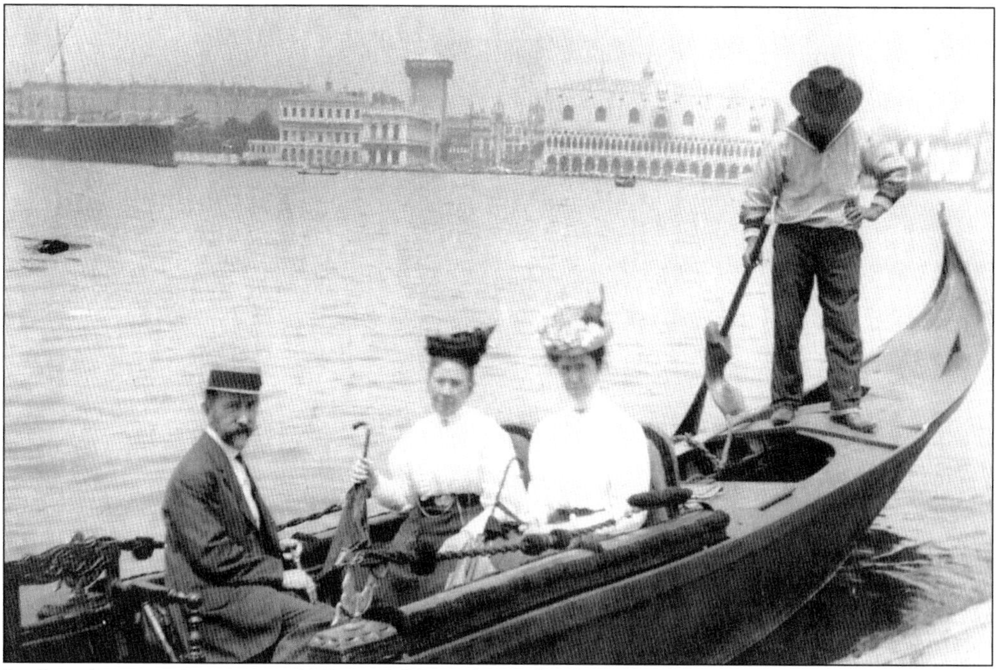

In this photograph, artist and Bloomfield resident Charles Warren Eaton is on the Grand Canal in Venice, Italy, in 1905, with his sister Charlotte Eaton Shaw and niece Grace Louise Shaw. Eaton lived for many years at 63 Monroe Place where he had his studio. Other Eaton photographs of picturesque locations are reproduced in this book, including many landscapes of local scenes and the Morris Canal.

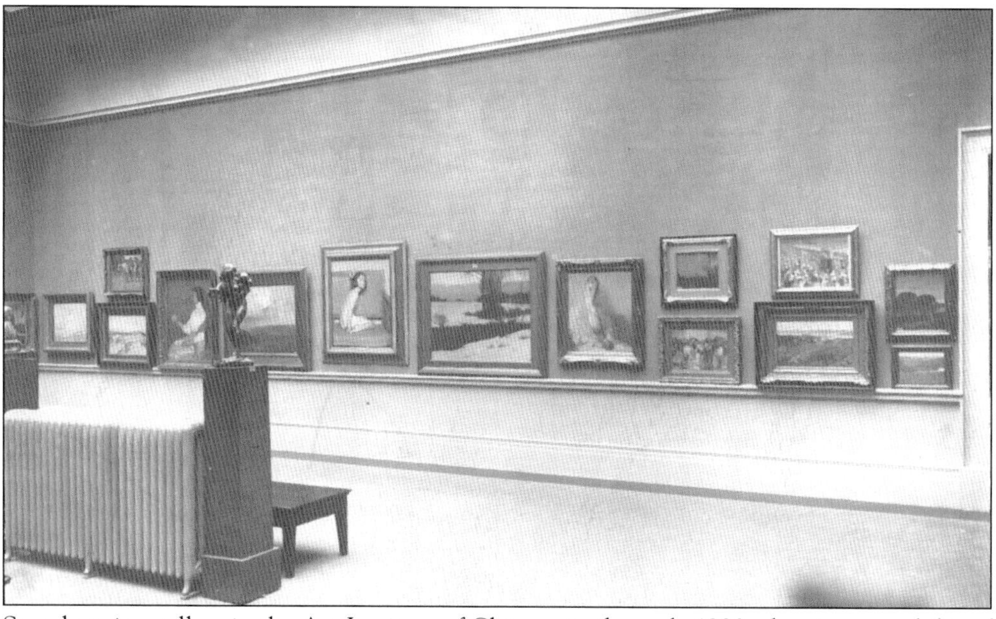

Seen here is a gallery in the Art Institute of Chicago in the early 1900s showing an exhibit of American paintings, including a landscape by Charles Warren Eaton (center). This painting, *Davey's Woods*, was given to the Bloomfield Library by the artist in 1925 and was included in the Eaton exhibit in the Montclair Art Museum in 1980.

Henry Vollmer's first excursion into the photography business came in 1888, the year of the great blizzard, when he worked for Helmuth Schumacher. He opened his first business in the town center at the corner of Washington Street and stayed there from 1900 to 1915. Vollmer then moved his studio, as well as his home, to 81 Monroe Place. He spent more than 50 years taking pictures in Bloomfield.

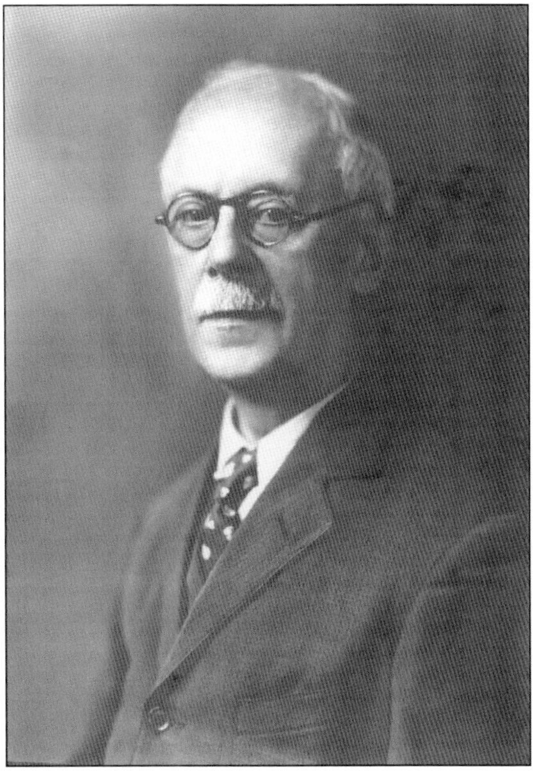

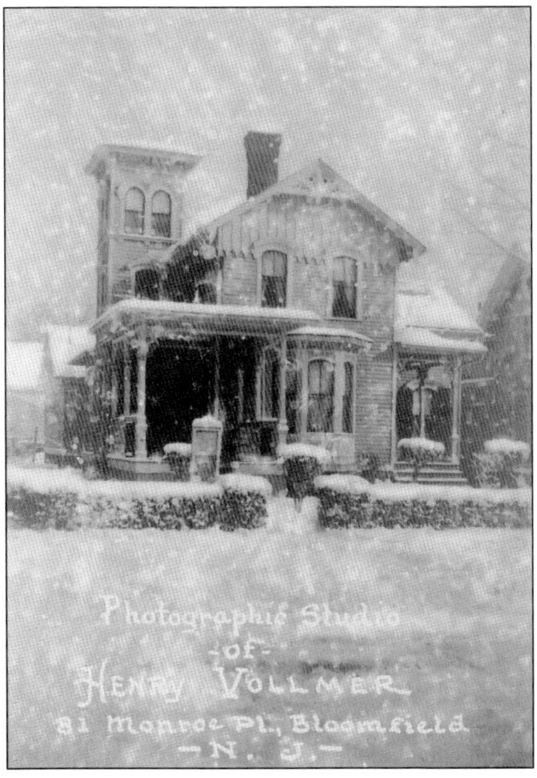

The portrait studio, a part of the Vollmer family's Victorian residence, provided a pleasant experience for clients. The layout included a comfortable reception room and convenient dressing rooms. Vollmer created special lighting and used quality equipment to produce outstanding results for five decades. The historical society is privileged to have several of the many photographs taken around town by Vollmer.

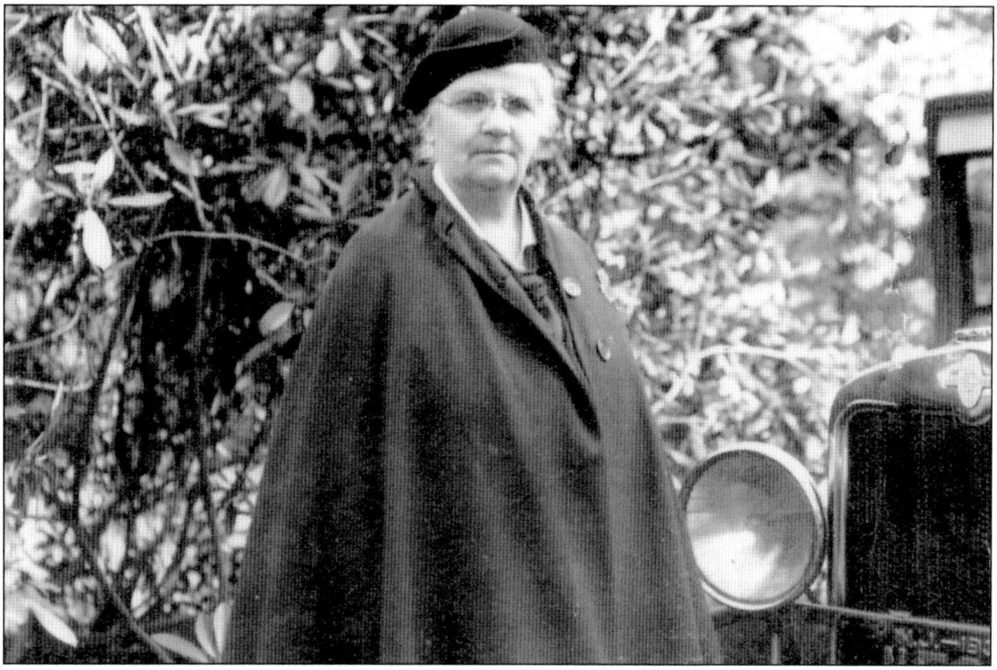

In 1935, Mary E. Dillon was the visiting nurse for the Bloomfield schools. The vehicle she used to get around town was a vintage 1927 Chevrolet. Her family originally lived at 17 Vine Street near the Morris Canal. They later moved to Clearview Avenue (changed to MacArthur Avenue during World War II) in the Watsessing section near the Westinghouse Corporation.

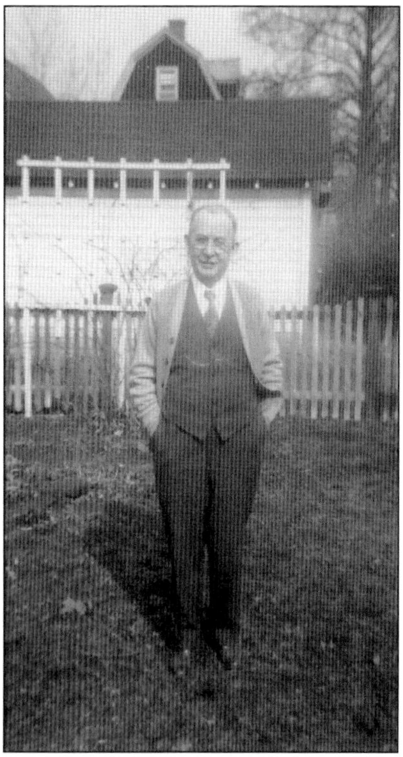

This photograph shows "Uncle Billy" McLaughlan in his backyard at 44 Walnut Terrace in 1944. McLaughlan, originally from Scotland, settled in Bloomfield and worked in the carpenter shop of the Oakes Mill for 35 years. His superb craftsmanship was much in demand, and he created many wonderful things from wood, ranging in size from glove stretchers to a large gazebo for the garden of his friend John A. Moran.

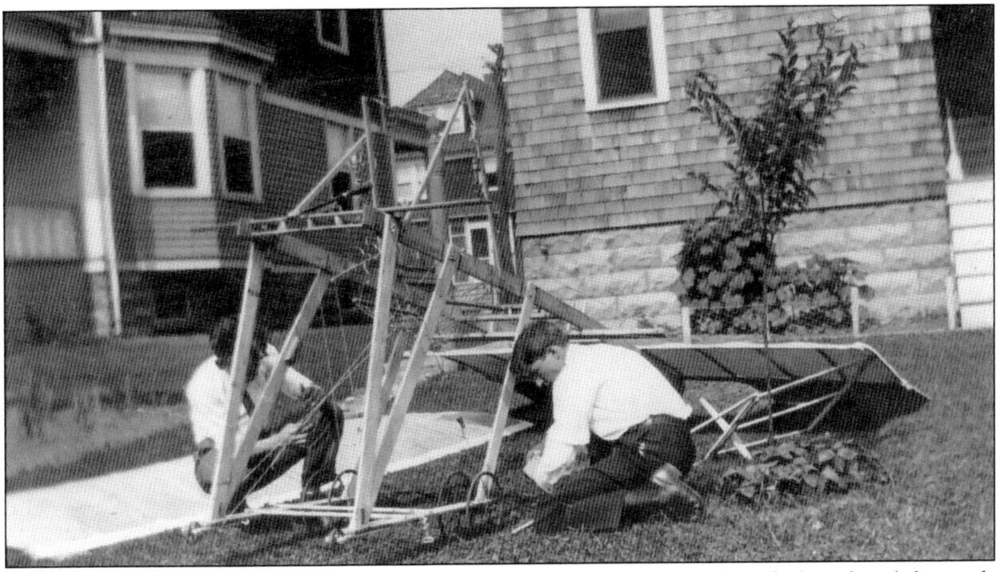

Launched on Sunset Avenue and flying toward Broad Street, the first flight of a glider with cockpit controls occurred in 1913. The pilot and builder of the glider was Leland Dorrothy of Stockton Street. He was 18 years old at the time of the flight. The glider, *Bald Eagle*, was built at home from readily available materials. Dorrothy is seen here (right) with his friend Capt. Charles Meyers.

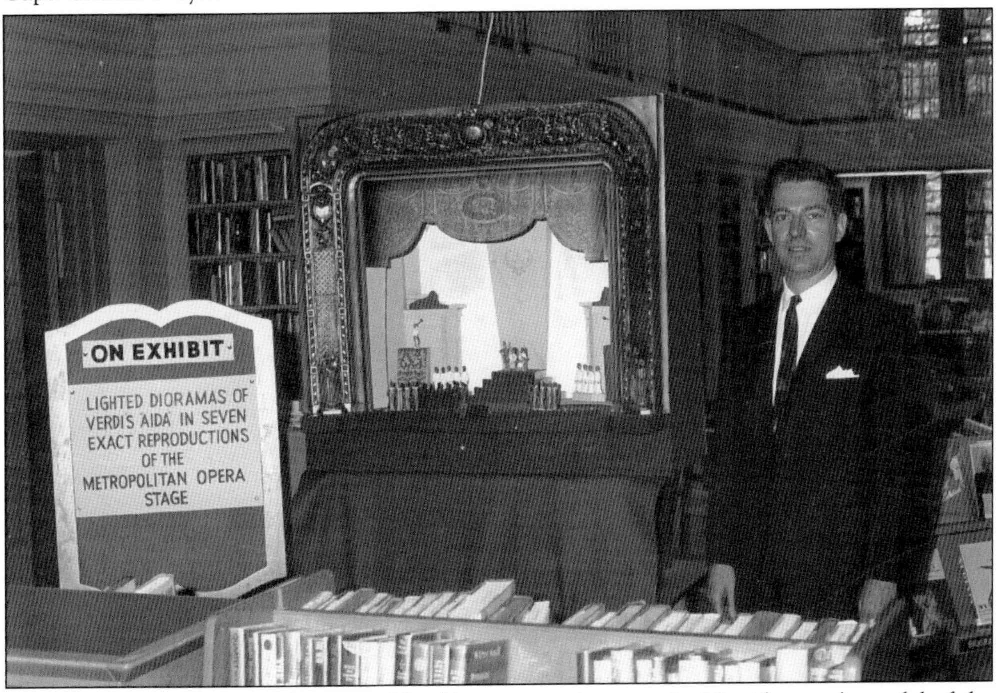

Howard S. Vogt, assistant director of the library, was photographed beside a scale model of the proscenium arch of the old Metropolitan Opera House in New York. This was one of five he commissioned from artists Robert Toth and James O'Toole. The models were exhibited in the library in April 1964, shortly after the famous opera house was demolished. Vogt later became director of the library.

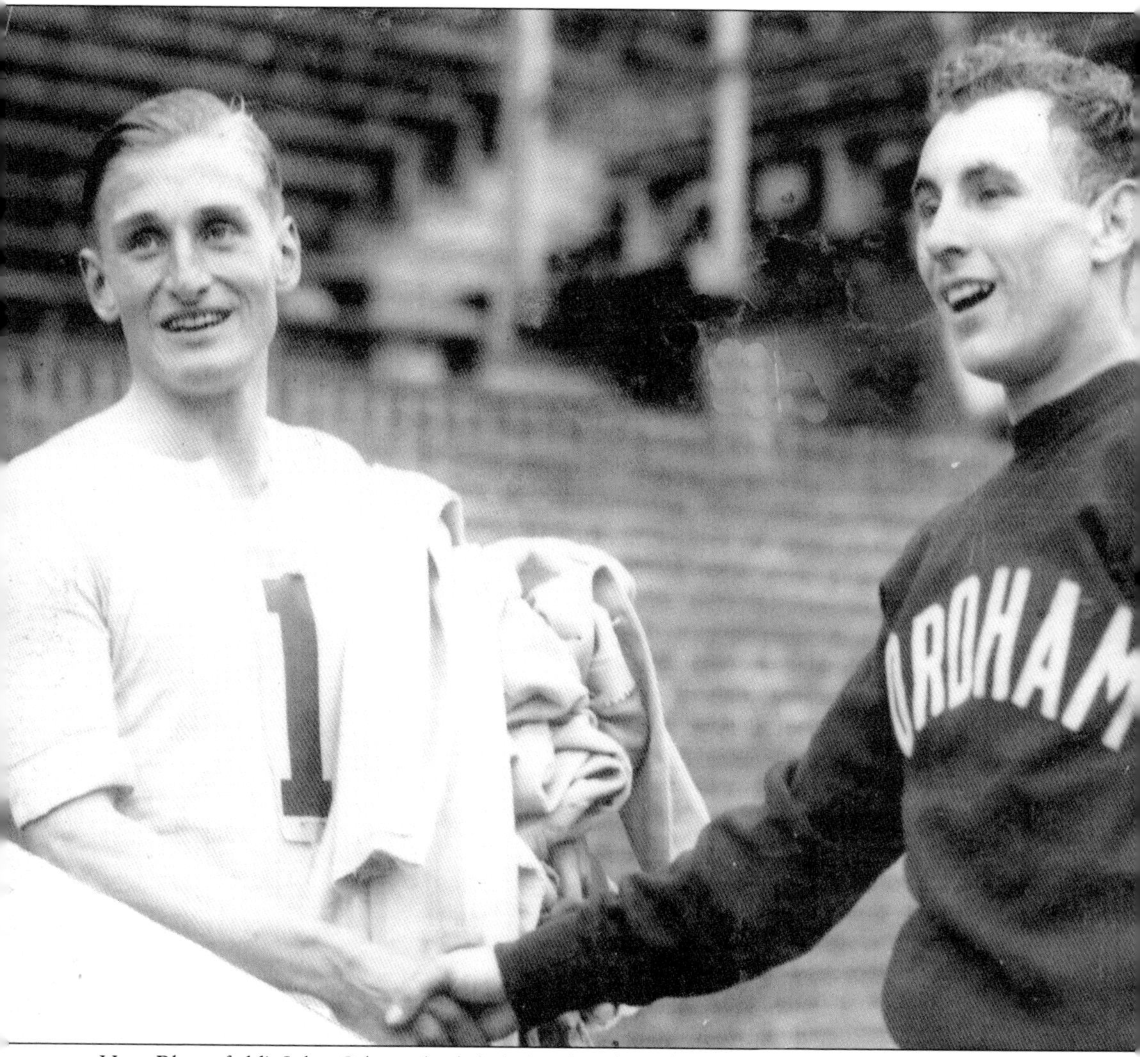

Here Bloomfield's John Gibson (right) shakes hands with Lord David Burghley, one of England's premier hurdlers, at the 1927 Penn Relays after Gibson defeated Burghley in the 400-meter hurdle race. At the completion of the race, the officials, ever mindful of royalty, told Burghley that they would disqualify Gibson because he was attending Fordham at night and give the race to Burghley. To his great credit, Burghley replied, "It doesn't matter when he is going to school. He won the race." It was Burghley's only defeat of that season in the United States. Gibson went on to set a world record of 52.6 seconds in the 440-yard high hurdles at the Olympic tryouts in Lincoln, Nebraska, later that summer and won a berth on the 1928 American Olympic team. The record stood for 15 years. The legendary Harry Coates was Gibson's coach.

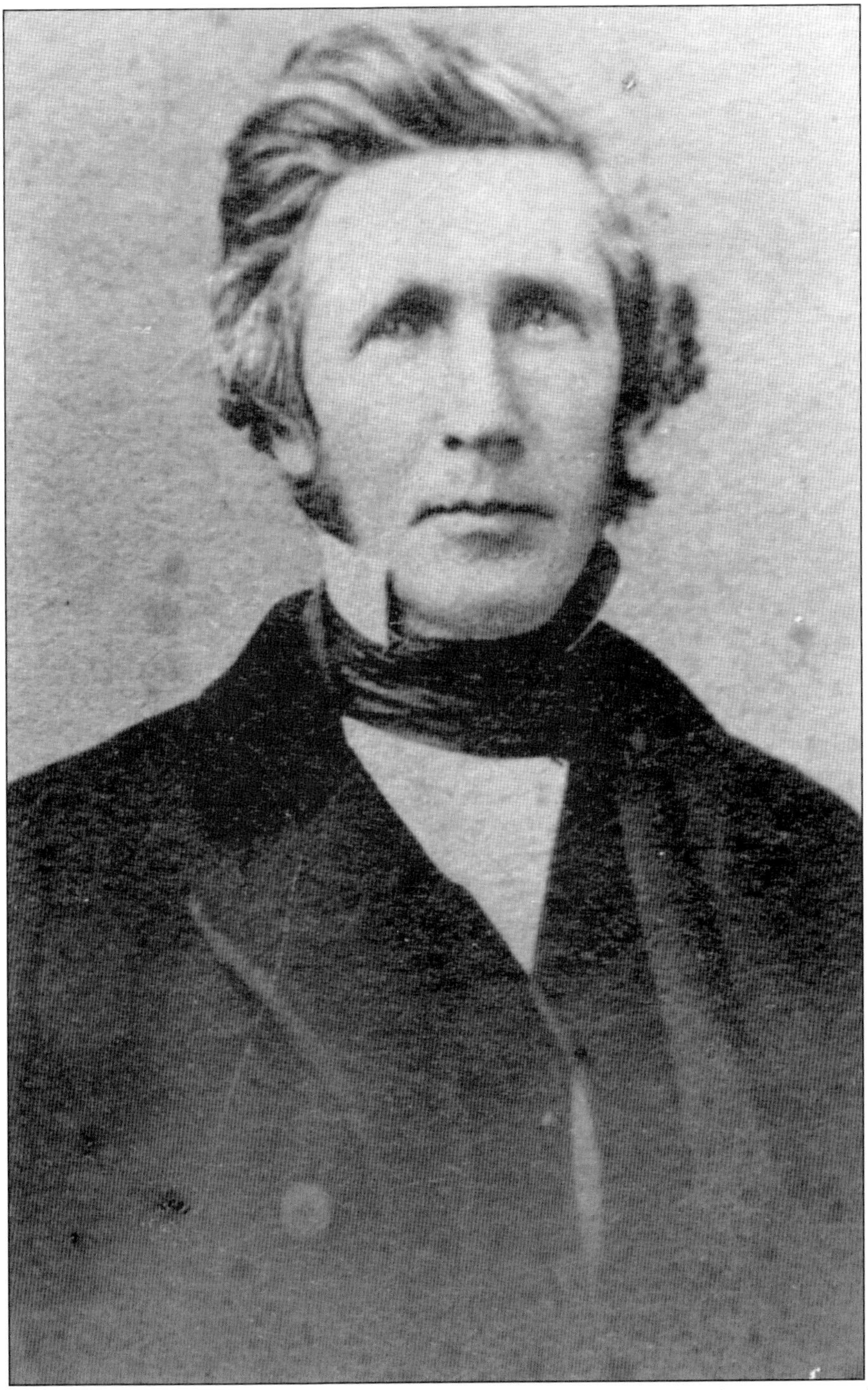

The early settlers followed ancient Native American trails to settle in the pleasant virgin forests of Stone House Plains. A look at any of the early maps of Bloomfield will show the northern part of the town consisting mostly of farmland until 1924. Large parcels of land in that area belonged to families with such names as Cueman, Garrabrant, Sigler, and Brokaw. This is a portrait of grandfather Joshua Brokaw.

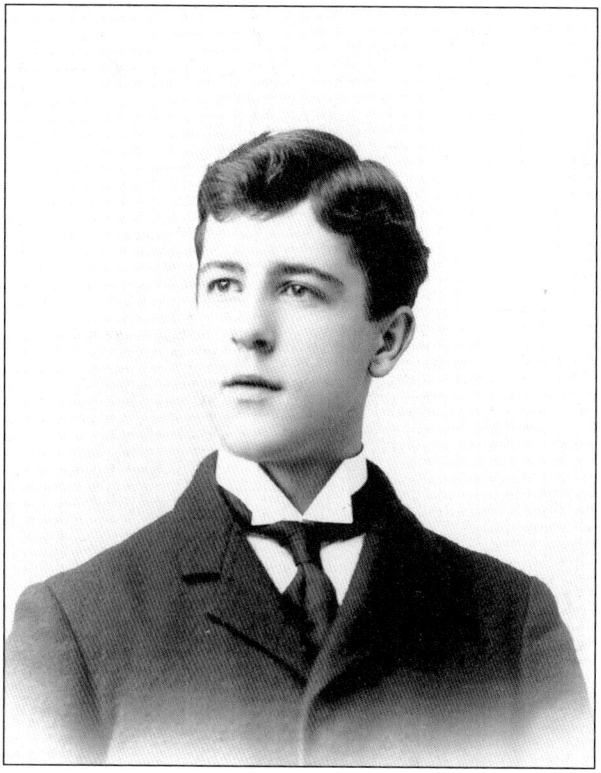

Fred Brokaw was born in 1876, probably in the house on Broad Street built by his great-grandfather Samuel Sigler in 1829. He married Mary Miller in 1899, worked the Brokaw farm in Brookdale, and continued to occupy the Sigler house until his new home at 1158 Broad Street was completed. A large part of his acreage was bought by Essex County in 1928 for the creation of Brookdale Park.

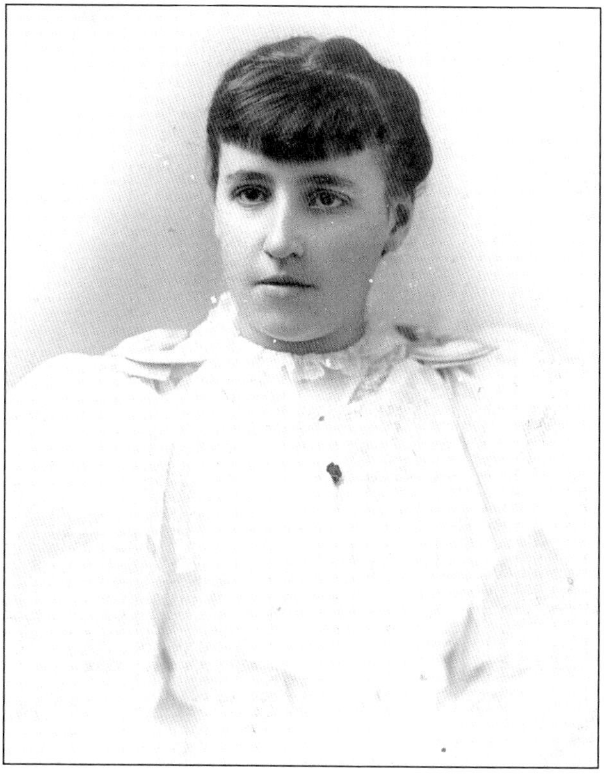

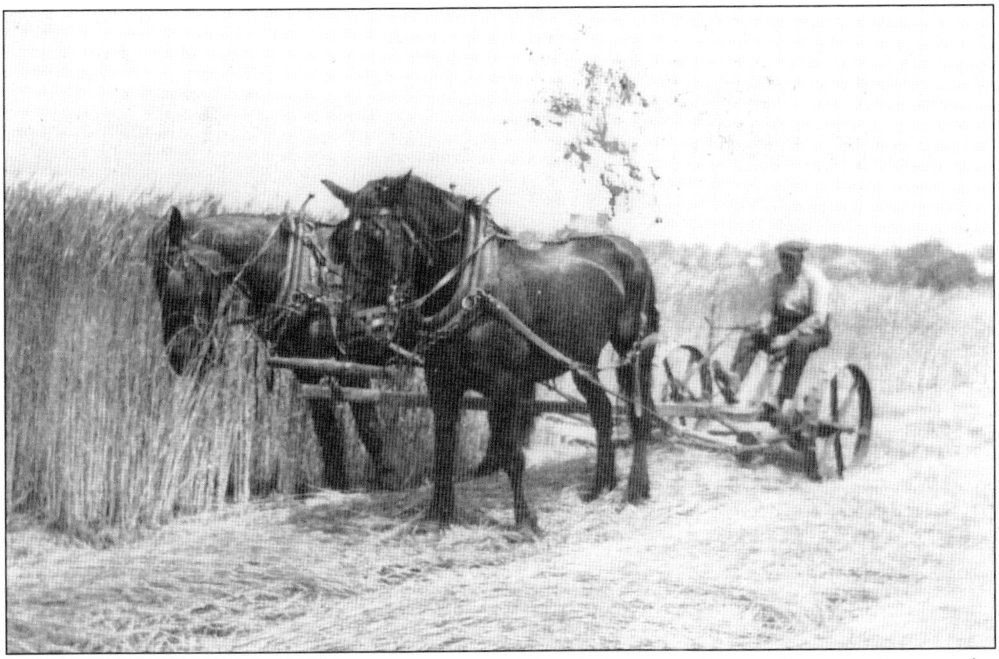

In this photograph, a horse-drawn reaping machine is in operation at harvest time on the Brokaw farm. The man in the driver's seat is probably Fred Brokaw, a large part of whose farm would become the site of Brookdale Park. The remaining land was then sold for development. Several farms were thus diminished in size, too much so to make them profitable.

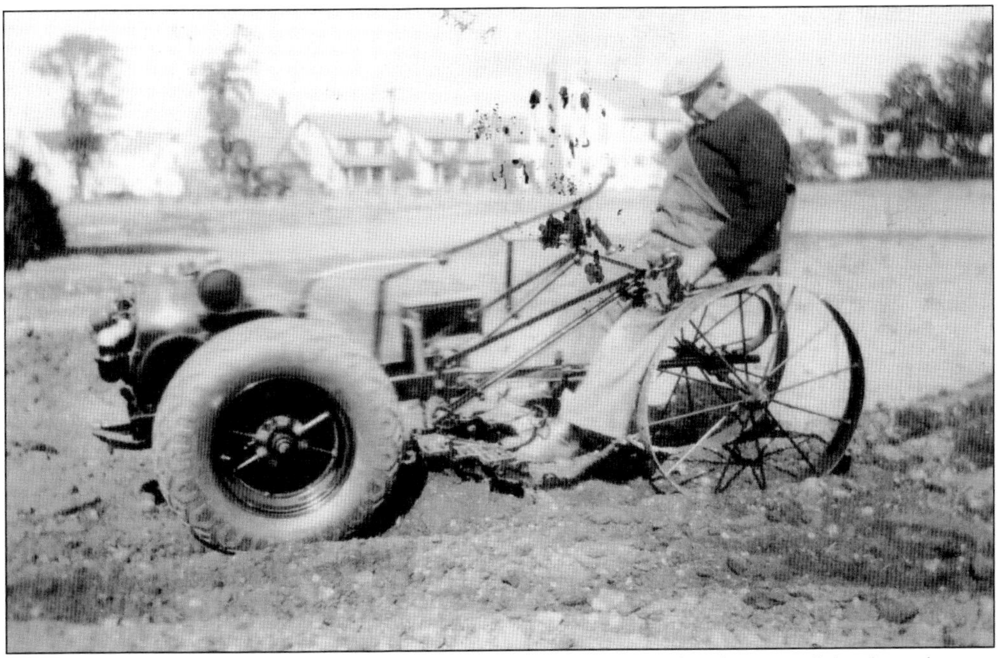

The county took the western part of the Brokaw farm for its park. The rest of the farm, having been in the Brokaw/Sigler families for generations, was developed into building lots and is now the site of houses on Parkview Drive, Aldon Terrace, Oakridge Road, Overlook Terrace, and Mountain Avenue. Fred Brokaw is pictured here on his tractor with Aldon Terrace in the background.

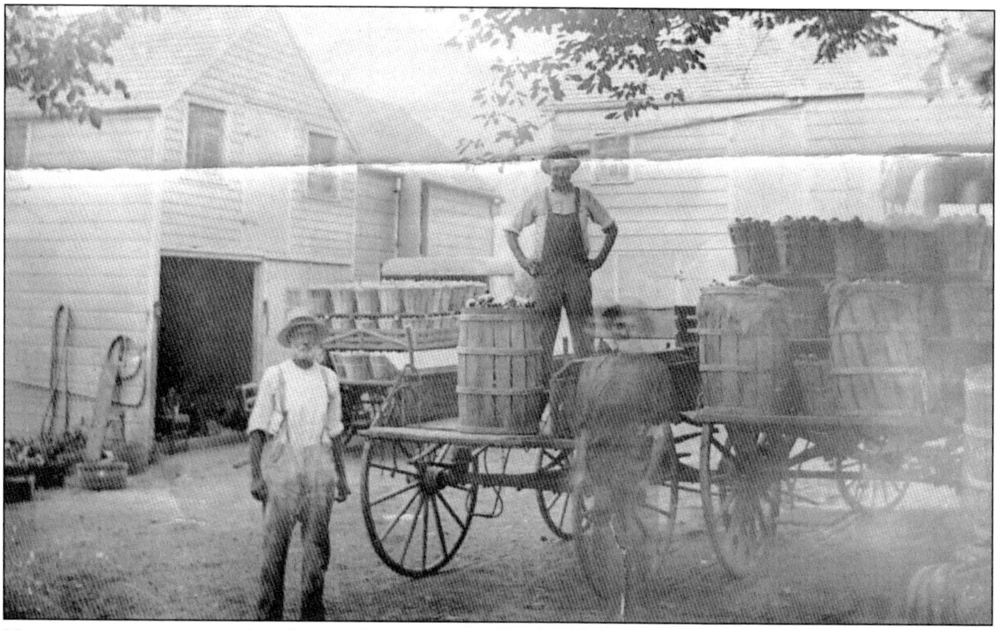

How many can remember horse-drawn wagonloads of melons, apples, and peaches winding their way down Broad Street and over Bloomfield Avenue on their way to the farmers' markets? Newcomers to Bloomfield will not know that until the 1950s there were still a few horse-drawn vehicles on the street. Brokaw farmhands are pictured here crating up produce on the family homestead where McLeod Road is today.

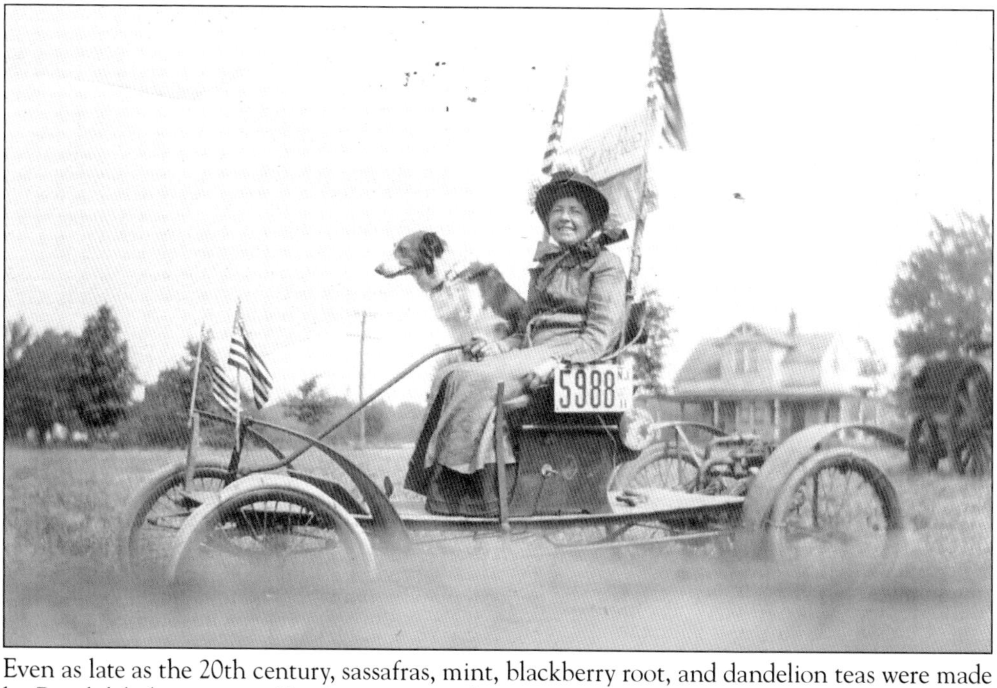

Even as late as the 20th century, sassafras, mint, blackberry root, and dandelion teas were made by Brookdale housewives. Fund-raising strawberry suppers for worthy causes were held on the side lawn of the old Brookdale firehouse. Mary Brokaw, wife of Fred Brokaw, is seen on the farm with a 1912 automobile the family enjoyed.

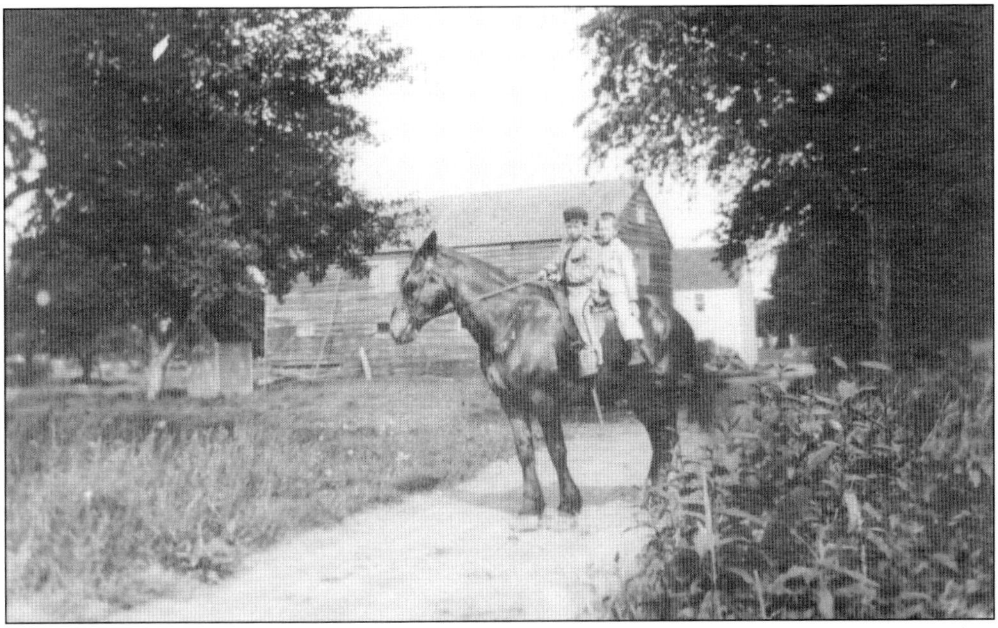

Although it is less than a century old, this photograph shows a rural Bloomfield that has completely vanished. In 1937, town ordinances declared that if citizens drove horses over eight miles an hour or lead their cows on the sidewalk, they broke the law and were subject to a fine. The young Brokaw boys saddle up on their father's farm, which was on Broad Street, across from Brookdale School.

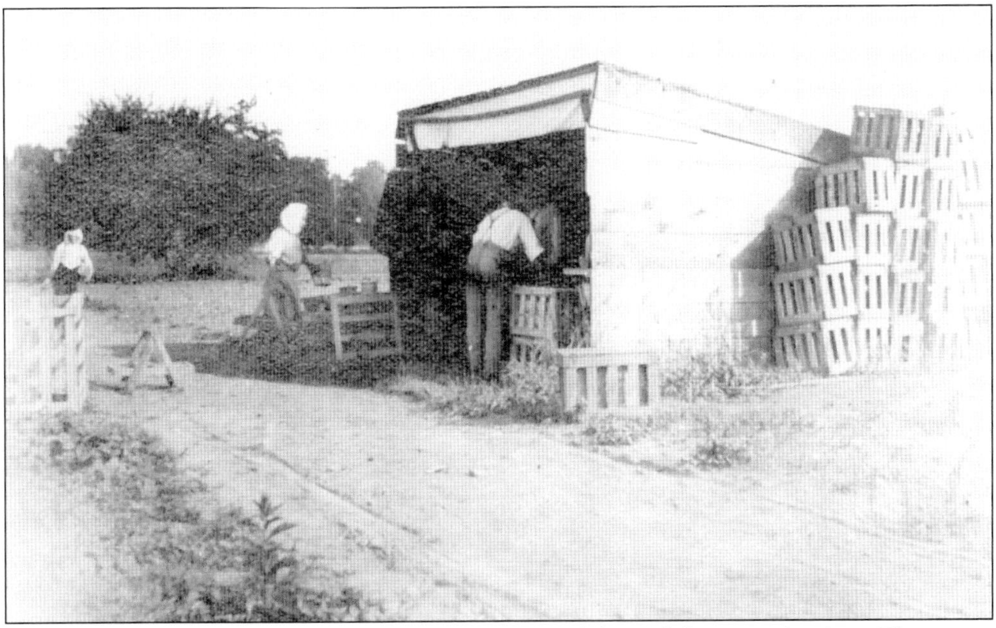

Brookdale farms produced excellent watercress, horseradish, cauliflower, and melons. There were farms that had large apple orchards for making cider known throughout the country. The best cider was made from two kinds of apples, Harrison and Canfield. Both seedlings had originated here. The produce stand is perhaps being supervised by the sunbonneted Mary Brokaw, wife of Wilber Brokaw.

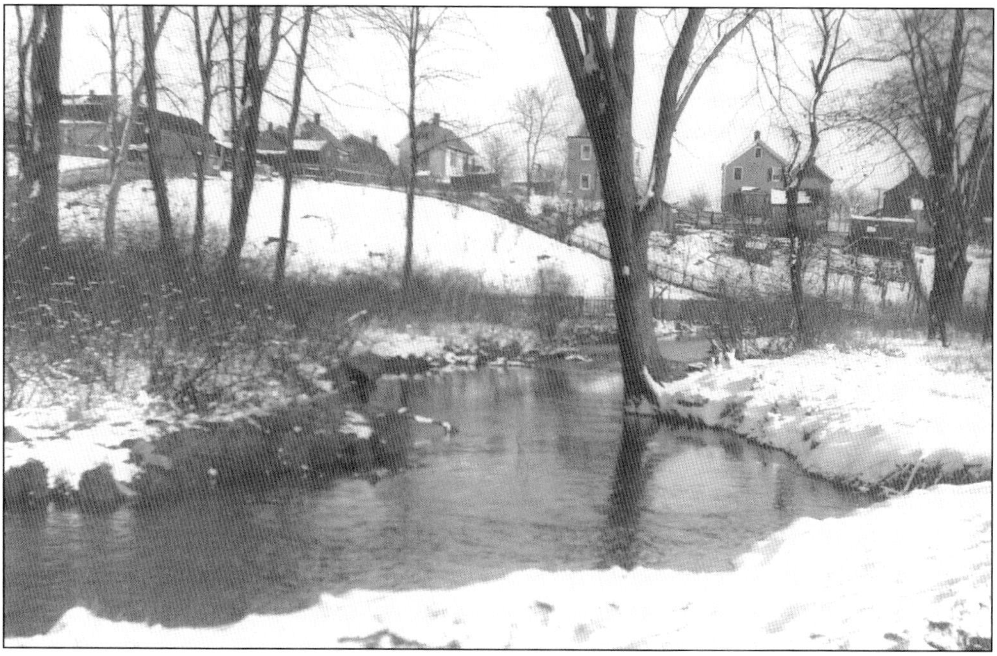

The Second and Third Rivers were important to the industrial development of Bloomfield. Manufacturing operations were located along the banks of these two sources of water and waterpower. This is the upper part of the Third River near James Street, just above the northern end of the millpond photographed by Charles Warren Eaton in the early 1900s. The houses in the background are located on Spring Street.

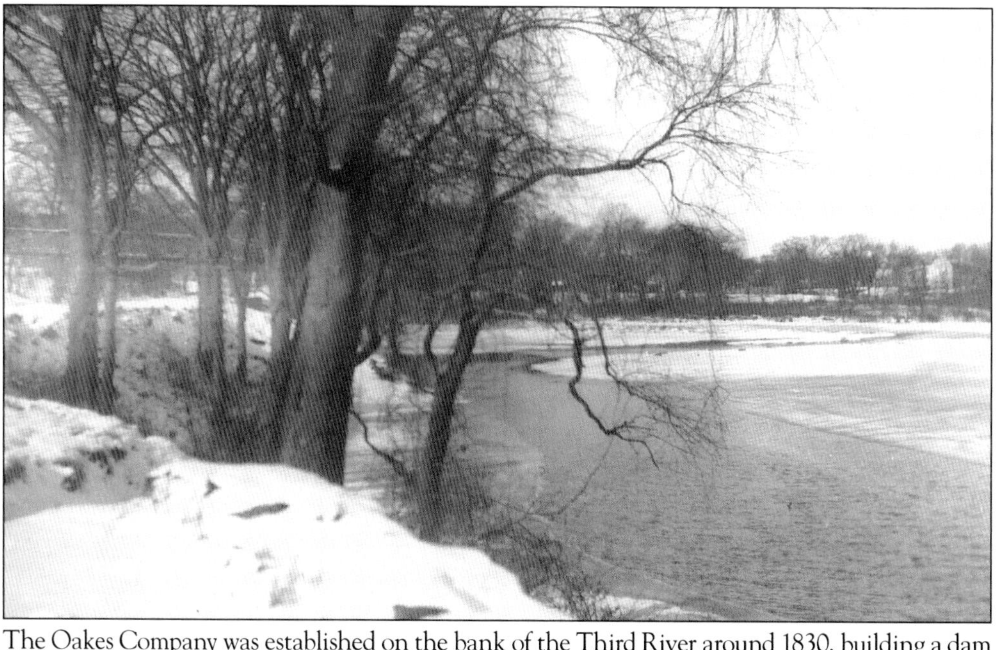

The Oakes Company was established on the bank of the Third River around 1830, building a dam and harnessing the river to drive a waterwheel and using water from the as yet unpolluted stream to process its wool. The Morris Canal and the Maple Street Bridge over it can be seen on the extreme left of the photograph. Later coal from the canal powered a steam engine at the mill.

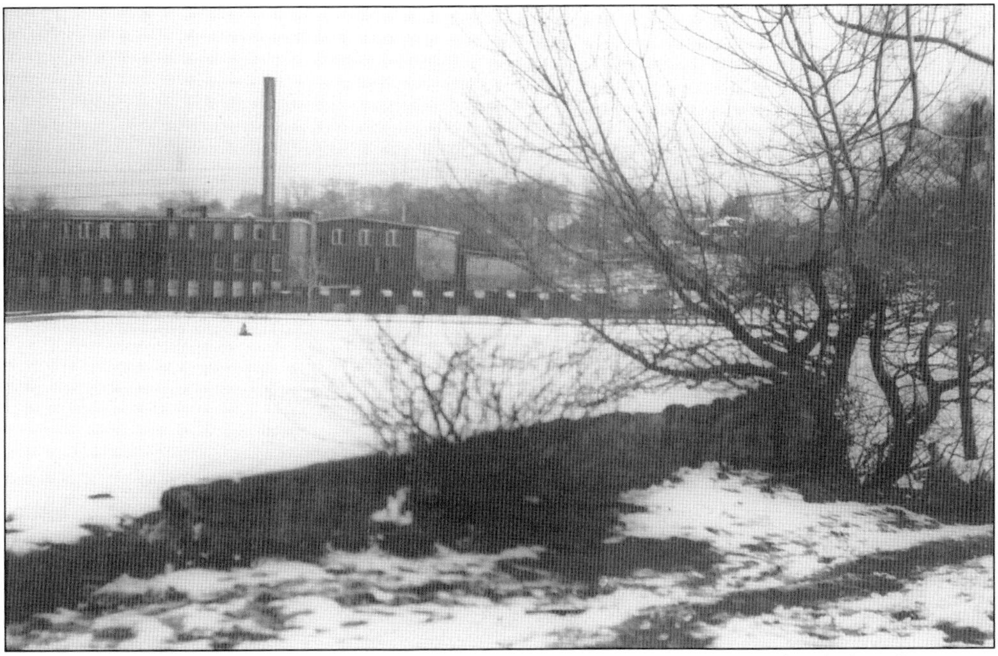

The tall chimney signals the end of the dependence on waterpower at the Oakes Company, but the pond remained for many years, still used as a source of water for dyeing wool. It was also enjoyed during the winter for ice-skating and, in the summer, for pleasure boating. This early-20th-century postcard of a rowboat on the pond is titled *Little Lake George*.

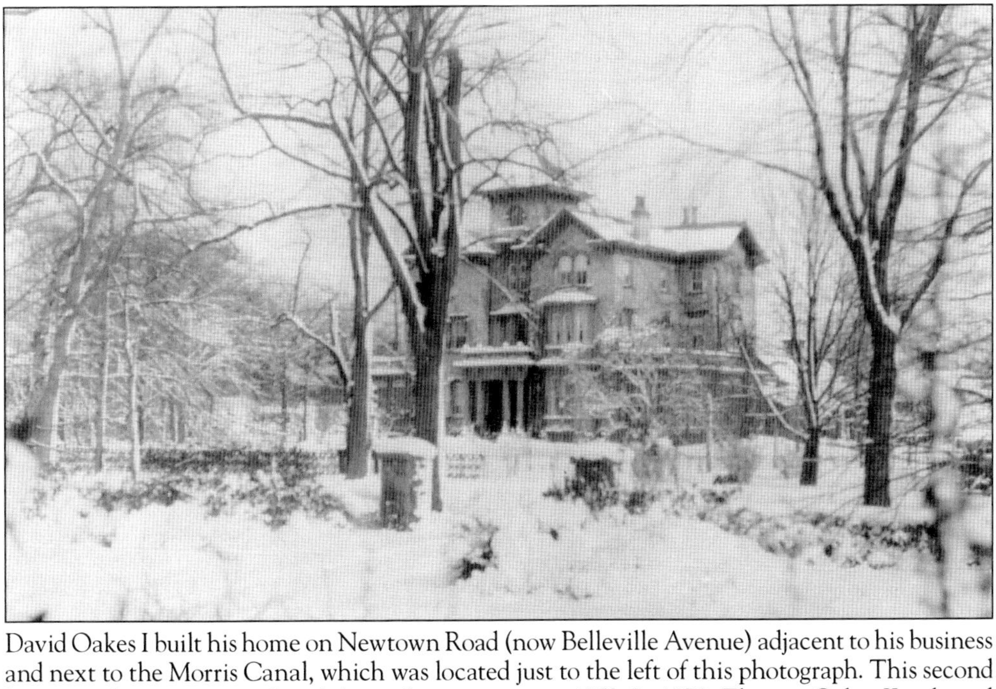

David Oakes I built his home on Newtown Road (now Belleville Avenue) adjacent to his business and next to the Morris Canal, which was located just to the left of this photograph. This second house on the property replaced the earlier structure in 1853. In 1878, Thomas Oakes II enlarged the house by adding the third floor and heightening the tower to four stories. It was demolished in 1943.

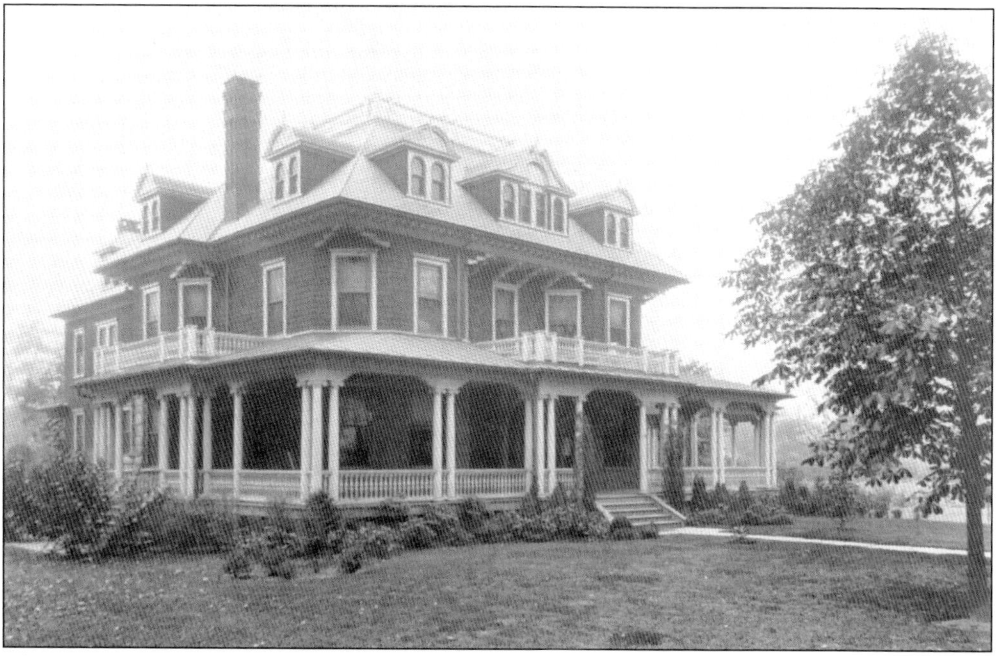

The second large house on the Oakes estate was built across Belleville Avenue in 1895 from designs drawn by Charles Granville Jones. The east side of the house was later altered by David Oakes II and Jean Oakes with the addition of a heated conservatory. This new room was used to raise plants during the winter and as a pleasant place for social gatherings in cold weather.

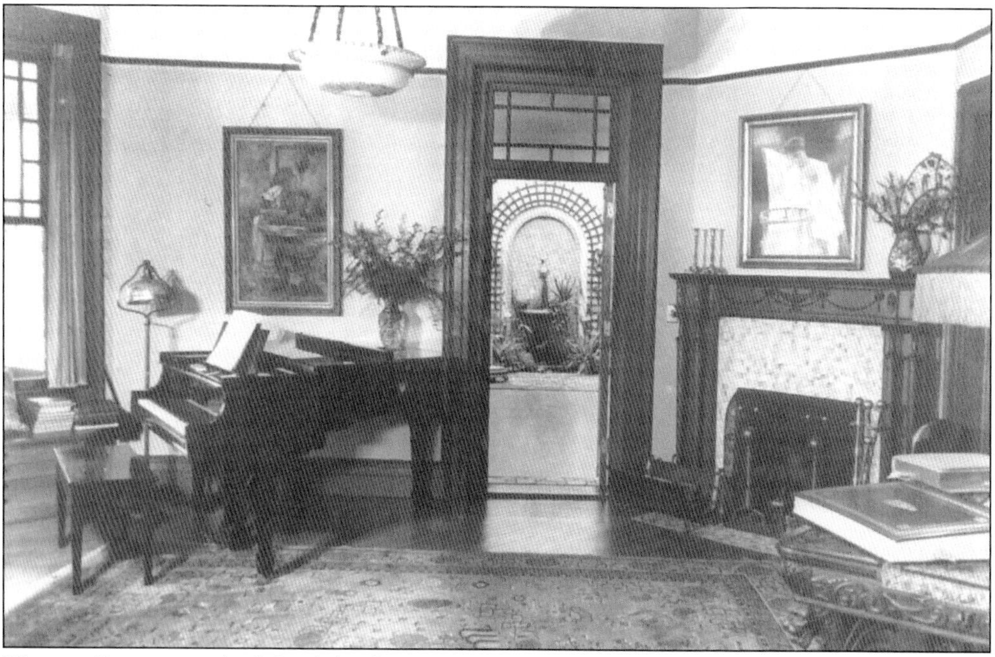

The small room on the left of the front entrance was used as a reception room, and, beyond, the fountain of the garden room can be seen. The bowl of the hanging light fixture is of carved alabaster, and the lamp in the corner is almost surely from Tiffany Studios. As designed by Jones, the rooms on the other side of the central hall were of this same size, with corner fireplaces.

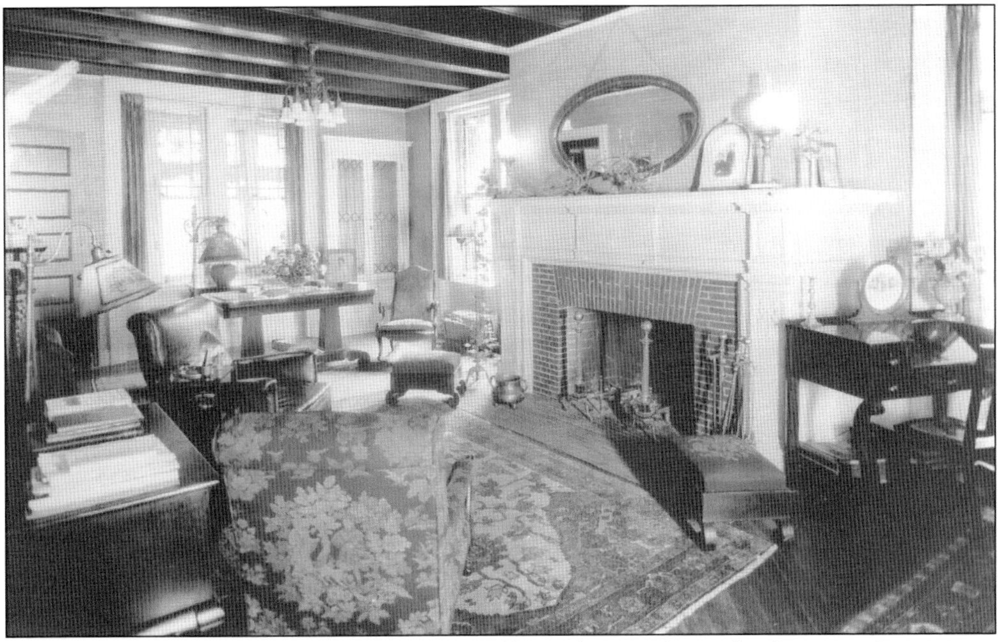

This large room was originally built as two smaller parlors similar to the dining and receptions rooms across the hall. David and Jean Oakes had the partition removed and the colonial fireplace installed when they moved in after their marriage in 1910. Most of the furnishings seem to date from the early 19th century and may have been originally used in the old homestead across the street.

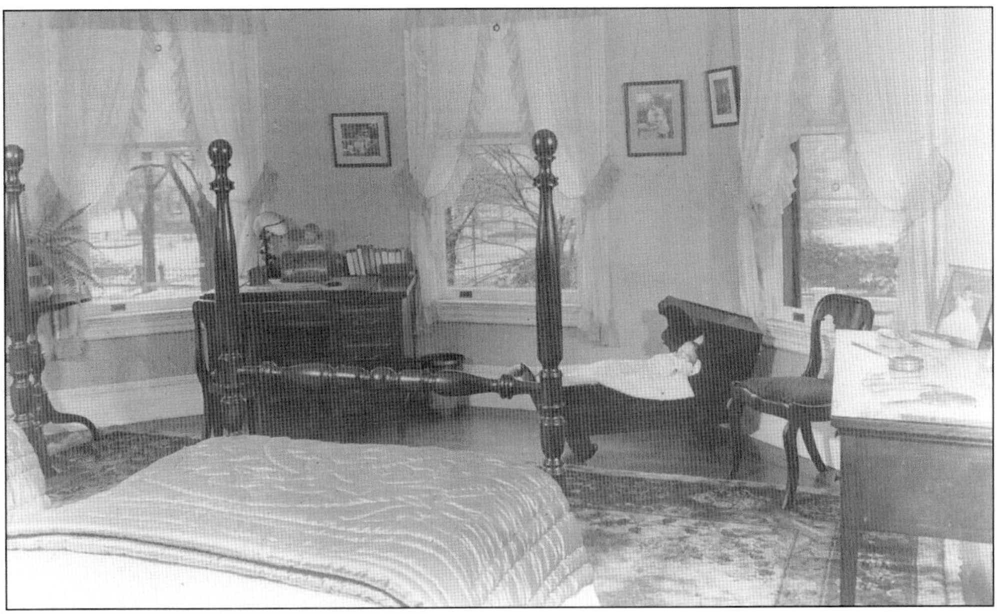

The northwest bedroom was also furnished with heirloom furniture, possibly from the homestead of 1853, just across Belleville Avenue. A glimpse of the old house (demolished in 1943) can be seen through the left-hand window. The cradle and tilt-top table may have dated back to the 18th century, and the chair was possibly made around 1840. This photograph may have been one of a series made in 1929.

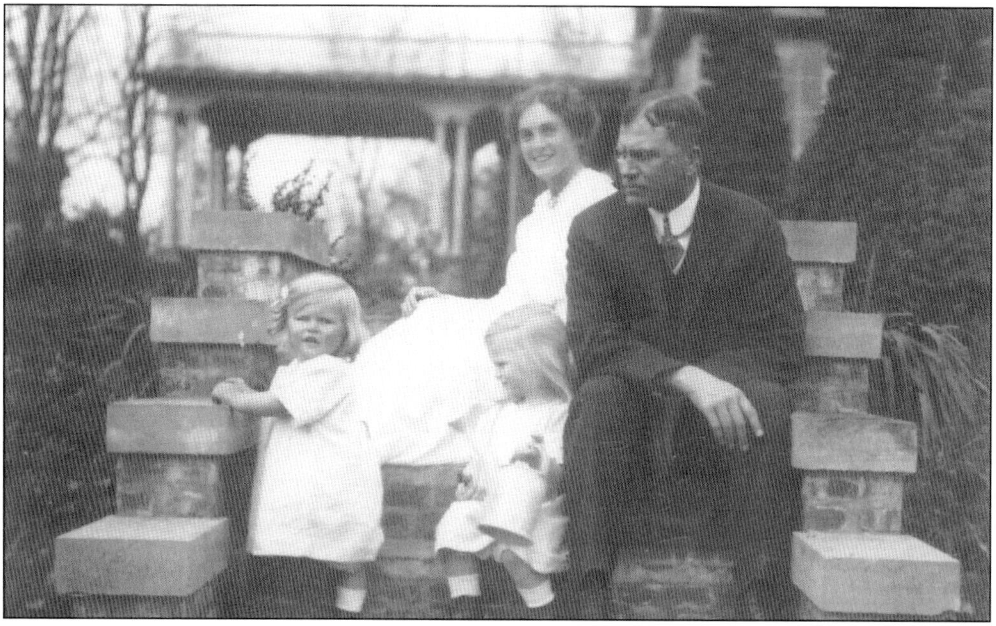

David and Jean Oakes and their daughters Juliet and Eleanor pose together on a warm spring day in the 1920s on the steps to the rear garden. The large porte cochere, a dominating feature of the house, is in the background. David Oakes's stand-up collar was in the height of fashion at that time. Two more children would come later: Jean and Thomas III.

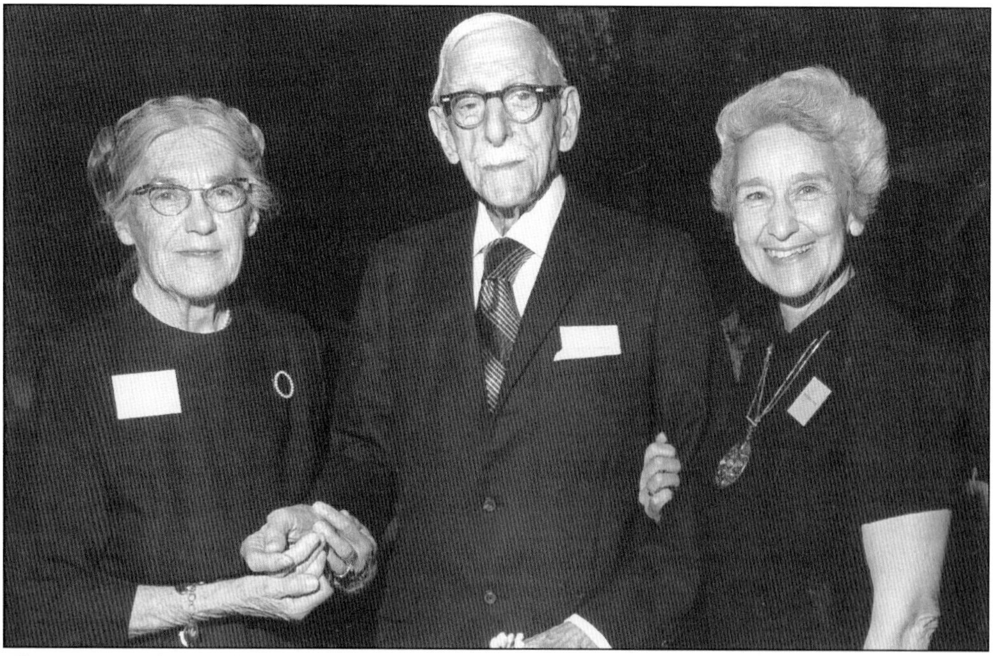

Three outstanding and venerable citizens of Bloomfield appear here: Jean Oakes (wife of David Oakes II), Addison Roubaud, and Mildred Stone. The group portrait was taken on April 6, 1971, to commemorate the 100th anniversary of the founding of the Bloomfield Savings Bank. The first meeting of the bank's board of managers was held at the home of the founder, Zophar B. Dodd, at the northwestern corner of Liberty and State Streets.

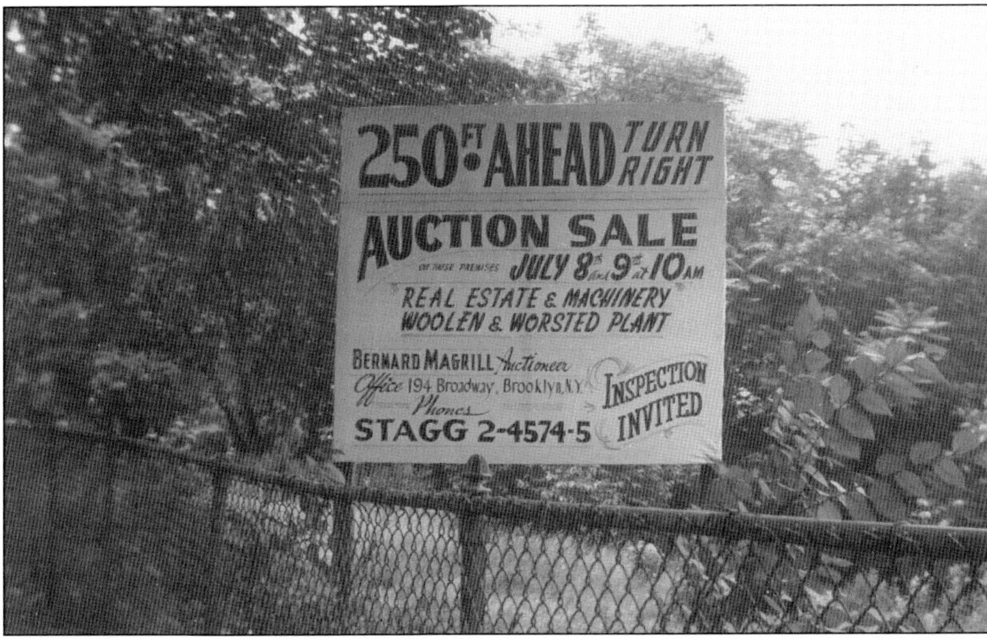

After the demand for woolen uniforms ended, following World War II, the Oakes Mill was faced with the development of new synthetic fabrics that would eventually make its product obsolete. In addition, manufacturing methods and machines were in need of modernization. It was time to sell the business that had been in the family for a century. This sign was posted on Belleville Avenue in June 1947.

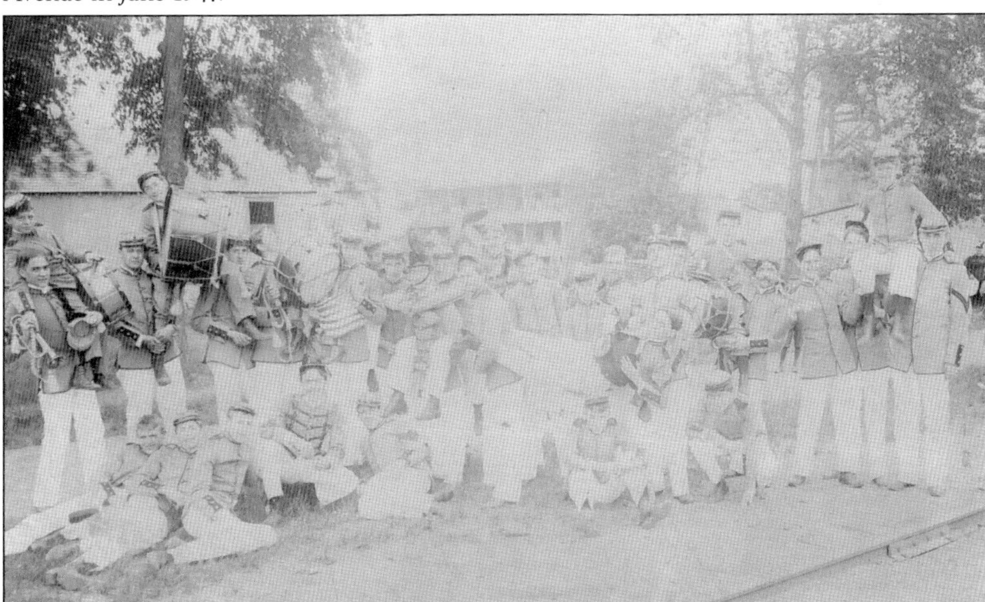

In the 1890s, Bloomfield was a typical small town. It gained some national attention when the newly elected Pres. William McKinley was presented with woolen material from Oakes Mill for his inaugural suit. Some large homes were seen, but farm wagons carrying horseradish, melons, and watercress still traveled to markets on a graveled Broad Street. The very lighthearted Bloomfield Cadet Corps poses for this photograph in 1896.

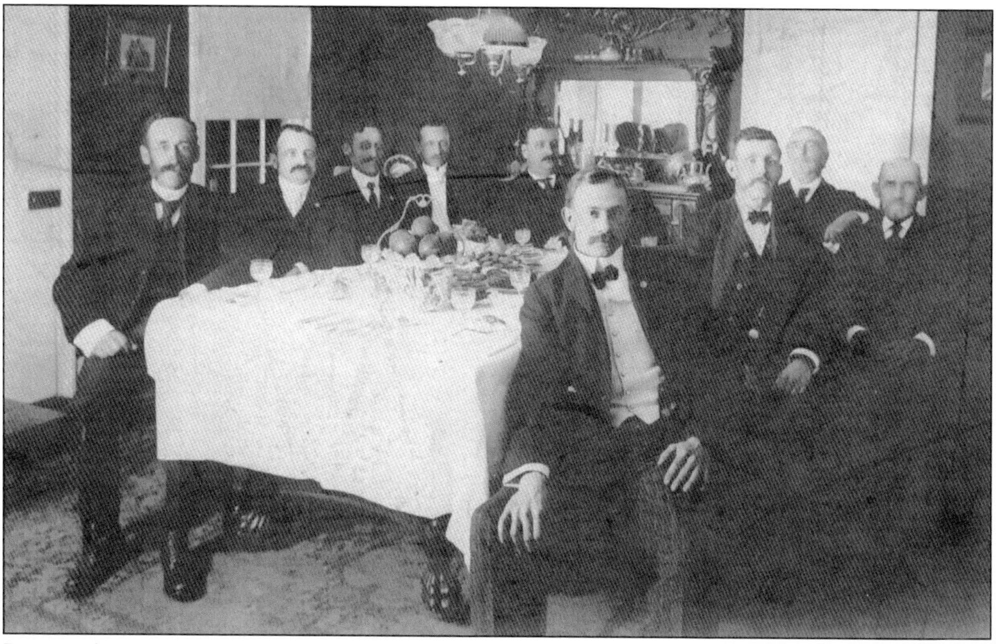

Even in the early 1900s, Bloomfield politicos met to discuss their views on local politics. Members of the Berkeley Club, including Herbert Farrand, Benjamin Baldwin, and Everett H. Brown, are shown at one of their meetings in 1901 in the first ward. Formed as a Republican social club, the Berkeleyites enjoyed many social get-togethers and meetings.

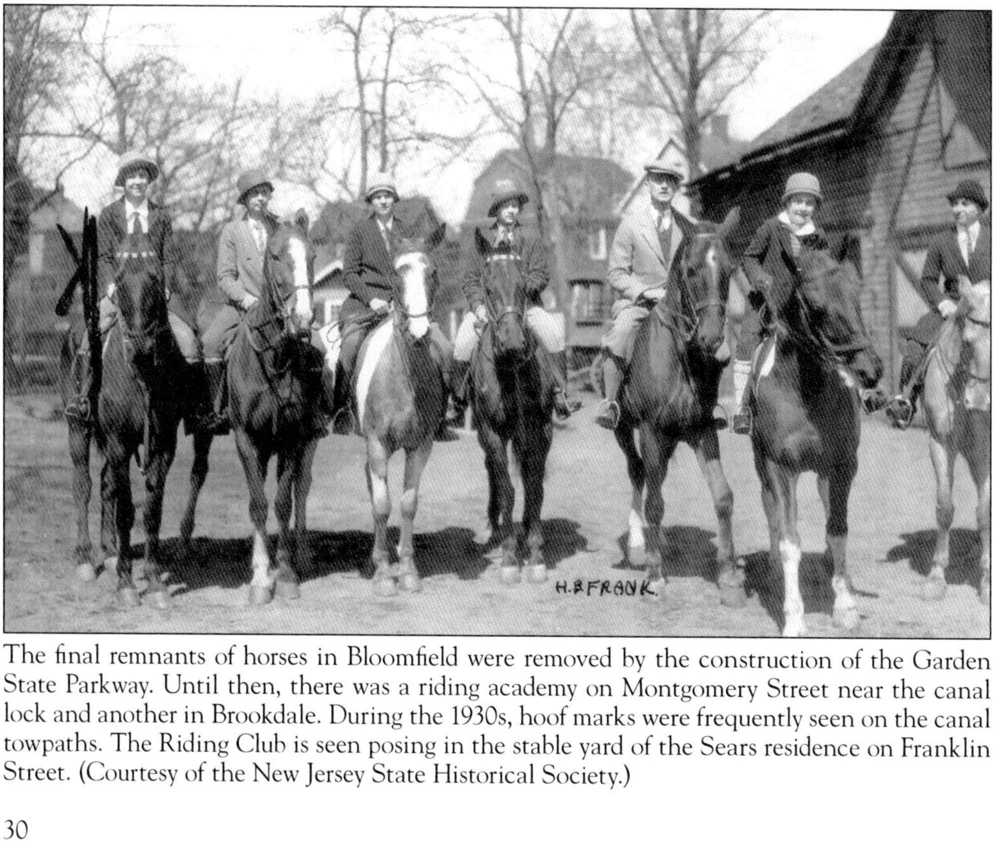

The final remnants of horses in Bloomfield were removed by the construction of the Garden State Parkway. Until then, there was a riding academy on Montgomery Street near the canal lock and another in Brookdale. During the 1930s, hoof marks were frequently seen on the canal towpaths. The Riding Club is seen posing in the stable yard of the Sears residence on Franklin Street. (Courtesy of the New Jersey State Historical Society.)

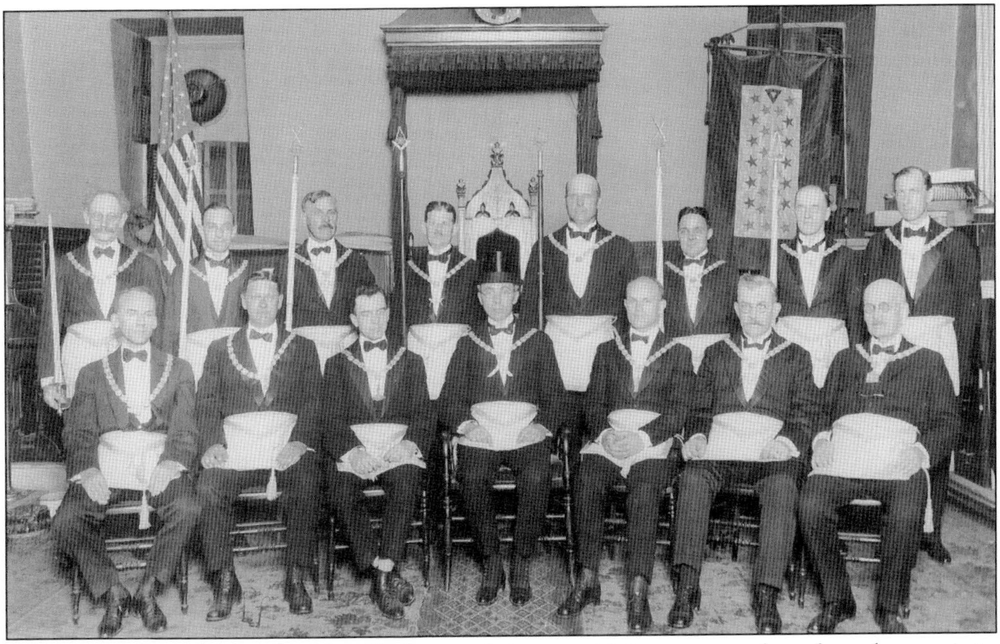

Officers of Bloomfield Lodge No. 40, Free and Accepted Masons, pose for a formal portrait in 1925, on the dedication day of their new building. Thirty years later, during the evening program in their lodge rooms at Broad and Liberty Streets, the burning of the mortgage for the Masons' building was celebrated with pride and satisfaction. It was the 130th anniversary of the lodge, one of the oldest organizations in town.

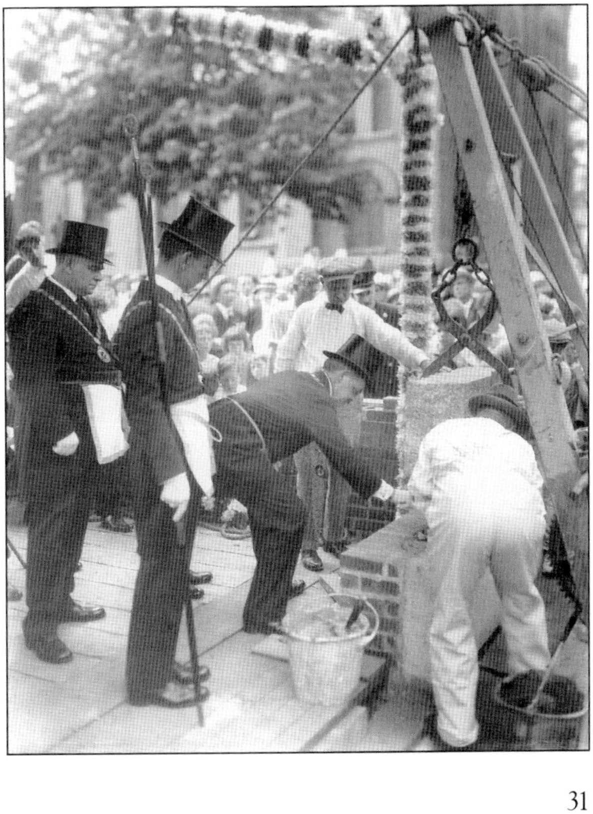

Initiated in 1824, the Masons found their old meeting place at 313 Glenwood Avenue too small to accommodate its membership by 1913. Edward Hughes, councilman of the first ward and treasurer of Sacred Heart Church, suggested that the property opposite the church at Broad and Liberty Streets be purchased. Amid impressive ceremonies, and 100 years after it formed, grand master Andrew Foulds laid the cornerstone.

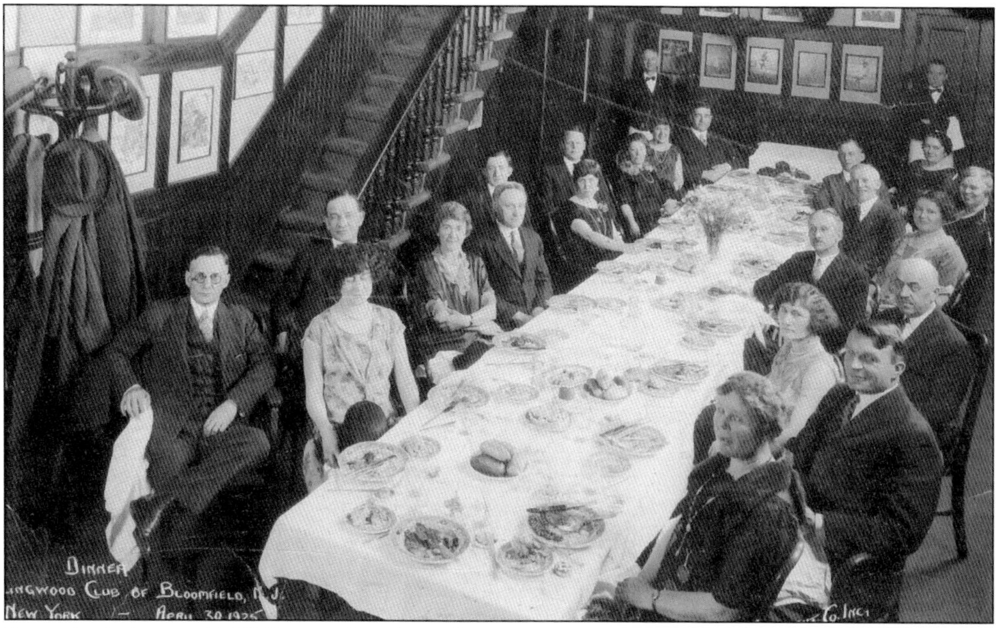

From Optimists to Odd Fellows to Knights to Lions to radios, stamps, poultry, and model airplanes, the town has always had an enthusiasm for sharing mutual interests. The library has a file with the names of more than 200 clubs and organizations, some with large memberships, some small. The Kindlingwood Club was formed by friends living in the Morton Street neighborhood. The club enjoyed years of having fun and playing bridge.

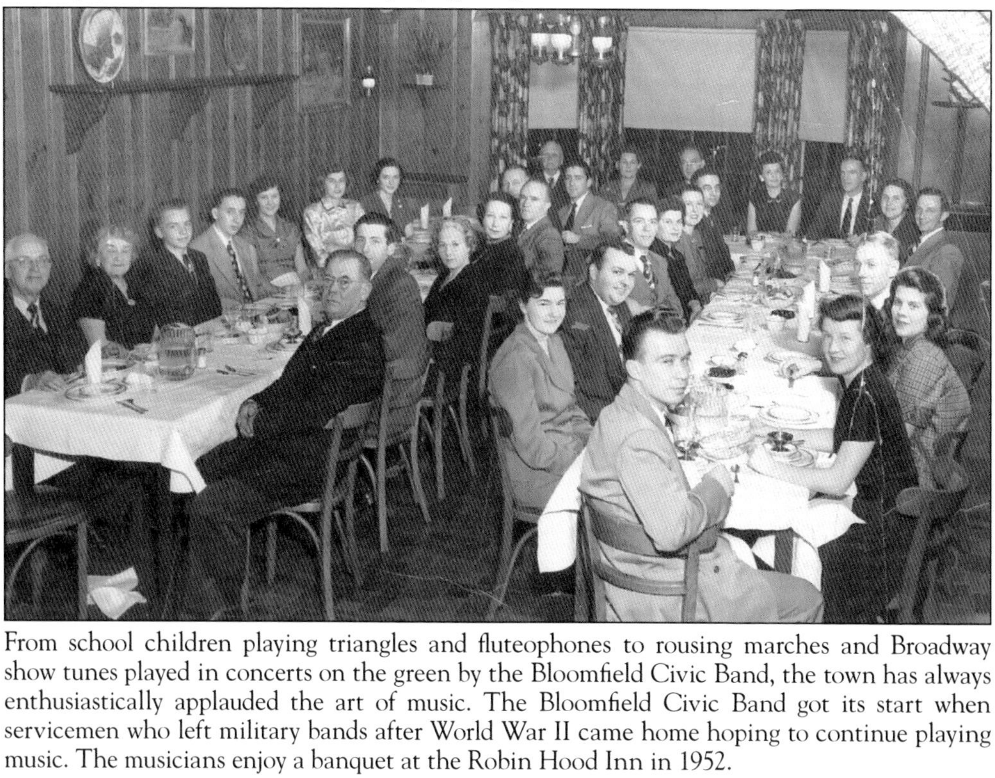

From school children playing triangles and fluteophones to rousing marches and Broadway show tunes played in concerts on the green by the Bloomfield Civic Band, the town has always enthusiastically applauded the art of music. The Bloomfield Civic Band got its start when servicemen who left military bands after World War II came home hoping to continue playing music. The musicians enjoy a banquet at the Robin Hood Inn in 1952.

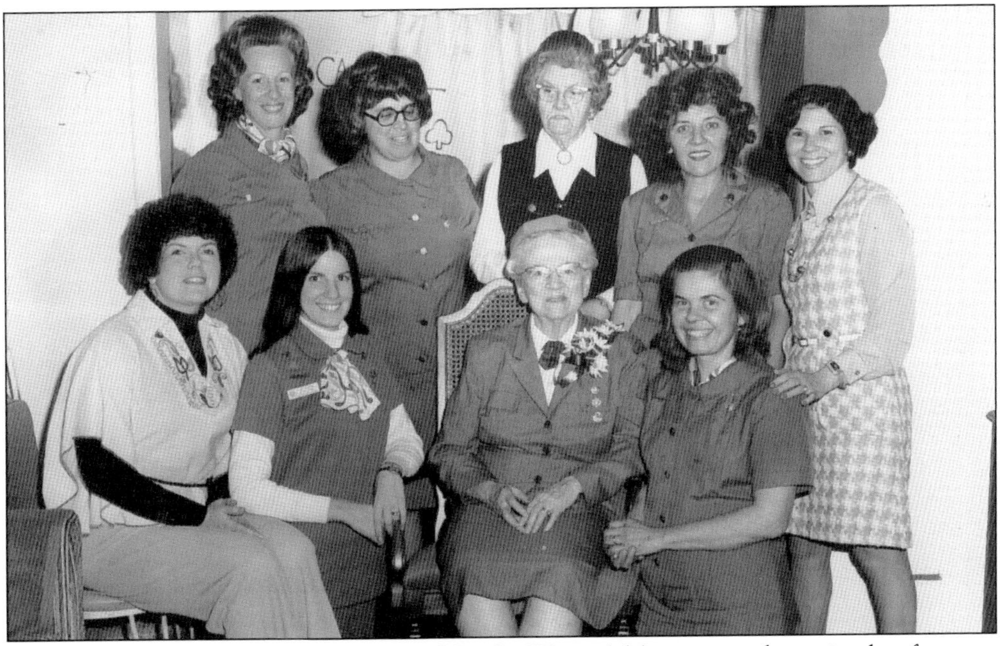

In 1976, Girl Scout leaders gather around Emilie Westerdahl at a party honoring her for more than 50 years of scouting work. Westerdahl was the beloved niece of watercolorist Anna Lindner. The artist depicted the growth of Westerdahl from her first Christmas to her adulthood, painting in vivid detail the life of a genteel family. In 1908, Westerdahl lived with her parents and aunt on Willard Avenue.

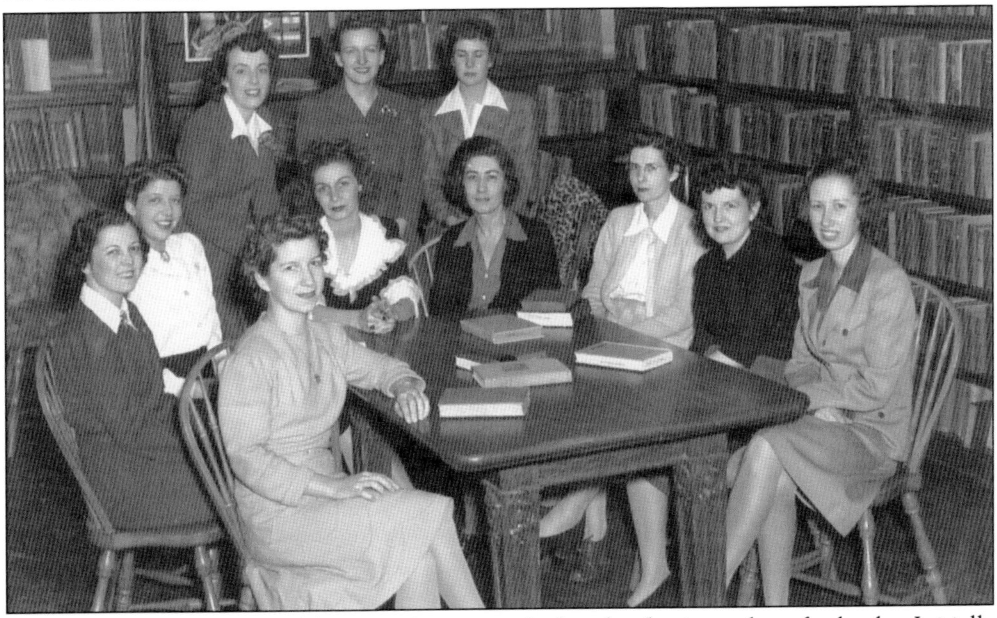

In 2006, the Fortnightly Club entered its seventh decade, sharing a love for books. Initially formed to encourage high school seniors to share their literary interest, the group met in the library at the invitation of the library staff. Through the years, members have come and gone, but the pleasure in reading remains vibrant. Greta Krantz (far right) is an original member of the group.

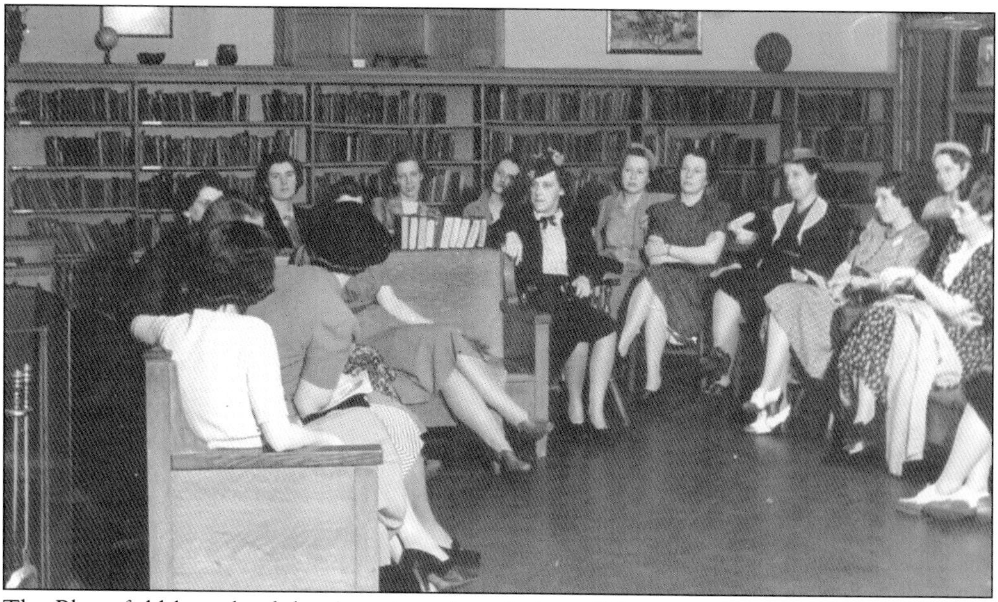

The Bloomfield branch of the American Association of University Women was organized in 1928 on the conviction that education is key to equality for women. The group cosponsored the important Friends of the Library. When the town closed its night school during the Great Depression, the American Association of University Women established an adult education program open to all county residents. During World War II, it offered child care services to mothers working in industry.

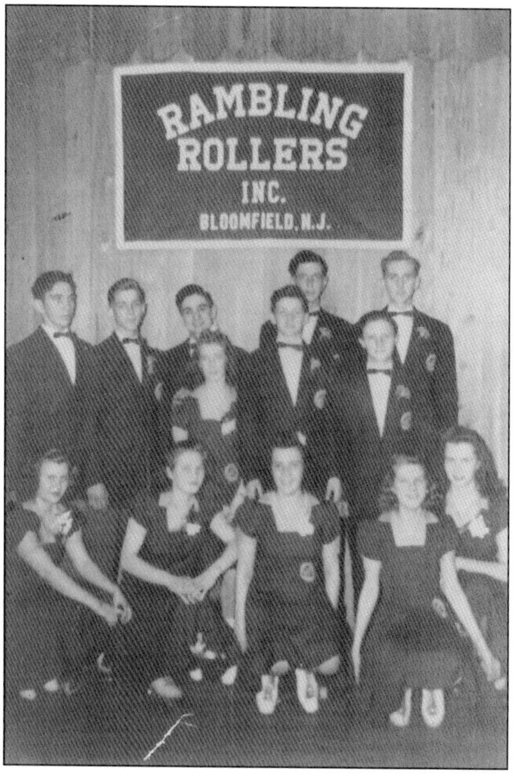

Back in the 1940s, before television and many family cars, people created much of their own entertainment. Roller-skating clubs were popular, traveling once a month to rinks in the area. One such group was the Rambling Rollers. They purchased uniforms through fund-raisers and got around in two or three jalopies owned by members. Ray "Rambling Ray" Neveil is in the top row, on the right.

Two

Homes and Churches

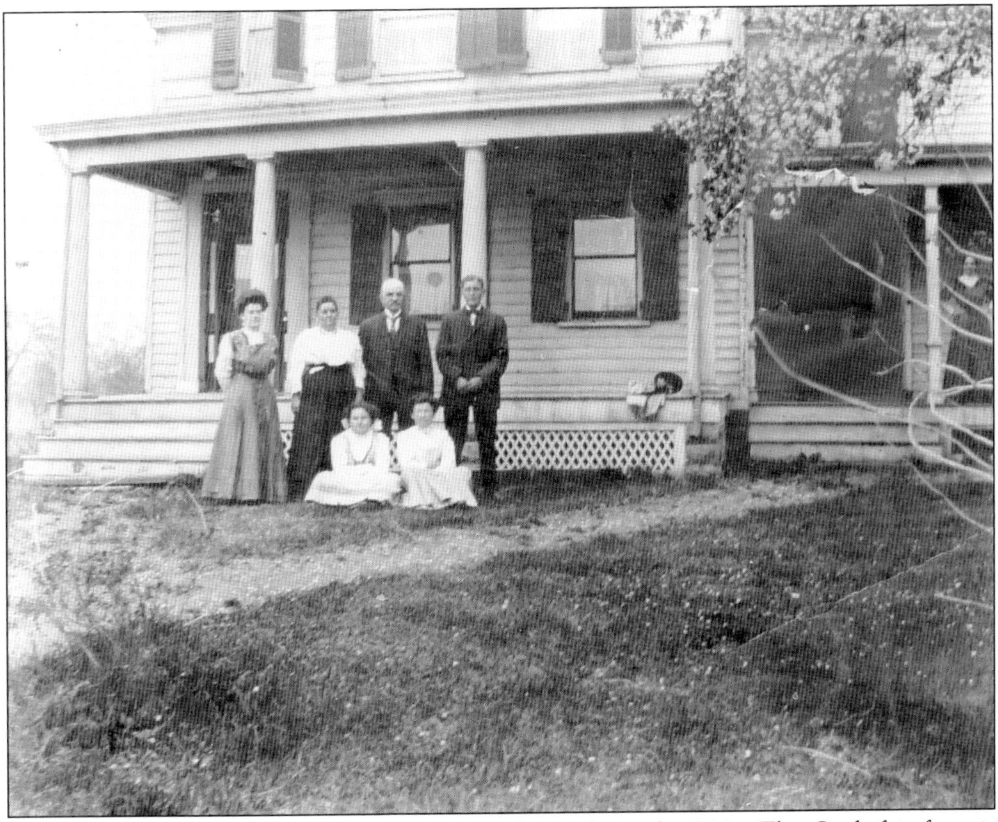

The first Cockefair house was built in Brookdale in the early 1700s. The Cockefair farm is supposed to have run from a ledge of rock in a field east of Broad Street to an oak tree near the corner of Broad Street and Watchung Avenue. In this photograph, taken around 1900, Mr. and Mrs. Alfred Cockefair and Mr. and Mrs. Sylvanus Cockefair pose in front of the homestead near Sunset Avenue, which is now gone.

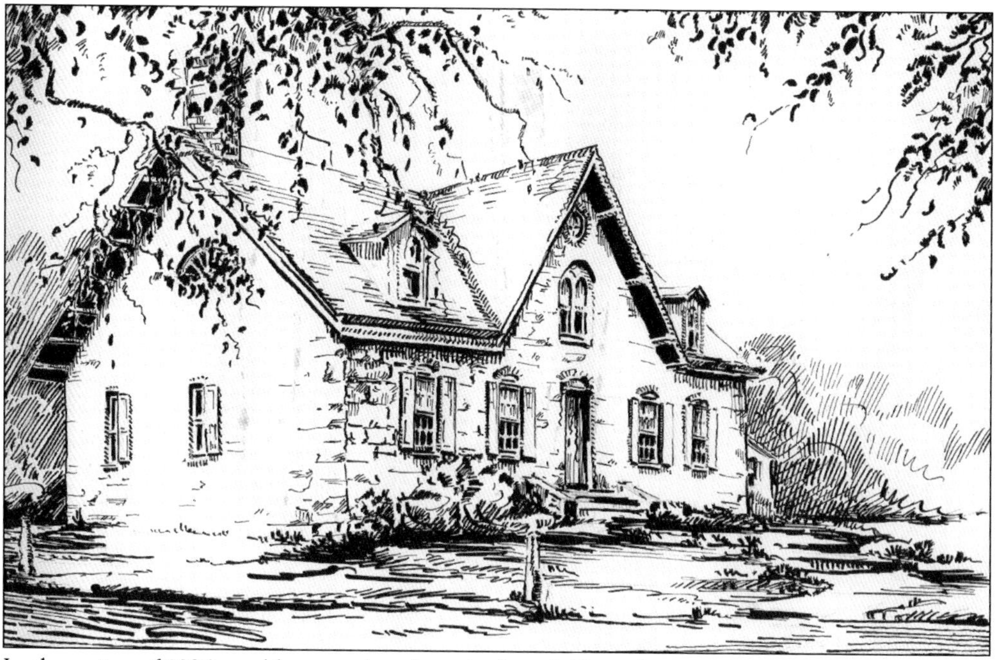

In the spring of 1936, a tablet was placed on the Joseph Davis house at 409 Franklin Street. The plaque indicated that the house was built in 1676. It was in this house that meetings were held to organize the First Presbyterian Church, and it was in this house that Gen. Joseph Bloomfield was received on the occasion of his visit here in 1797. (Drawing by Herbert Fisher.)

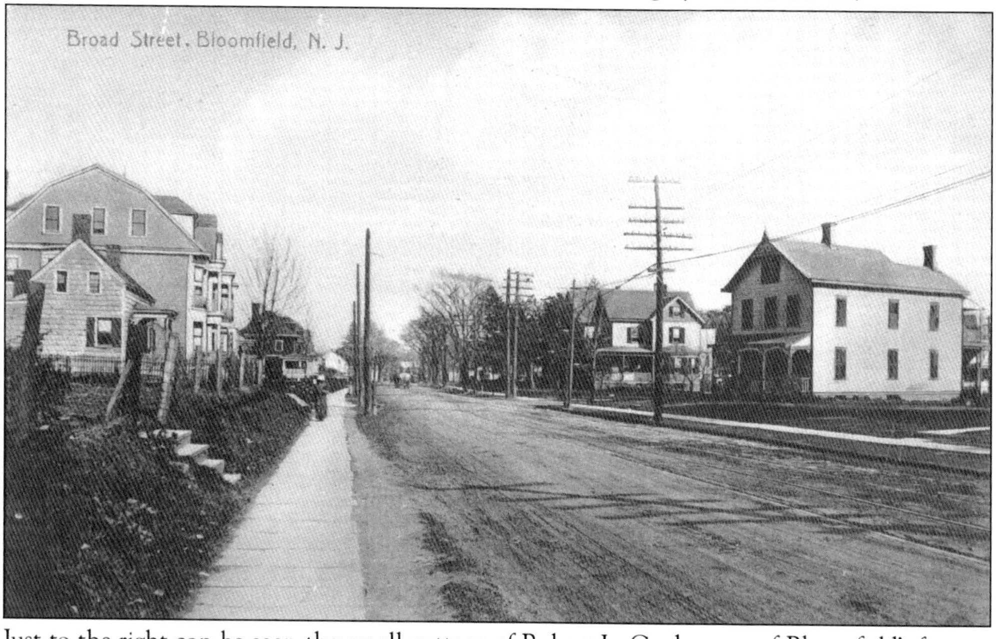

Just to the right can be seen the small cottage of Robert L. Cooke, son of Bloomfield's famous educator Harriet B. Cooke. It has since been replaced by an early-20th-century development, Broad Terrace. The large residence to the right, owned by Robert Orr in 1906, still stands near the corner of Almira and Broad Streets. The Nevada diner and parking lot occupies the property just beyond.

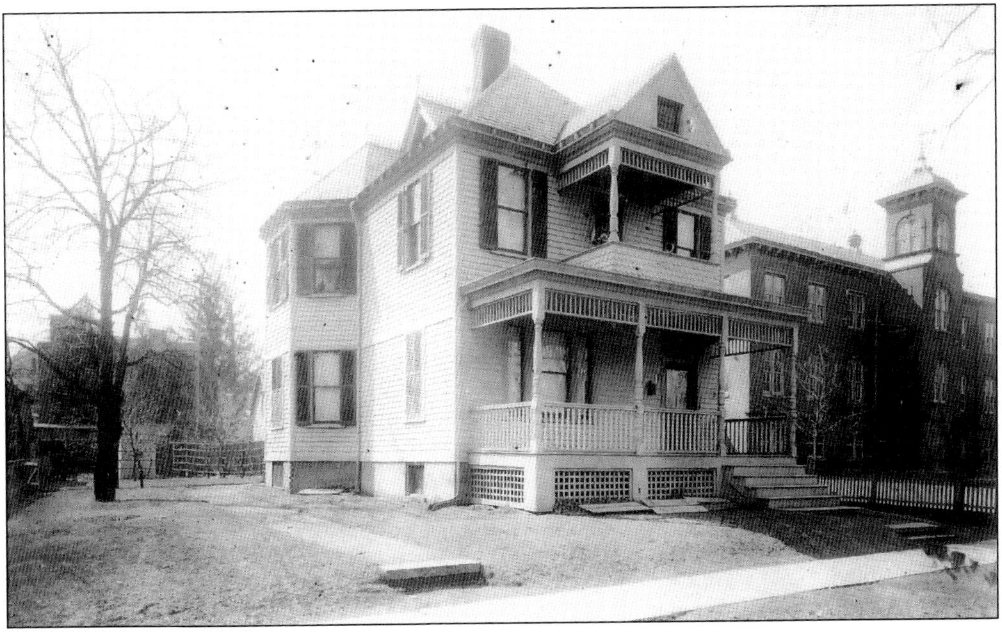

The *Bloomfield Citizen* wrote in 1887, "A new house and attic cottage, representing a very neat appearance, is going up on Belleville Avenue, next to the public school building. The owner is Frank M. Hinkle, who intends to occupy it as his residence when completed." The architect and builder was George W. Cadmus. Cadmus was a descendant of the original settlers.

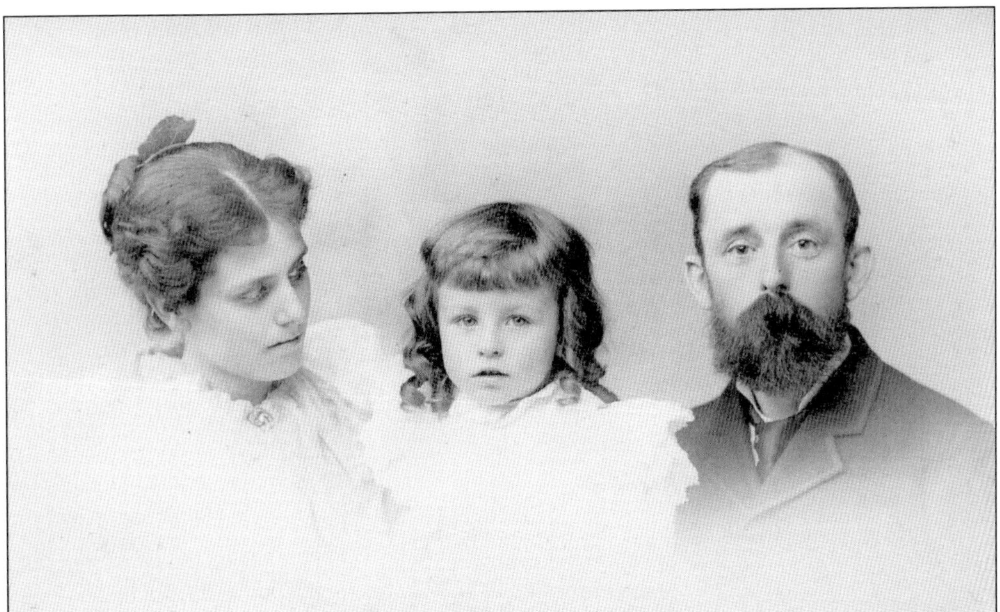

Frank Hinkle (right), Minerva Cadmus Hinkle (left), and their son, Edgar, were photographed in 1895. Minerva's father, architect George Cadmus, built their home on land belonging to William Cadmus. After the death of her husband Frank, Minerva married Elia Ewan. She and her son are buried with her first and second husbands in adjoining Hinkle-Ewan plots in Bloomfield Cemetery.

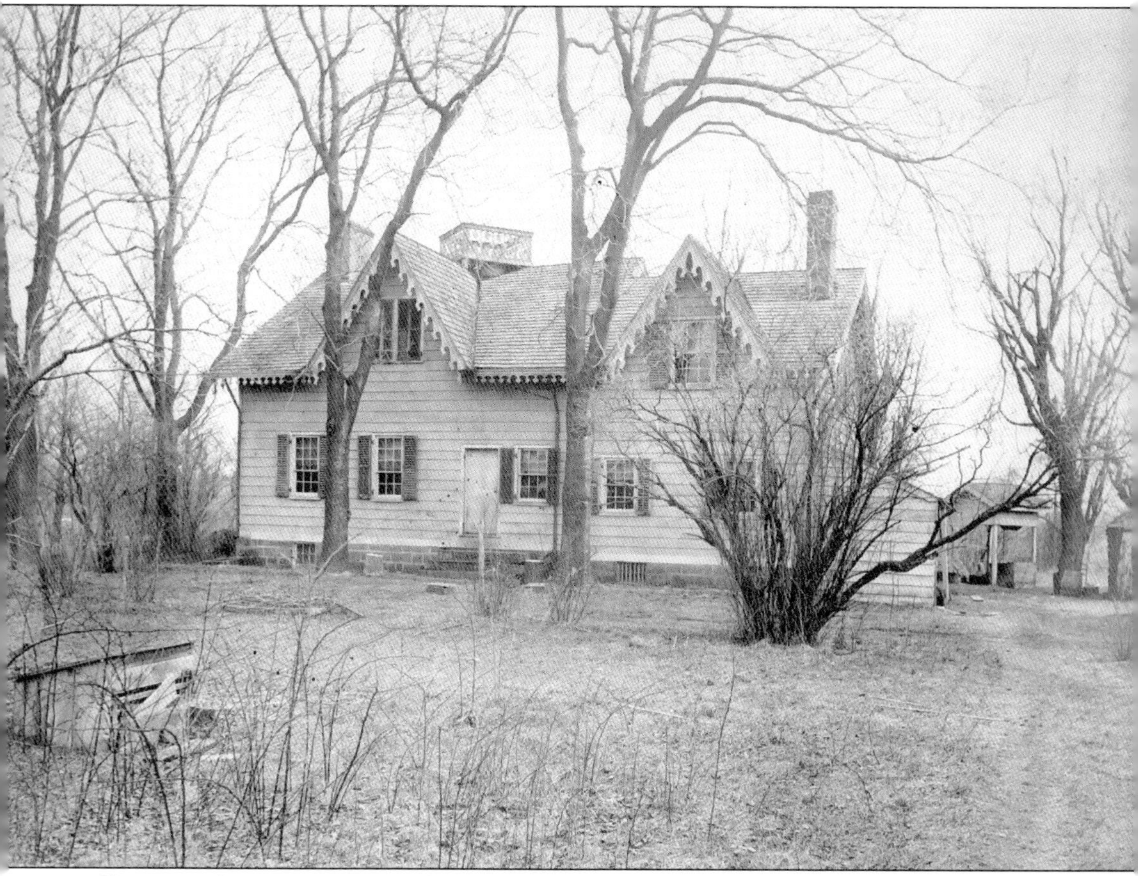

Shown on the 1856 map as Dodd property, these houses from the early 1800s had become the home of J. B. Robinson by 1888. They were located at the corner of Bloomfield and Watsessing Avenues, now the site of the Job Haines home. They were removed around 1900, when they obstructed the modern improvement of Bloomfield Avenue.

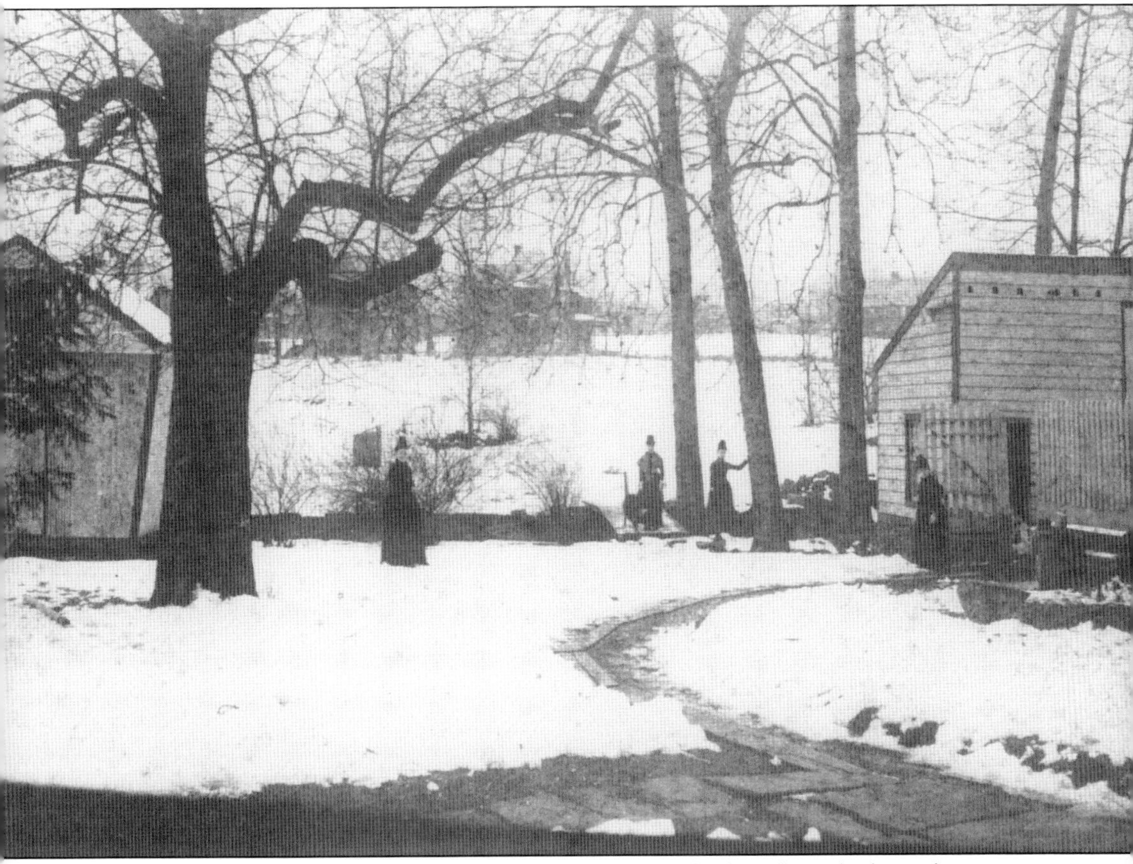

Several members of the Bromley family are shown in their backyard overlooking the property of Rev. J. S. Gallagher. The small wooden bridge right of center spanned Tony's Brook, the boundary line of the Cadmus property. The Gallagher residence is seen in the background. Clark Street was at one time the entrance to this estate. Although built in Bloomfield, this property became part of the new town of Glen Ridge in 1895.

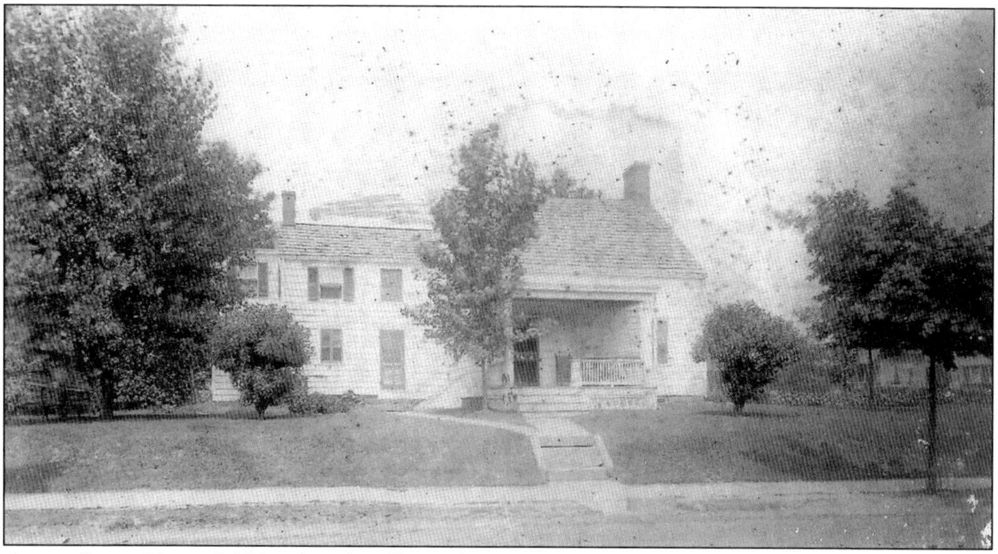

A significant Bloomfield landmark still standing on Broad Street, although encroached on both sides by business enterprises, is the old Ball house, which dates from the 1700s. Isaac Ball gave five acres of the burying ground, the first part of the present 20-acre Bloomfield Cemetery, to the Presbyterian Society about 1796. A second floor has been added to the right-hand side since the early 1900s.

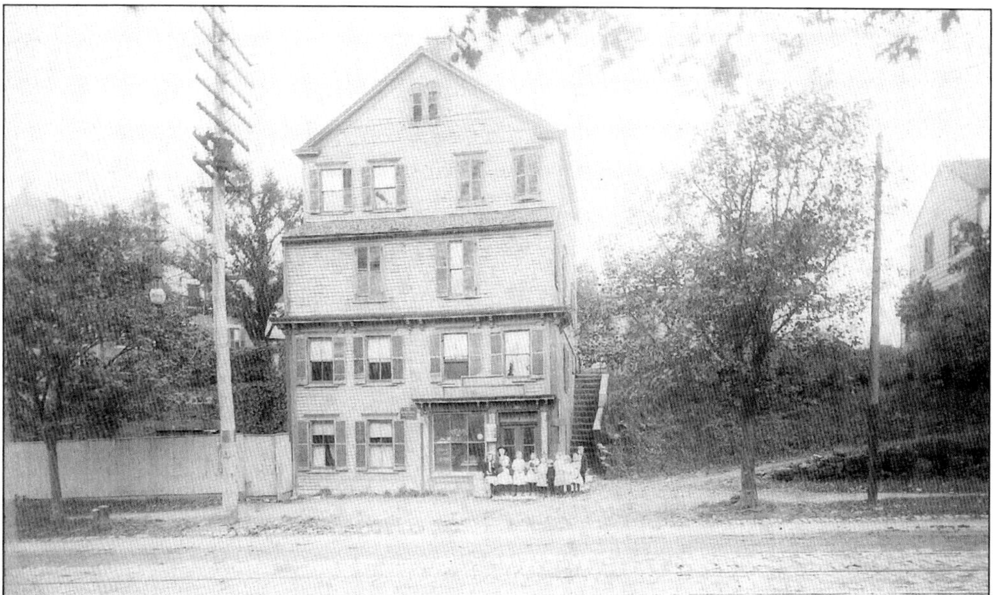

In 1891, grading machines were tested in preparation for the leveling of some streets that were considered traffic hazards. A troublesome intersection was the corner of Bloomfield Avenue and Dodd Street. A building near this corner was left high and dry when the grade level was dropped about 20 feet, so two stories were inserted under the old structure. The original ground level can be seen in the background.

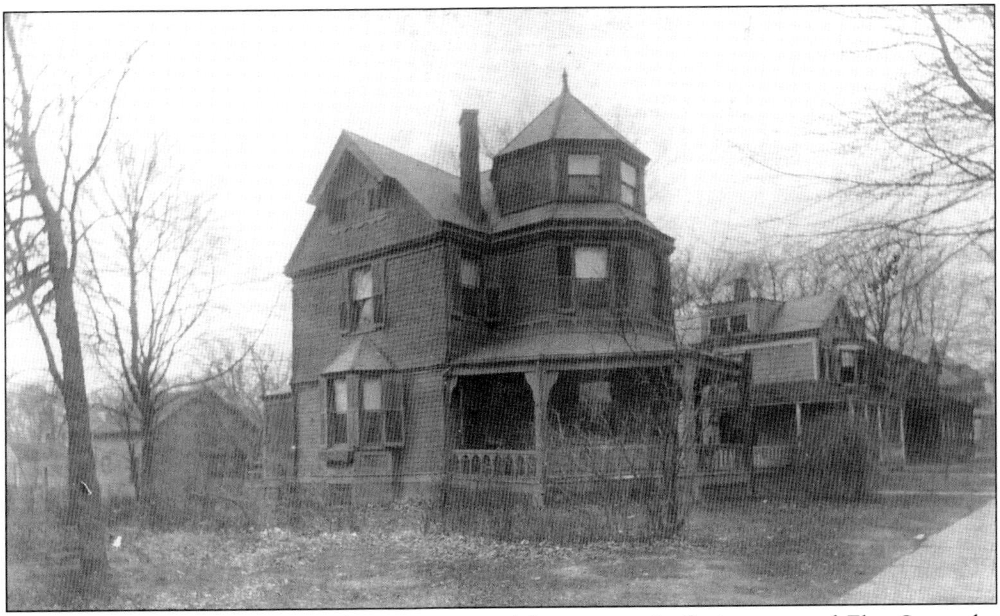

Dating from 1886, this unusual semi-octagonal house was built just east of Elm Street by Richards Kingsland Schuyler, a cousin of the noted Revolutionary War general Phillip Schuyler. Two other Schuyler houses can be seen on the right side of the photograph. In the 1920s, four modern houses were built on the former Bourne property, and this side of the house, which was recently restored, is no longer visible.

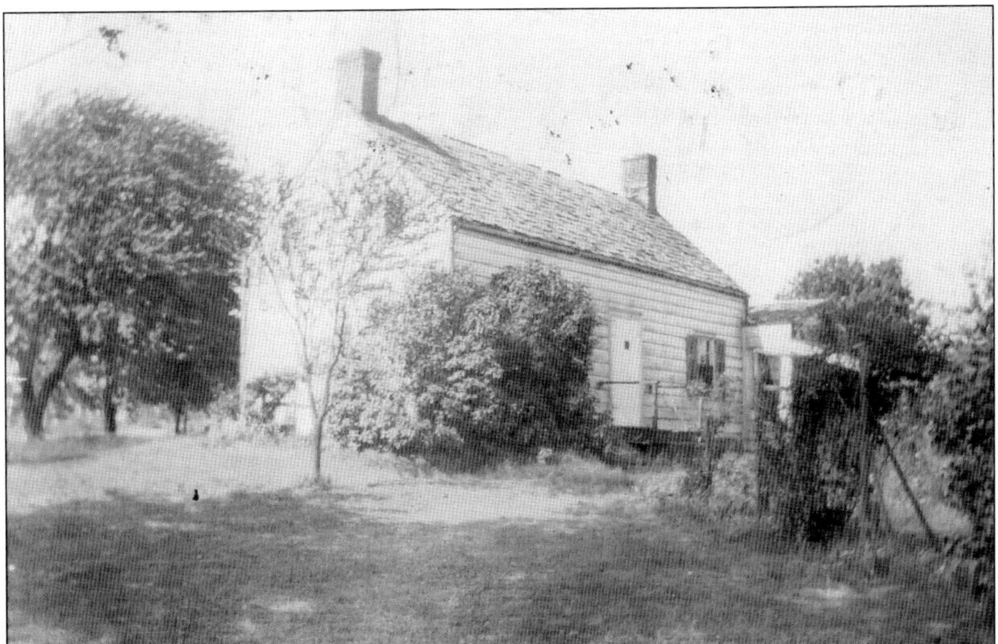

Here is the old Powelson house at 595 East Passaic Avenue that was built before the Revolution and was one of many homes in the area raided by the British. The name Powelson is an English derivation of the Dutch patronymic for "the son of Paul." At one time, there was a well in front of the house, but this was covered over when sewers were installed in the area.

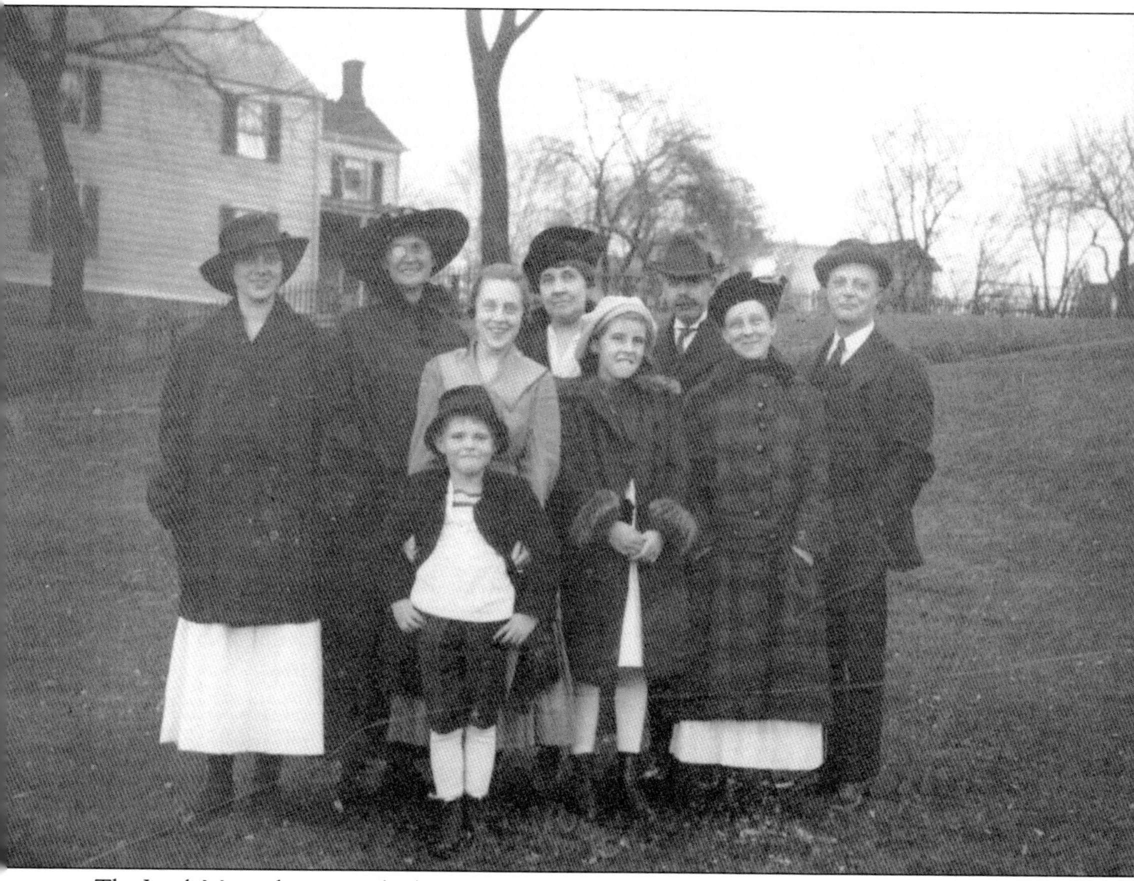

The Jacob Morris house was built in 1822 on a portion of the old Morris plantation, which covered several acres in the Bay Avenue area. The Third River flowed gently by. Farther north were the Morris mills, the dams, and the millponds. The house was torn down in 1960 to make way for a group of apartment buildings. Here descendants of the family posed on the lawn in 1917.

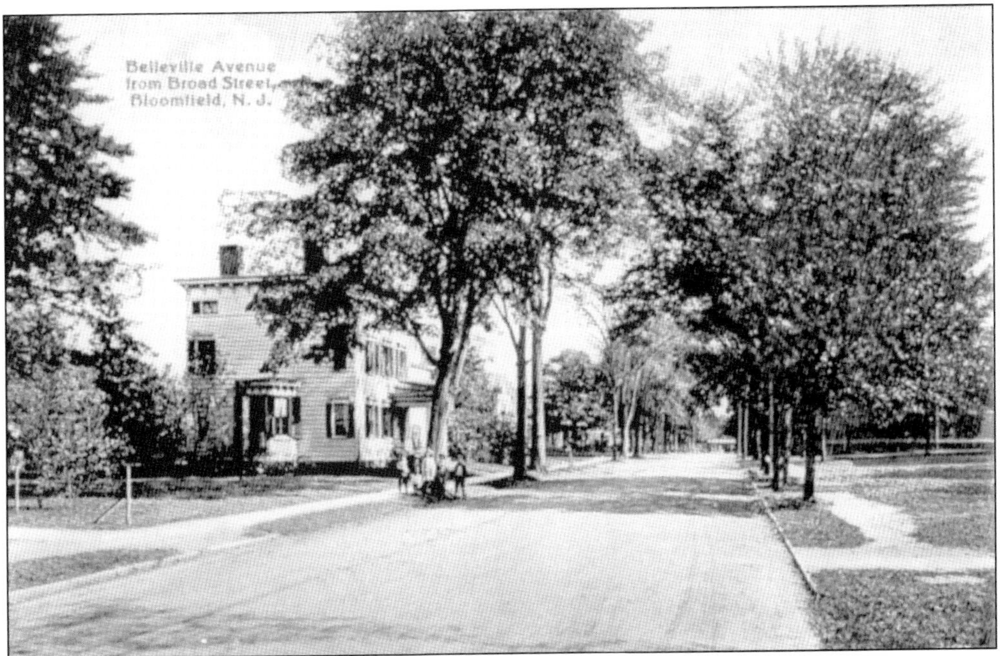

The large house to the left is the 1850s addition to the 18th-century Baldwin-Bradbury house, still standing today. The large vacant lot on the northwest corner is now occupied by a four-story brick apartment house. The grounds of the 1875 high school, built from designs by architect Joseph Kingsland Oakes are across the street. The Erie Railroad bridge is in the distance.

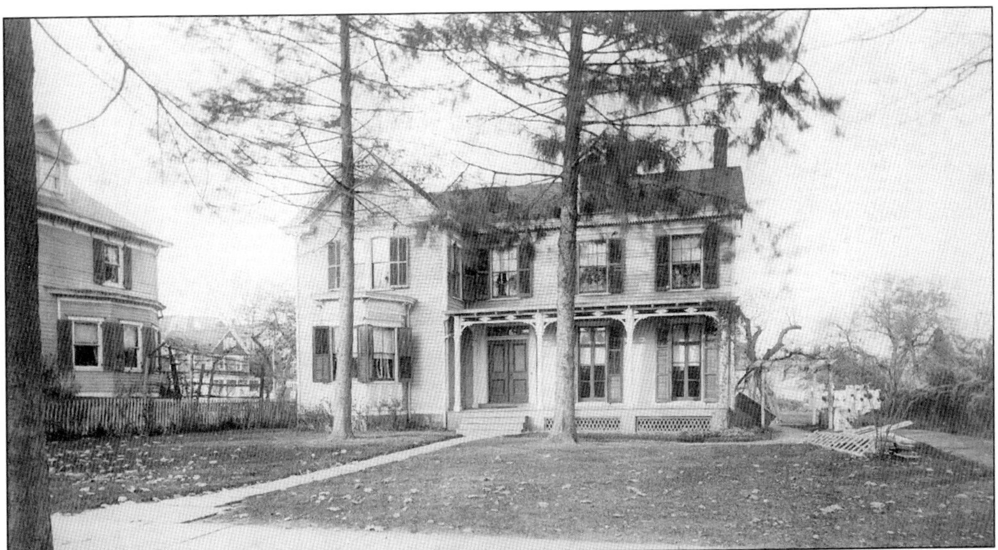

A house at 63 Park Avenue is shown as it appeared in 1910. The information on the photograph says, "old but comfortable." It is believed to have been designed by architect George W. Cadmus around 1880. The house to the left is still standing. There is a trio of four-story brick apartments to the right that date from the mid-1920s when developers came to Park Avenue.

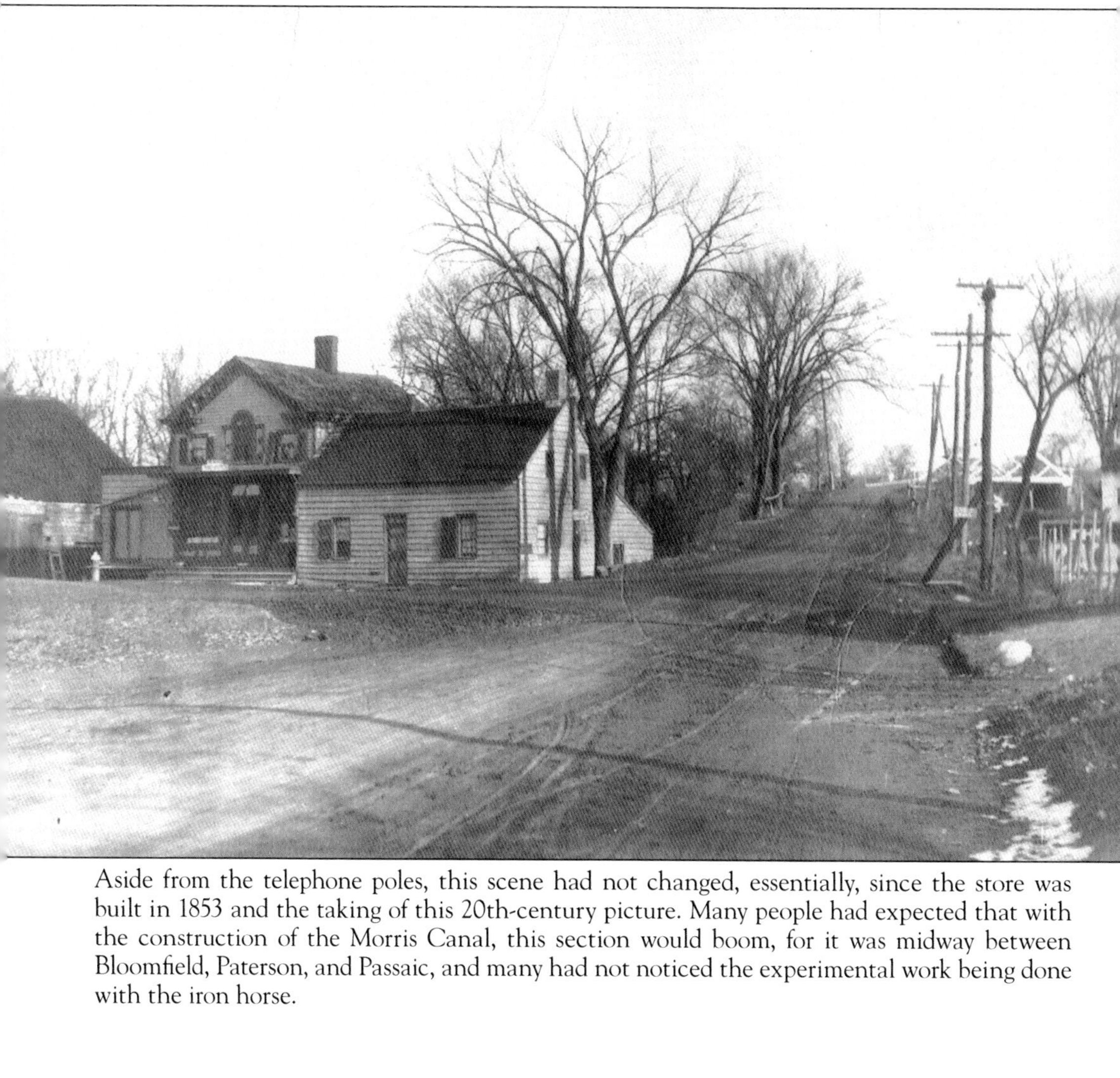

Aside from the telephone poles, this scene had not changed, essentially, since the store was built in 1853 and the taking of this 20th-century picture. Many people had expected that with the construction of the Morris Canal, this section would boom, for it was midway between Bloomfield, Paterson, and Passaic, and many had not noticed the experimental work being done with the iron horse.

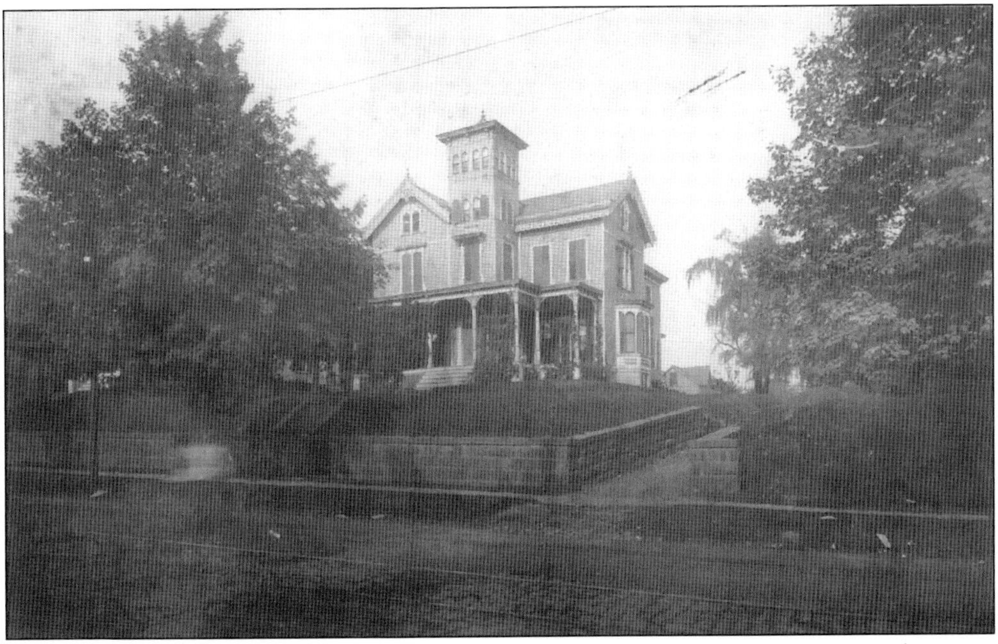

One of the most imposing residences in town was the Italianate Hampson home at 271 Bloomfield Avenue. Its tower had been modeled on the mid-19th-century Osborne house on the Isle of Wight. James Hampson was in the hat business with Samuel Ellor and was connected with Mayor George Peterson and the Dahl family of Peloubet Street. Although the house was demolished around 1941, the stone retaining wall remains today.

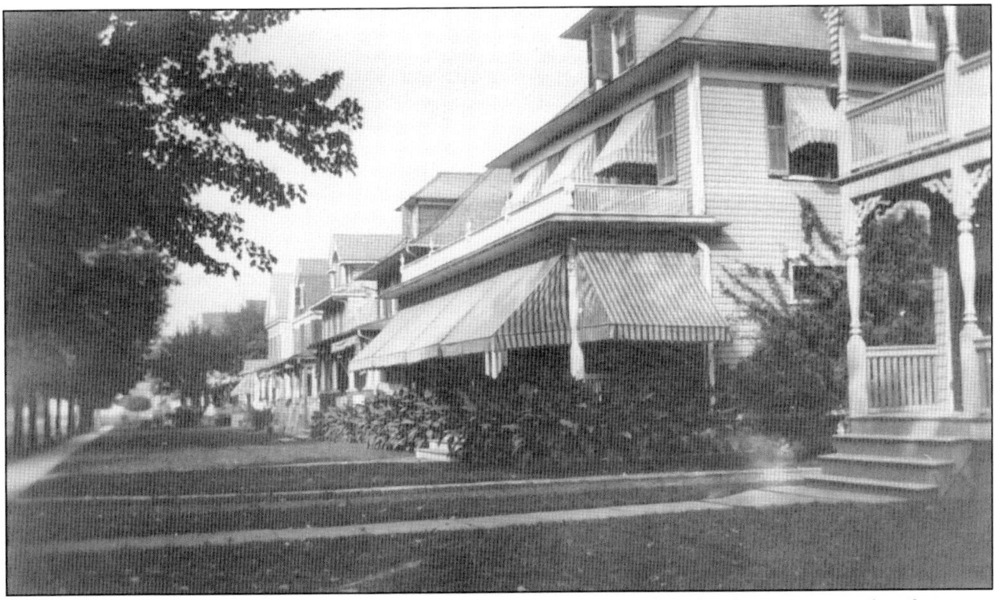

Before the days of air-conditioning, it was necessary to swathe the house in yards of canvas awnings to control the heat. William Keyler, proprietor of the old Scherff's Drugstore and local undertaker, owned this handsome establishment at 163 Thomas Street. He obviously appreciated ornamental plants, surrounding his front porch with unusual plantings. The house still stands today, without awnings, which seem to have entirely disappeared from Bloomfield.

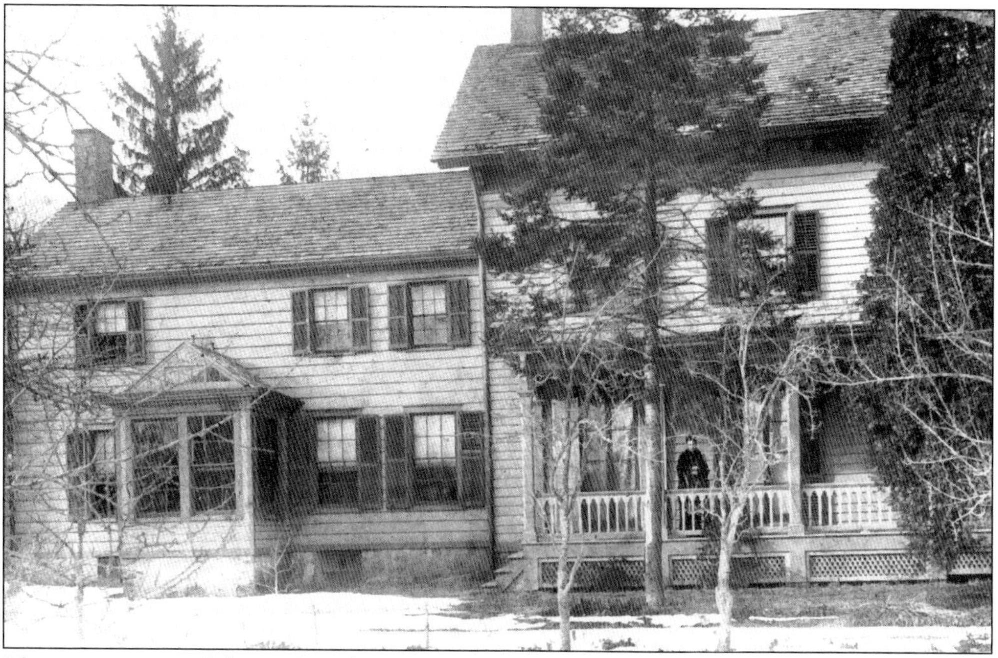

The rear section of the Cadmus/Bromley house on Bloomfield Avenue is believed to be the 18th-century portion of the house. The larger 19th-century addition, toward the right, may have been designed by architect Joseph Kingsland Oakes, who lived directly across Bloomfield Avenue. The last surviving relative of Rosetta Bromley Westlake moved out of the home in the early 1900s, after which it was abandoned.

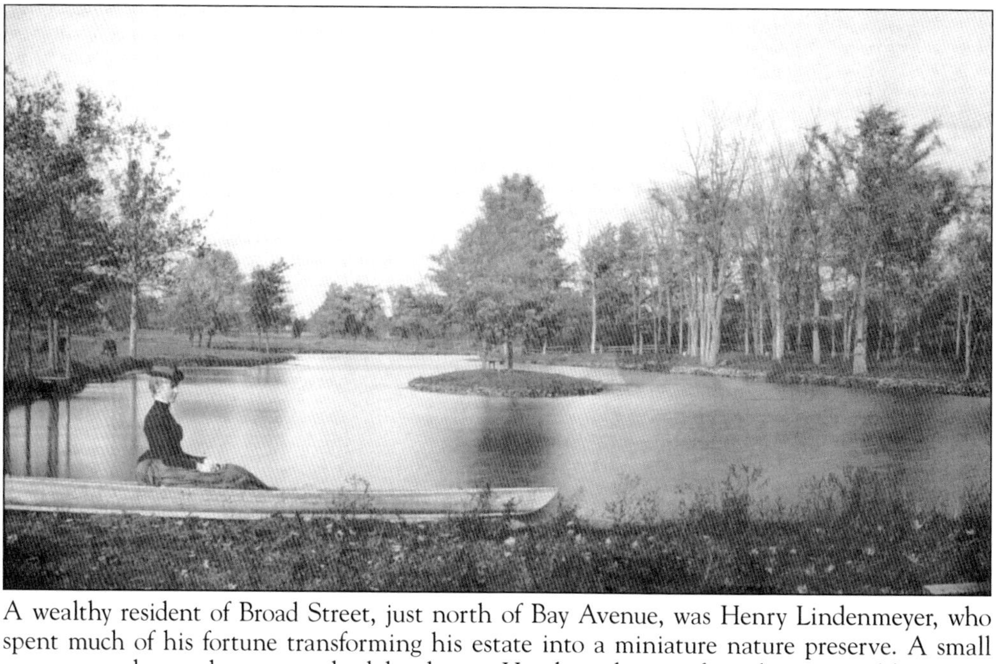

A wealthy resident of Broad Street, just north of Bay Avenue, was Henry Lindenmeyer, who spent much of his fortune transforming his estate into a miniature nature preserve. A small stream was dammed to create the lake shown. He planted rows of maple trees and his estate became a bird sanctuary. With the march of progress, all of this has disappeared. (Courtesy of the New Jersey Historical Society.)

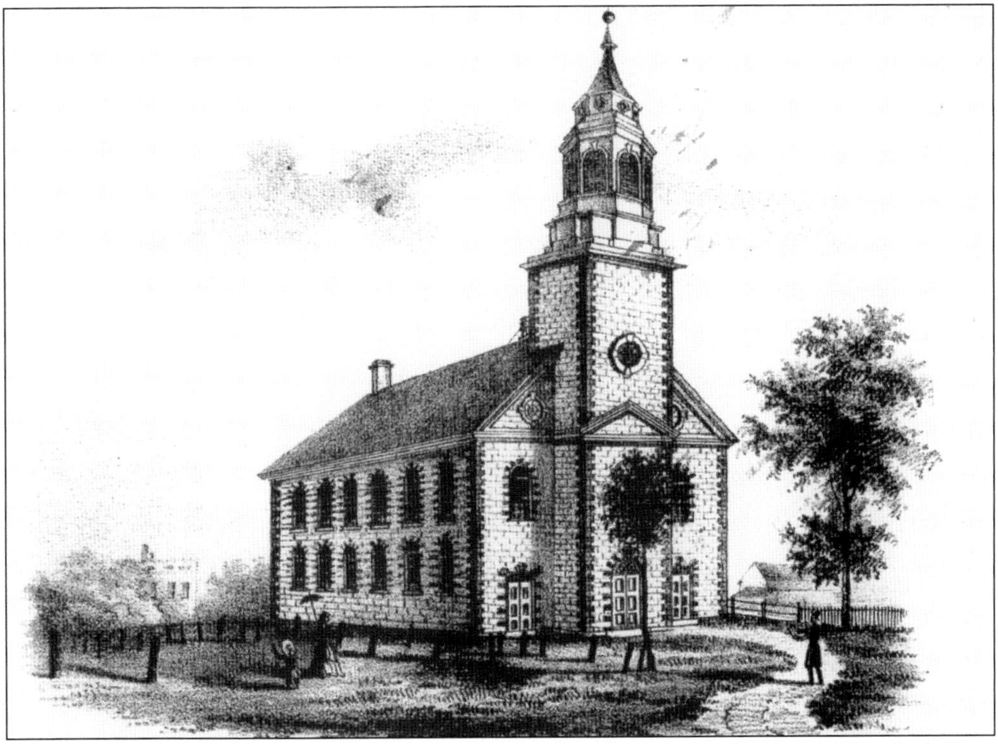

Of Bloomfield's many houses of worship, the original is the First Presbyterian Church, known as the "Old First Church on the Green." Just 18 years after the Revolutionary War, the New York Presbytery granted permission for organization of a church in the township. The spirit of patriotic pride succeeding the Revolution led the congregation to honor Gen. Joseph Bloomfield by choosing his name, calling its church the Presbyterian Society of Bloomfield.

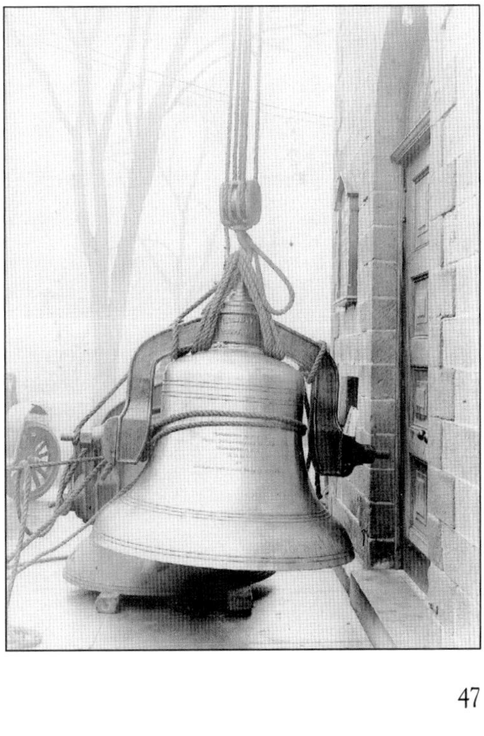

The same patriotic spirit inspired a successful campaign to purchase land fronting the church. Church building began on a knoll facing the field that soon became known as the common or the green. Old First was constructed of brown freestone, and the mortar that cemented it was purchased with Gen. Bloomfield's gift of $140. The 1930 photograph captures the occasion when the church prepared to raise a new bell.

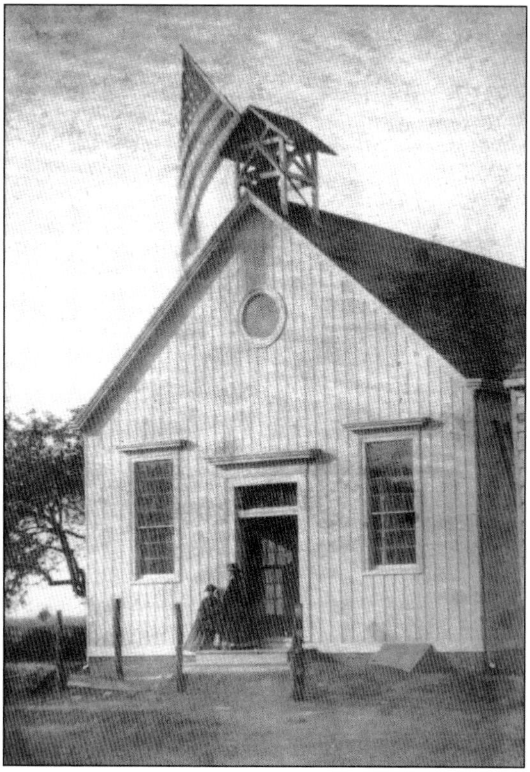

In 1851, thirteen Baptist Church members got together to form the First Baptist Church. This 1864 photograph shows one of their temporary places of worship, Franklin Hill School. Financial stress did not stop them from engaging ministers and building a structure near Watsessing Lake. In 1910, the beautiful present church was built. (Courtesy of the New Jersey Historical Society.)

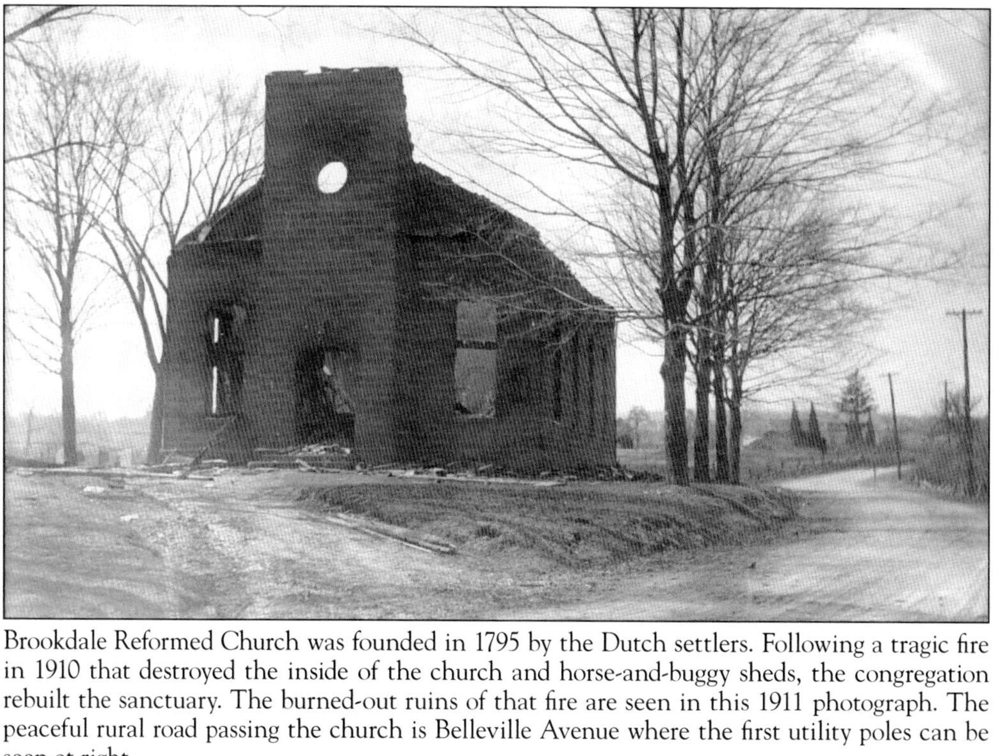

Brookdale Reformed Church was founded in 1795 by the Dutch settlers. Following a tragic fire in 1910 that destroyed the inside of the church and horse-and-buggy sheds, the congregation rebuilt the sanctuary. The burned-out ruins of that fire are seen in this 1911 photograph. The peaceful rural road passing the church is Belleville Avenue where the first utility poles can be seen at right.

The Watsessing United Methodist Church or the "Little Church in the Woods" was dedicated in 1872. In 1924, fire destroyed the parish hall, but the determined congregation rebuilt the following year. For many years, Watsessing has been represented in the Methodist hymnal by "Diadem," composed by townsman James Ellor.

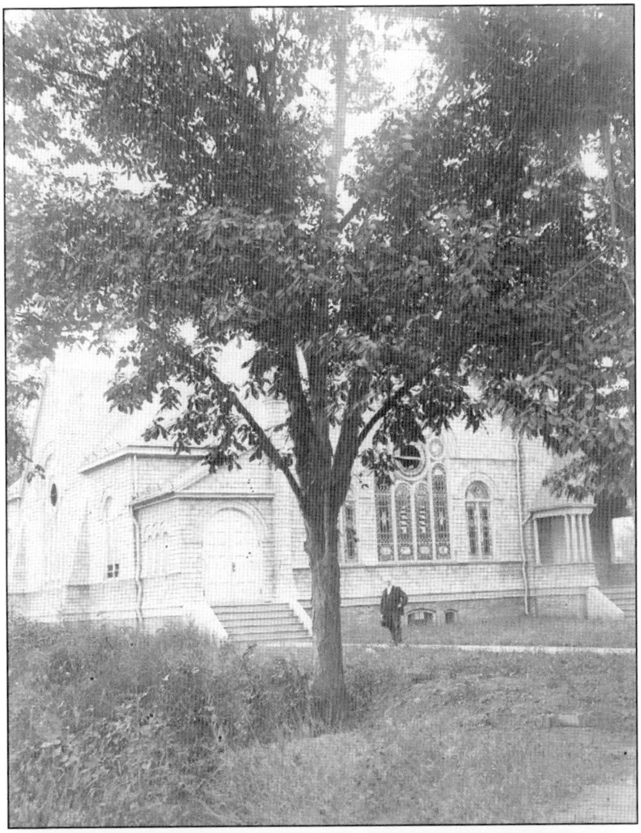

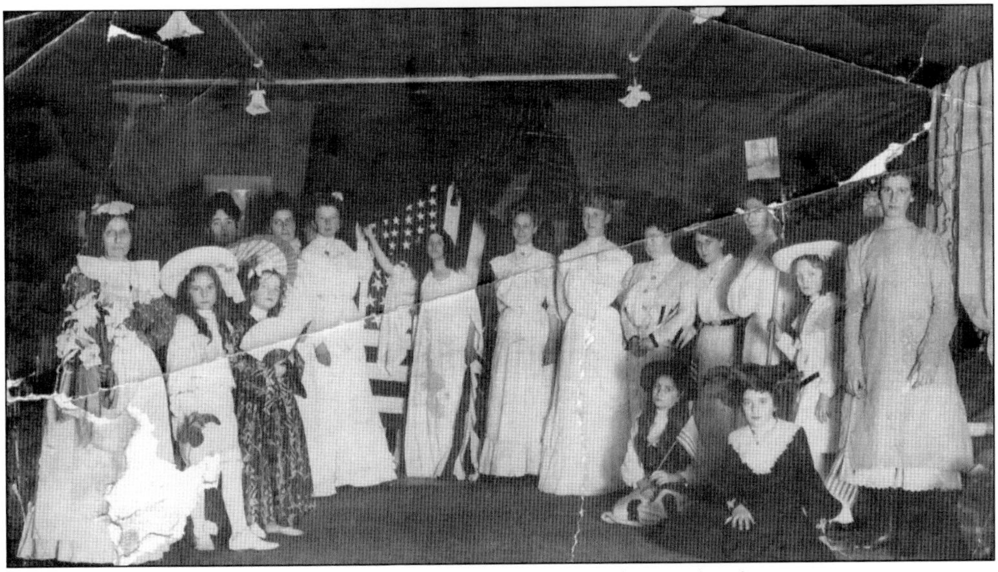

In the pre-television and cinema era, people were required to make their own entertainment, and Bloomfield's churches were the scene of amateur plays and musicals. This curtain call, dated about 1907, was taken in the parish hall of the new Church of the Ascension on Montgomery Street. Built in 1902 as a parochial mission of Christ Church, it was originally lit by gas. The electric lights seen here appear to be newly installed.

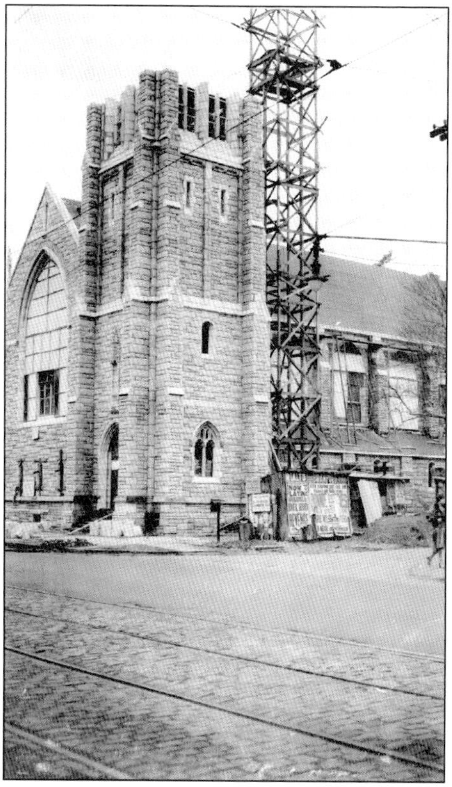

The Methodist church was founded on Bay Avenue in 1832, but the area was as yet undeveloped, and in 1853, a new site near the center of town was purchased on the west side of the green at the corner of Park Street. The brick structure, later considered unsafe, was abandoned and the present edifice of Gothic design was erected. This 1920s photograph shows the building nearly completed.

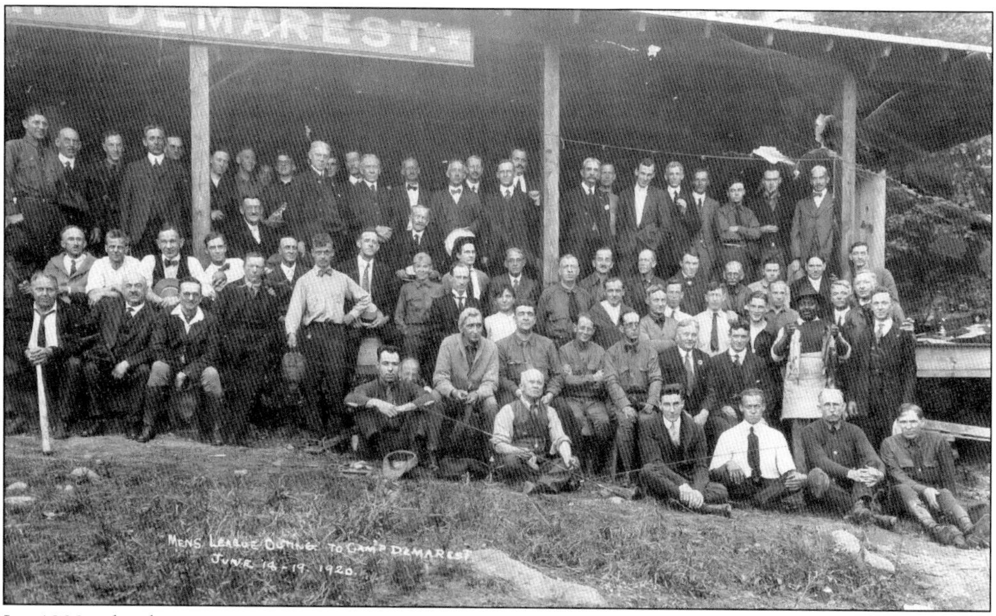

In 1892, the brownstone Westminster Presbyterian Church on the corner of Fremont and Franklin Streets was erected. Ten years later, James N. Jarvie built as a memorial to his parents the building known as Jarvie Memorial Hall, which also housed a public library. In 1920, the Men's League enjoyed an outing to Camp Demarest in Butler. Five-time mayor Charles Demarest is seated second from the left in the second row.

Sacred Heart Church, at the corner of Broad Street and Liberty Street, was dedicated in 1892, accomplished through the brilliant work of Rev. Joseph Nardiello. This 1900 print from a glass plate negative is believed to be the first taken of the Broad Street front after the church was completed. Note the gas lamp, wooden fence, and stepping stones.

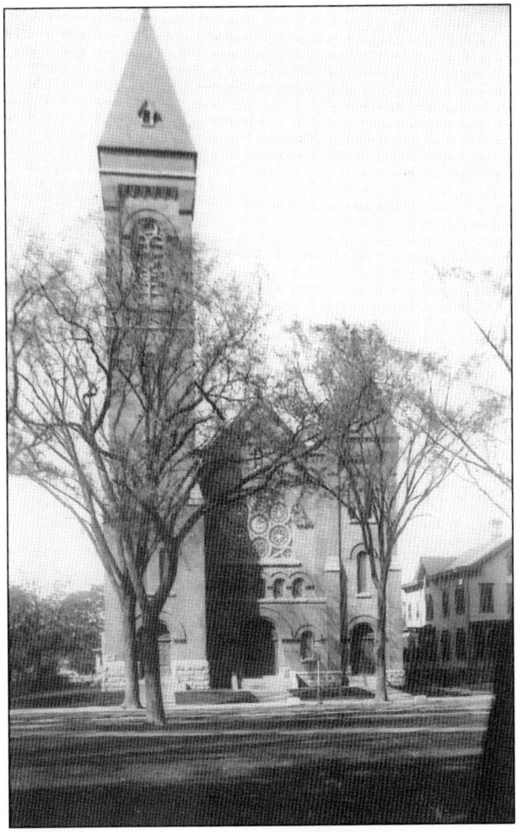

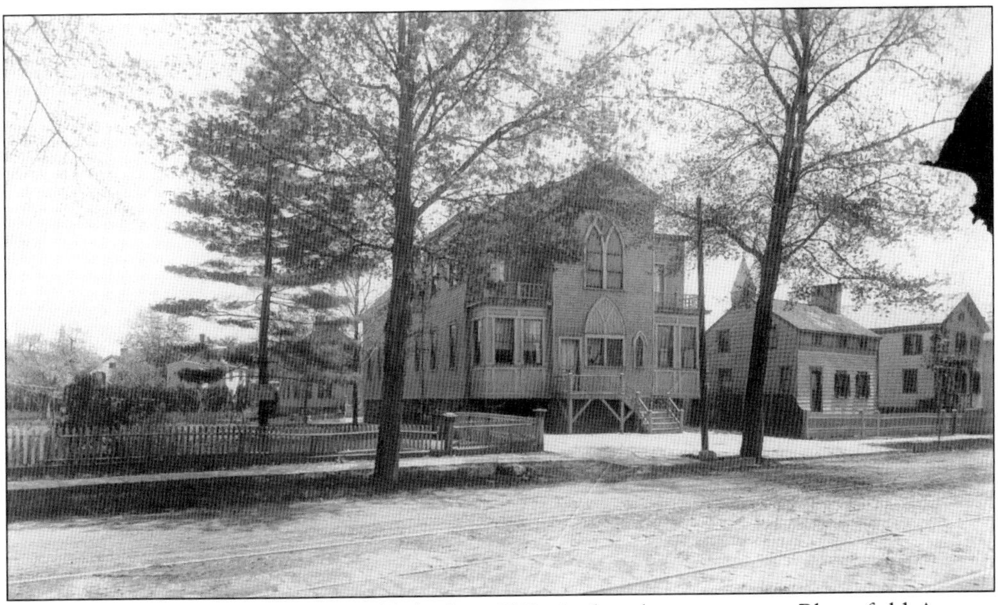

The Sacred Heart Church was established in 1878. A church structure on Bloomfield Avenue was dedicated that year. This was used until 1892 when the present church was built. At that time, the original wooden church was converted into a lyceum for the parish's young men and women. It was razed in 1922 when Sacred Heart School was erected on the property.

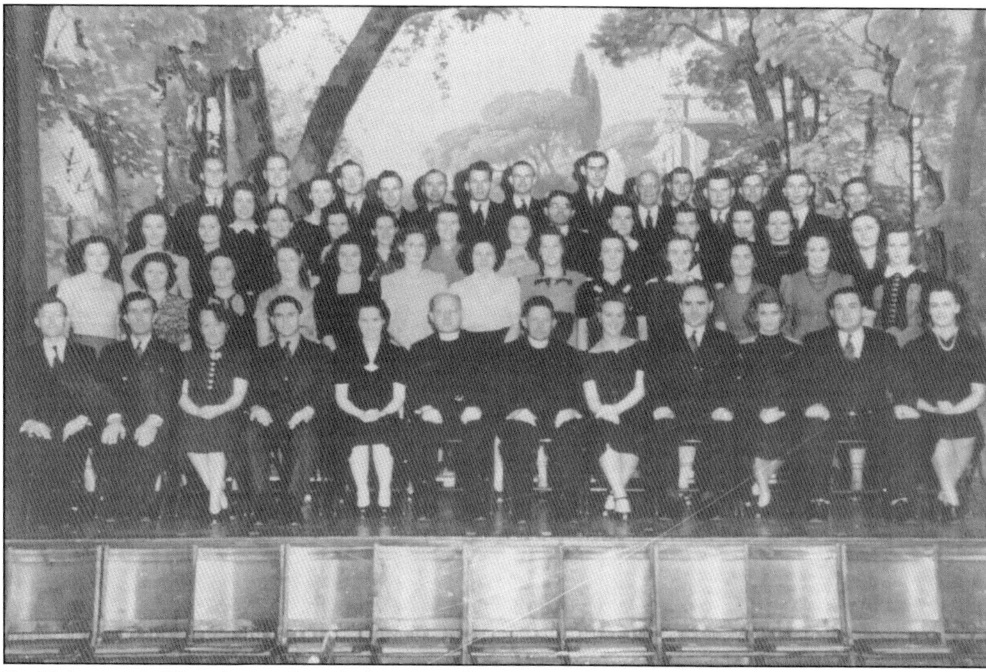

St. Valentine's Church was founded in 1898 for the nearly 100 Polish families of Bloomfield and Newark with the purchase of the Hope Chapel on Hoover Avenue. The move to its present site was made eight years later. In 1924, a school was built containing classrooms and an auditorium. It is here the church choir of 1939 poses with its director and Msgr. Bronislaus Socha.

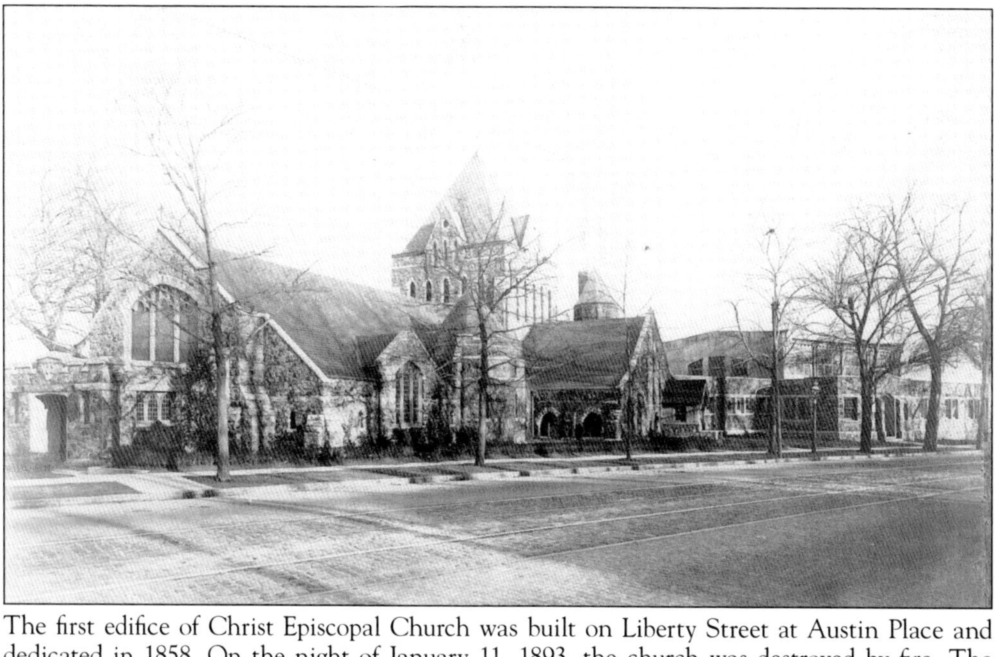

The first edifice of Christ Episcopal Church was built on Liberty Street at Austin Place and dedicated in 1858. On the night of January 11, 1893, the church was destroyed by fire. The church merged with St. Mark's Society of Glen Ridge and built its present stone structure in 1894. The photograph shows the trolley line tracks of the Newark to Caldwell route on Bloomfield Avenue.

Three

COMMERCE AND THE CANAL

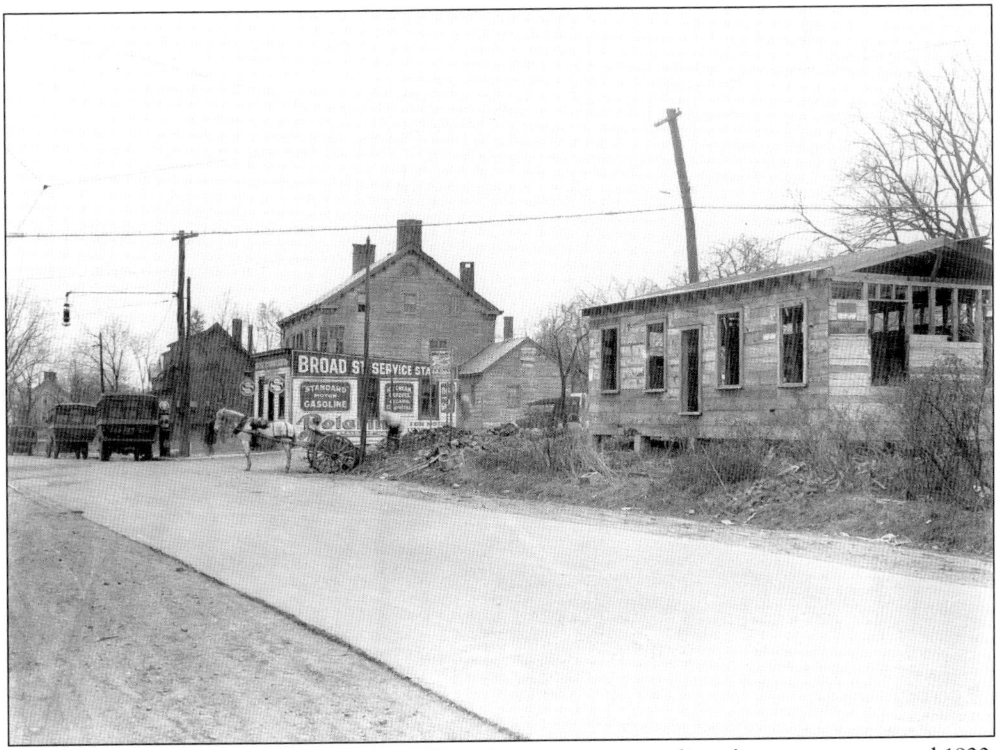

The now busy corner of Broad Street and Bay Avenue presents a dismal appearance around 1920. The large house, left of center, had been a stately residence owned by James Morris. This area had been known as the Morris neighborhood, and the family had held reunions in a nearby grove for many years. Two public service buses stand in front of the gas station at the old Morris house.

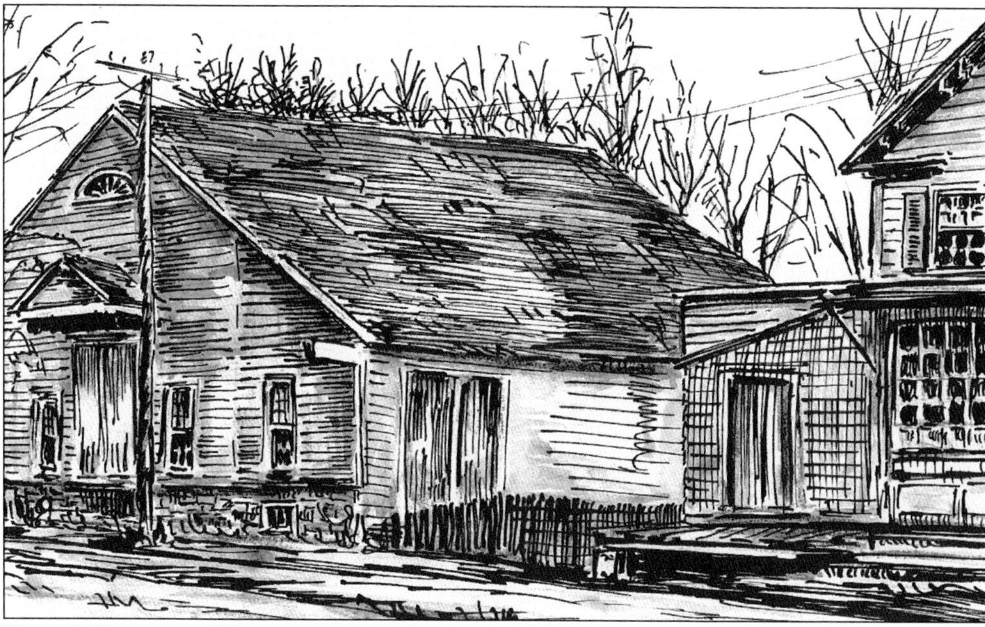

Bloomfield was a well-known cider-producing area up until almost the 20th century. There was a small cider mill on almost every farm and a distillery on every fifth or sixth. This old cider mill was built about 1820 by Tunis Garrabrant at the junction of Broad Street and West Passaic Avenue. The mill made Jersey Lightning and shipped it on the Morris Canal. (Watercolor by Herbert Fisher)

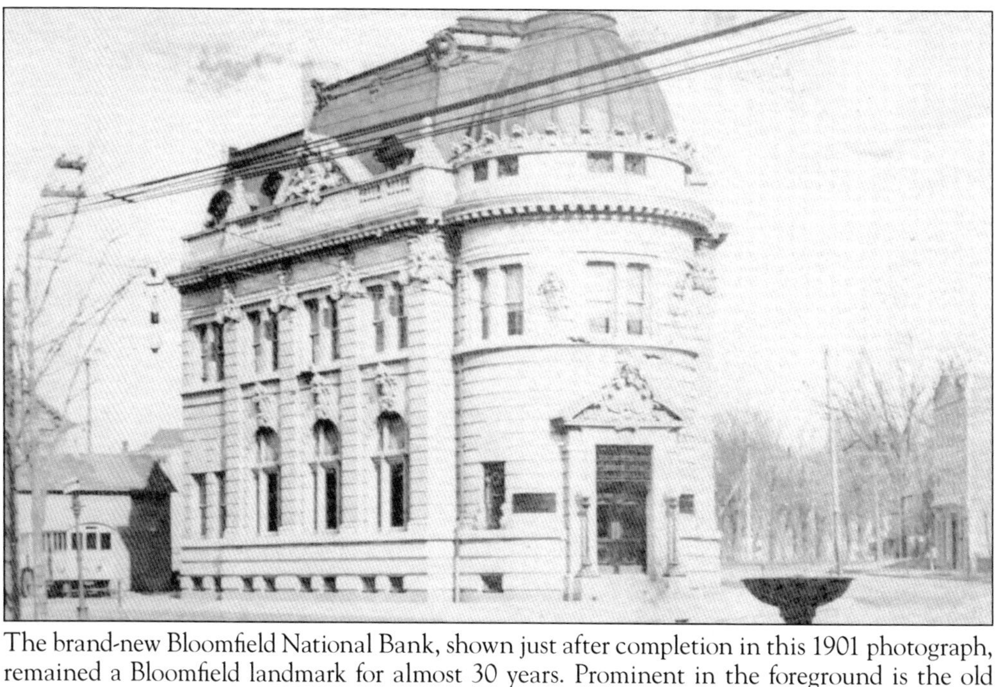

The brand-new Bloomfield National Bank, shown just after completion in this 1901 photograph, remained a Bloomfield landmark for almost 30 years. Prominent in the foreground is the old five corners watering trough, reminding one that the motive power of over a century ago was measured in real horsepower. In the background are a streetcar, the American House Hotel on Broad Street, and not a pedestrian anywhere.

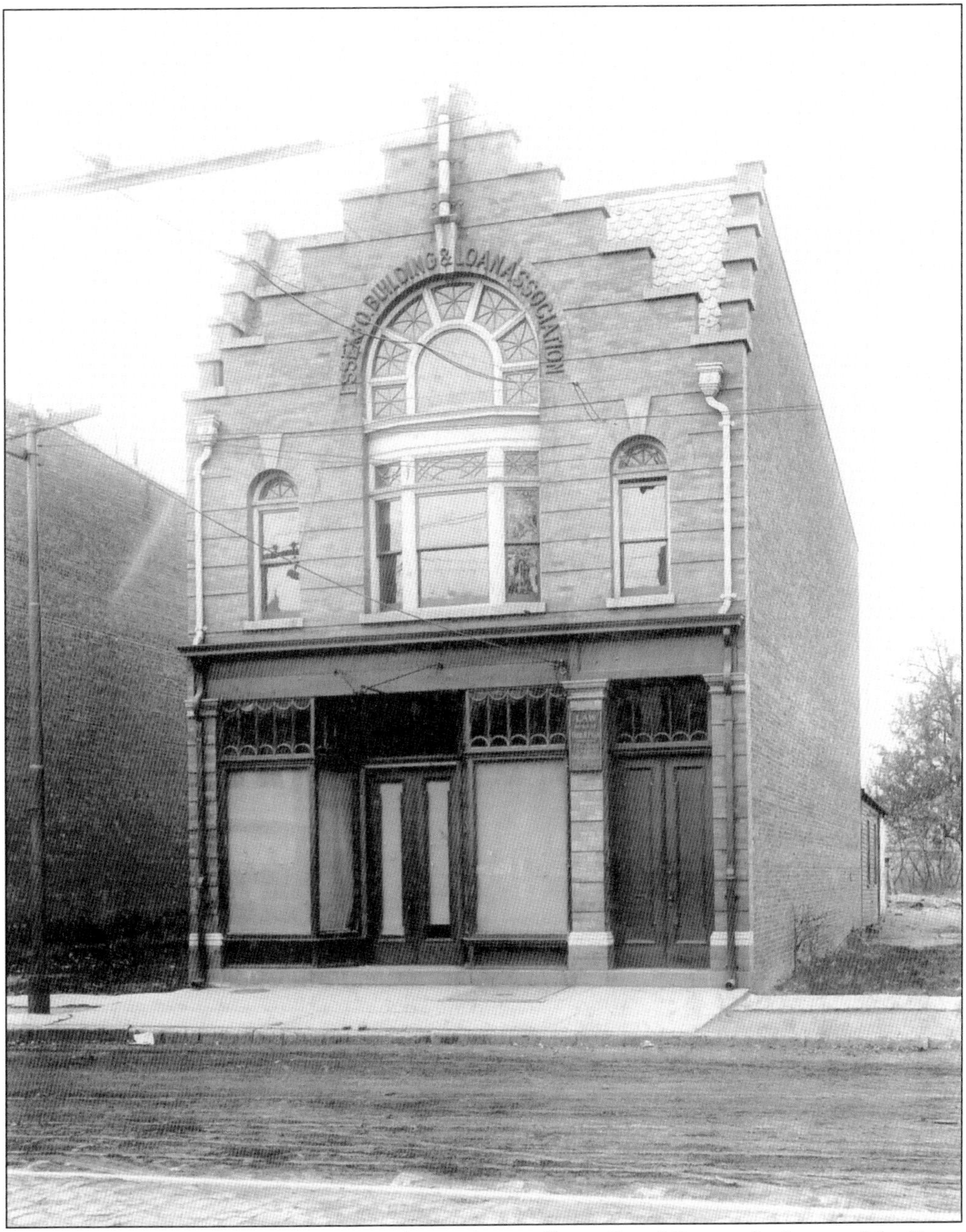

A new structure in the Romanesque style stands proudly on Broad Street: the home of the Essex Building and Loan Association. One of the organizers and the president of this enterprise was former mayor George Peterson. He emigrated from Denmark at the age of 25 and began working at the Peloubet Organ Company. The building still stands at 20 Broad Street. (Courtesy of the New Jersey Historical Society.)

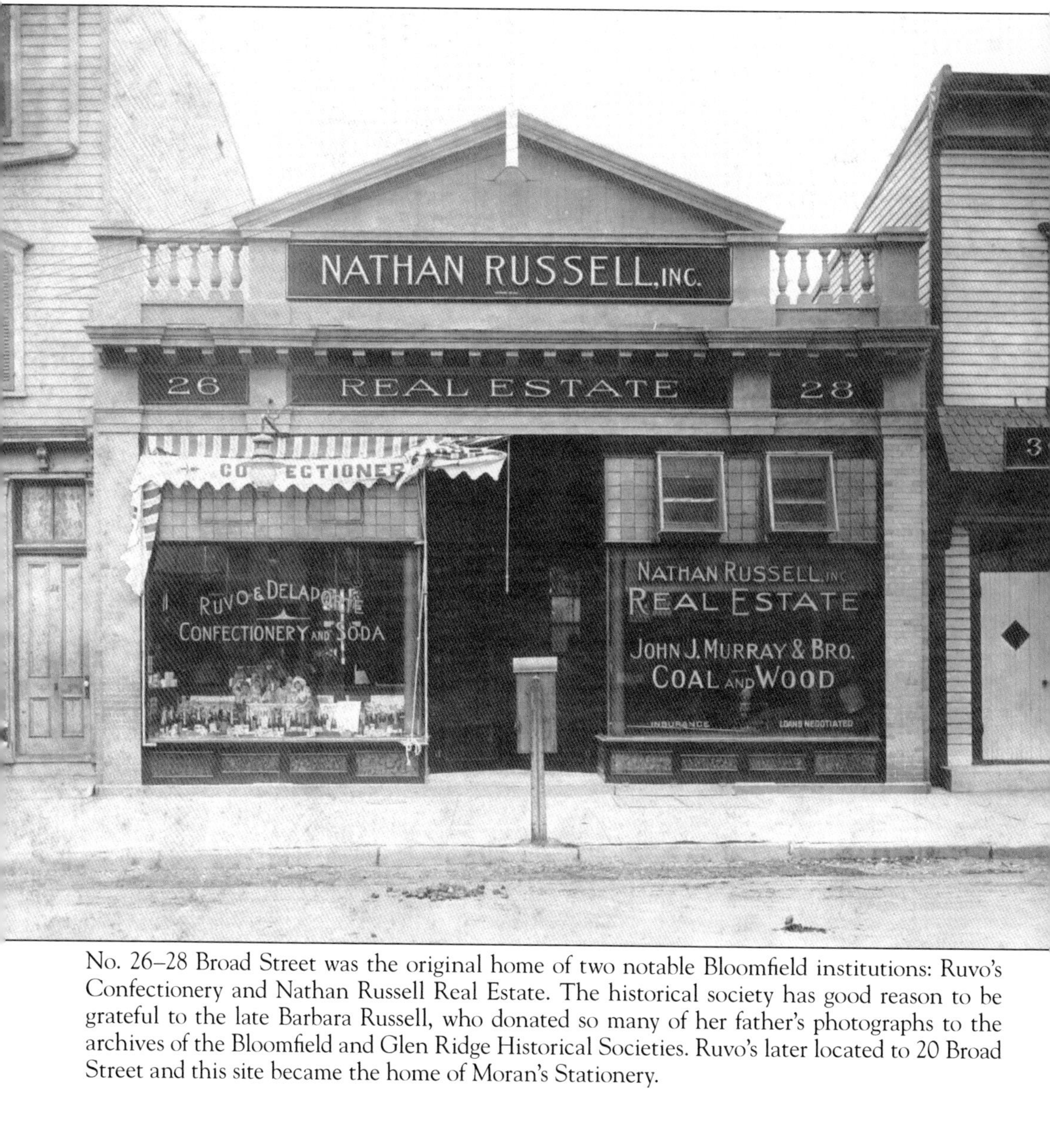

No. 26–28 Broad Street was the original home of two notable Bloomfield institutions: Ruvo's Confectionery and Nathan Russell Real Estate. The historical society has good reason to be grateful to the late Barbara Russell, who donated so many of her father's photographs to the archives of the Bloomfield and Glen Ridge Historical Societies. Ruvo's later located to 20 Broad Street and this site became the home of Moran's Stationery.

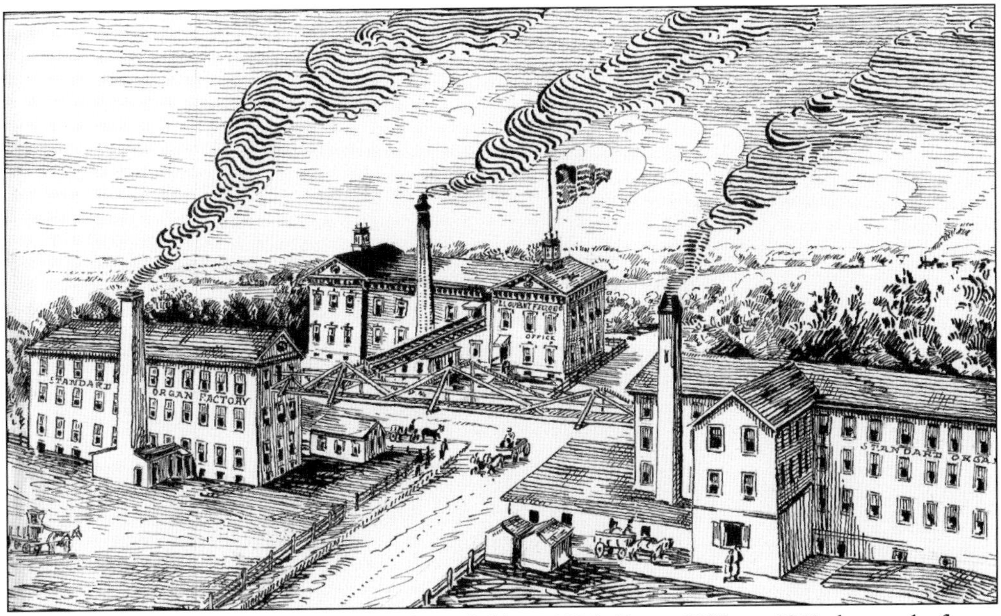

Louis Chabrier Peloubet arrived in Bloomfield in 1836. From 1837 to 1841, he made flutes, piccolos, clarinets, and other small musical instruments in Pierson's Mill on Myrtle Street. Soon after, Peloubet moved to Orange Street where he built his own factory and began to manufacture melodeons and reed organs. The largest industrial plant in town in 1883 was the Peloubet, Pelton Standard Organ Company. (Drawing by Herbert Fisher.)

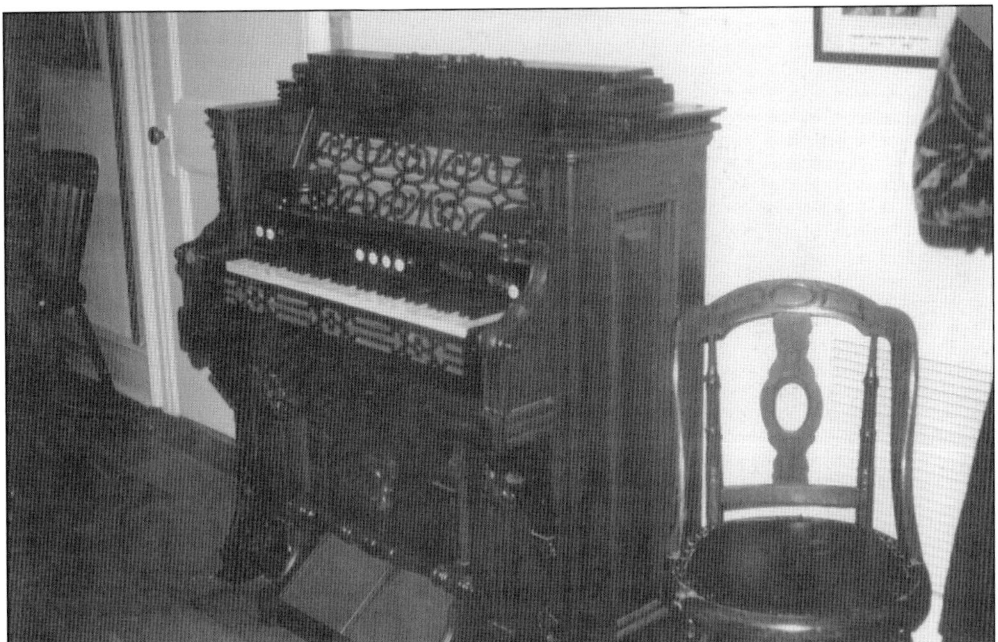

One of the earliest gifts to the new historical society museum was from Sadie Nicholl, whose father, James Nicholl, worked at the Peloubet factory and may have had a hand in the creation of this instrument. The derelict organ was completely renovated at the expense of Sadie Nicholl. Repairs included a new bellows and replacement of missing reeds and lost ivory keys.

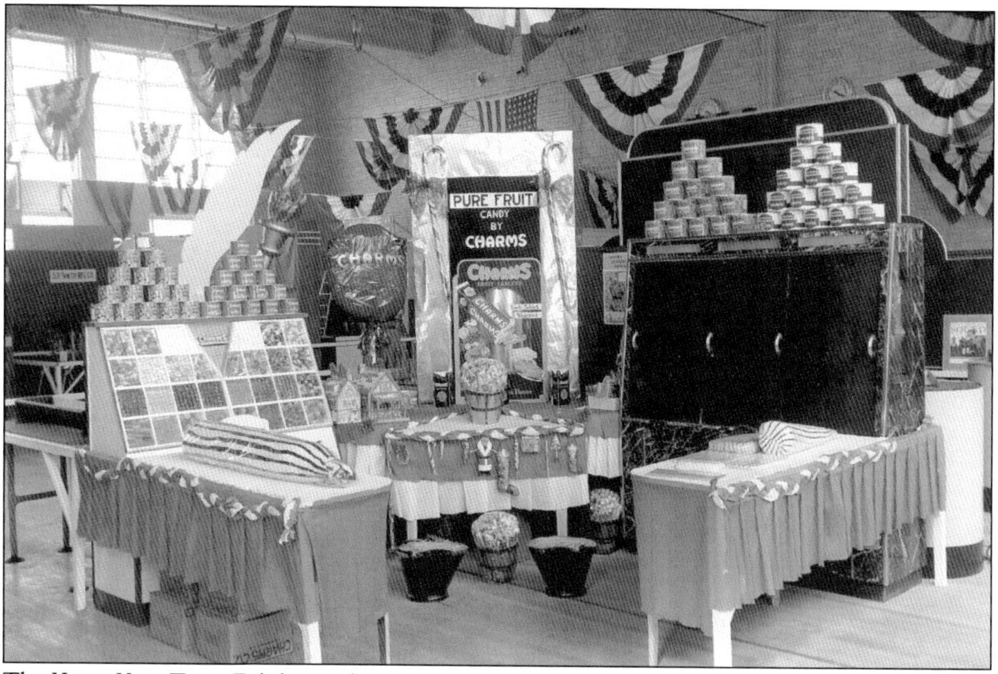

The Know Your Town Exhibit in the new 1939 junior high school featured displays of Bloomfield's leading industries, of which there were many. One of the favorites with both kids and adults was the Charms Candy Company on Bloomfield Avenue at Grove Street, which produced 50,000 pounds of the sweet stuff every day. The company relocated to a new plant in Freehold in 1973 and is now in Tennessee.

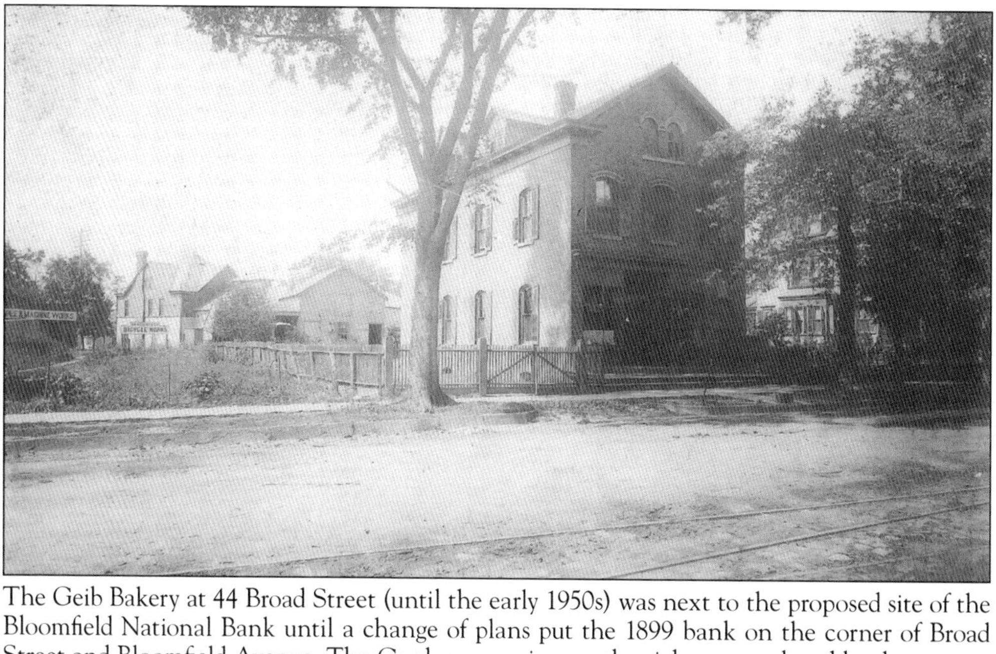

The Geib Bakery at 44 Broad Street (until the early 1950s) was next to the proposed site of the Bloomfield National Bank until a change of plans put the 1899 bank on the corner of Broad Street and Bloomfield Avenue. The Gardner mansion on the right was replaced by the present Park Building (once the home of Lipton's) in the 1920s. The buried trolley tracks often reappear during street repairs.

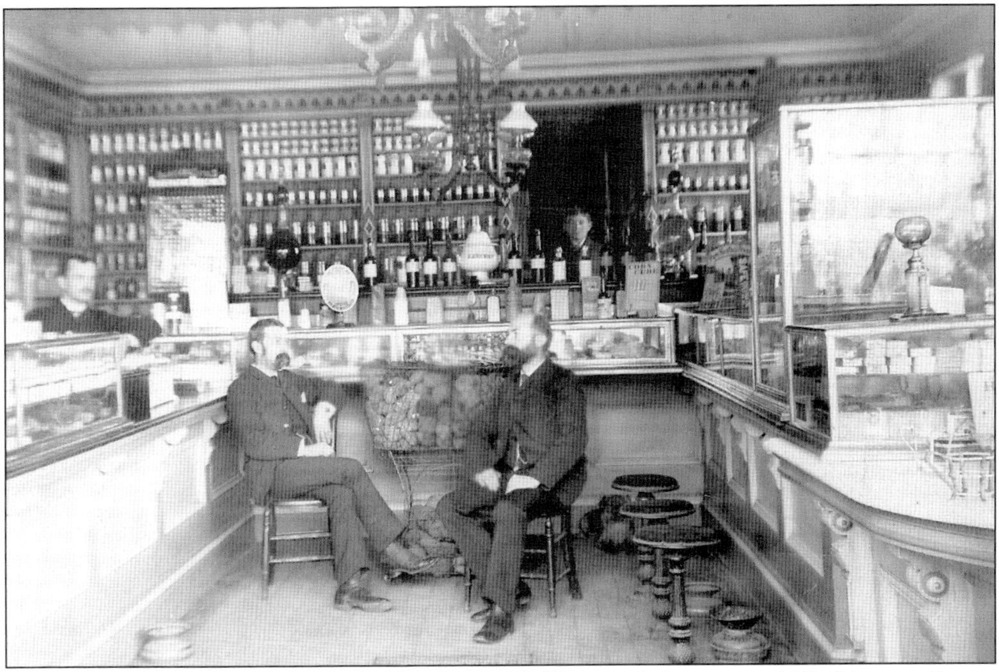

Located for more than 100 years at the corner of Glenwood Avenue and Washington Street, Scherff's Drugstore was a Bloomfield Center landmark. In this photograph, dated 1882, one can see jars of drugs that were compounded to the doctor's prescription by the skilled hands of the proprietor. There were also leeches for erasing black eyes from Saturday night donnybrooks at Bloomfield Avenue and Orange Street. The "gaslights" are oil lamps.

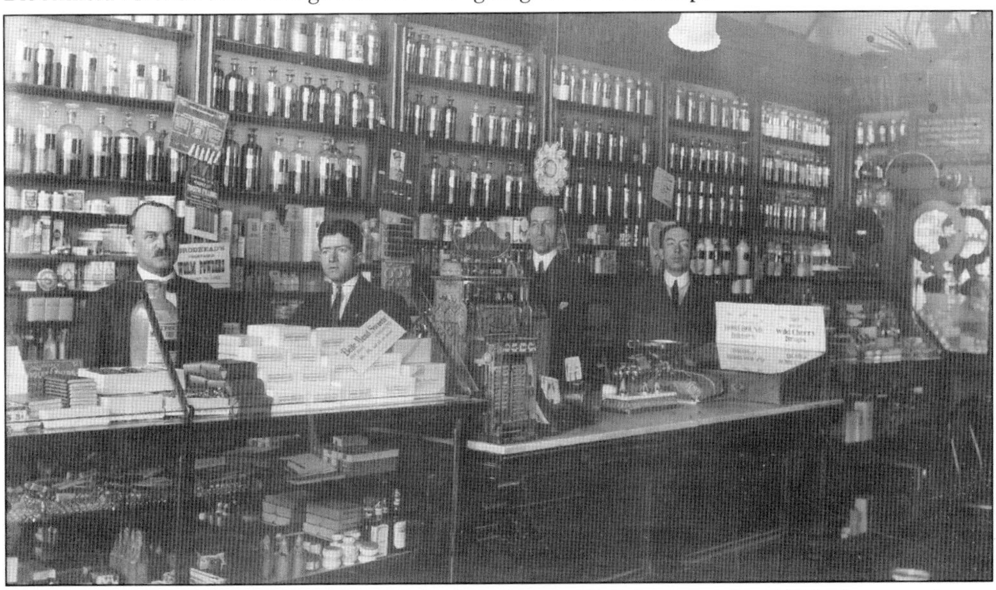

The passing of almost 30 years has made few changes. By the time this 1908 photograph was taken, Scherff's became Keyler's. The rows of jars are the same, customers (now clean shaven) are different. It is possible that the gentleman nearest the camera is Keyler himself, who lived within walking distance at 163 Thomas Street, and there is a big improvement: electric lights have come to Bloomfield.

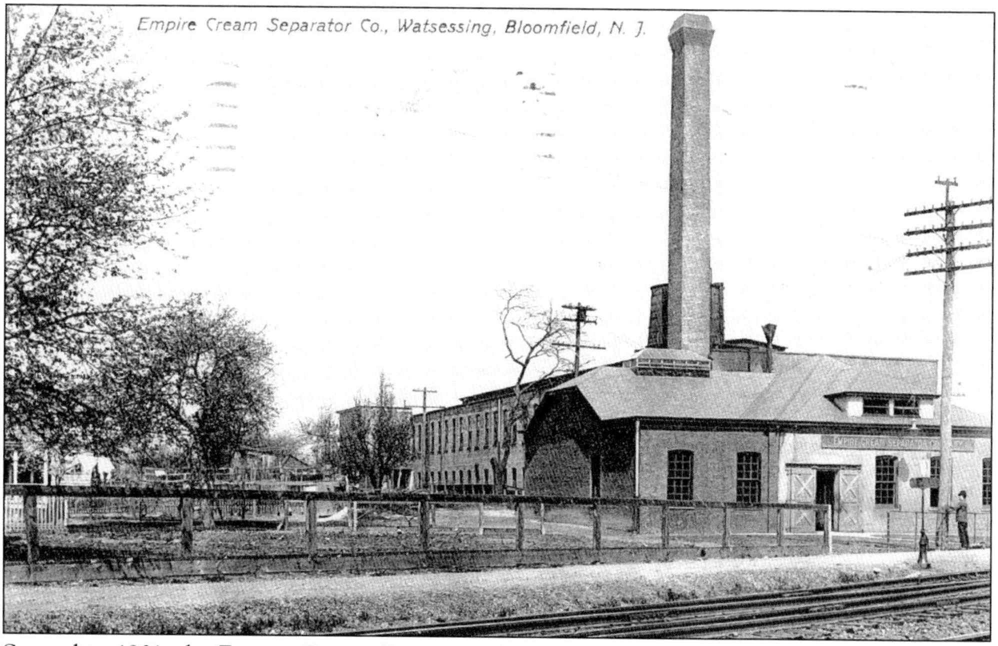

Started in 1901, the Empire Cream Separator Company employed over 300 skilled workers by 1910. The company, near Willow Street, used water drawn from artesian wells sunk deep into the Passaic River basin, which underlays Bloomfield and from which most water was drawn before 1910. Empire machines once helped produce the finest grade butter in the world.

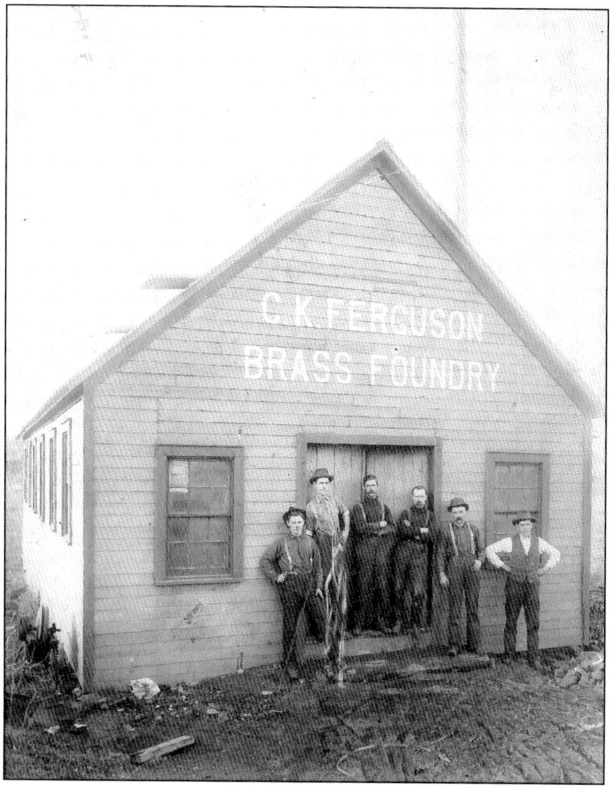

The first mention of the Charles K. Ferguson Brass Foundry on Lake Street (formerly located along the eastern shore of Lake Watsessing) was in the *Saturday Gazette* of April 4, 1874. This photograph may have been taken shortly thereafter because it shows only one building and a staff of only six men. The rather unsubstantial structure seems to have been built out of odds and ends.

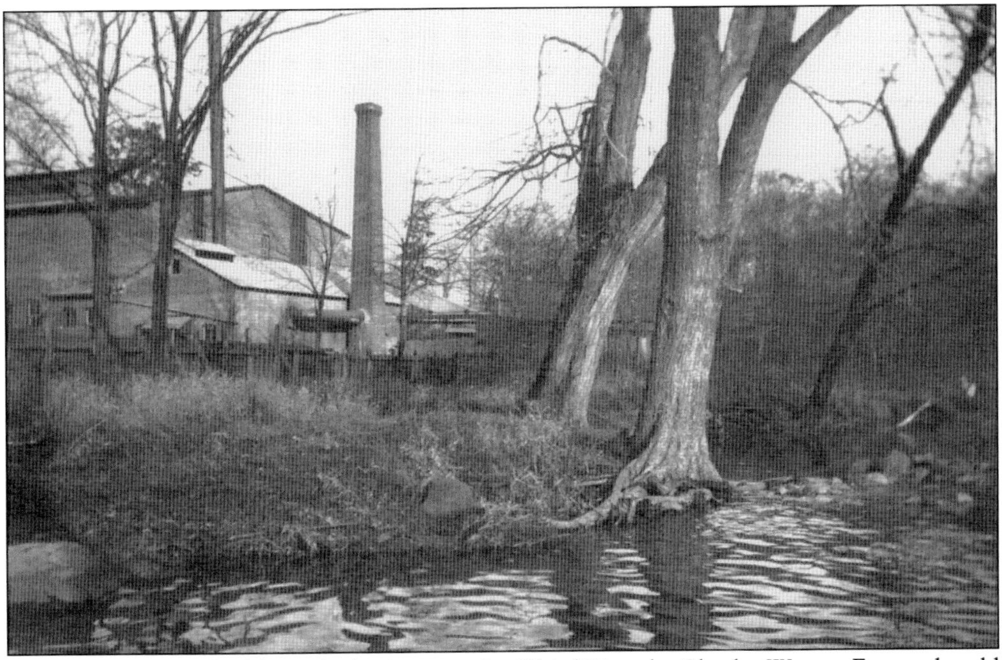

Probably photographed from the bridge over the Third River by Charles Warren Eaton, the old buildings of the Davey Trunk Board mill have seen a lot of history. Although it was in operation until the mid-1930s, the buildings are already looking run-down, and the company is probably considering abandonment of its Bloomfield operation, which did indeed happen in 1937.

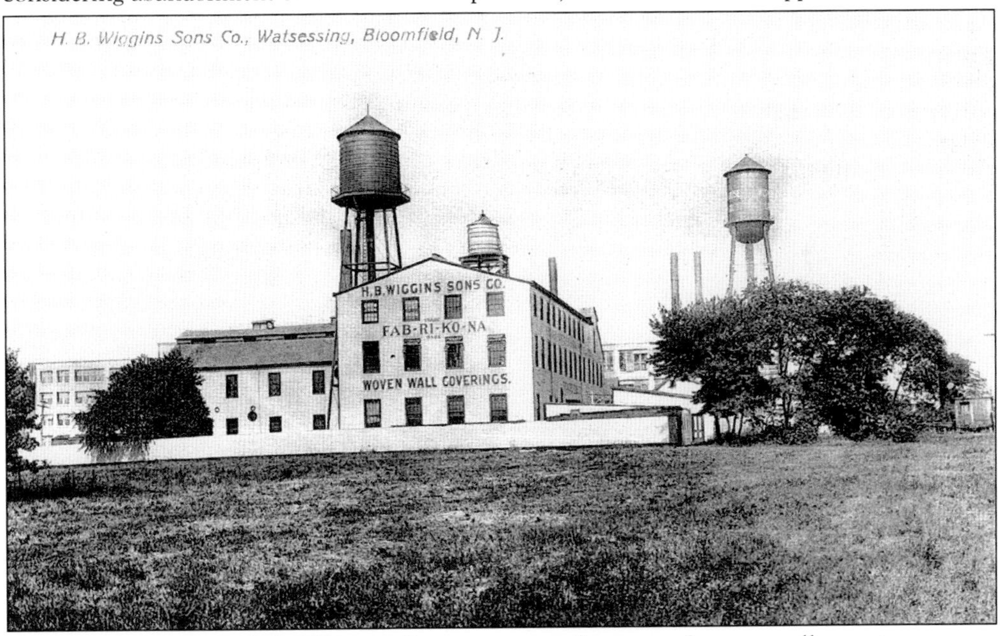

The frame structures of the Wiggins Company, manufacturers of woven wall coverings appear in this photograph. A fire later damaged the abandoned buildings and they were demolished. Also gone are the reinforced concrete walls of the neighboring Westinghouse Corporation seen in the background. The entire Wiggins plant, including the grassy area in the foreground, has been blacktopped.

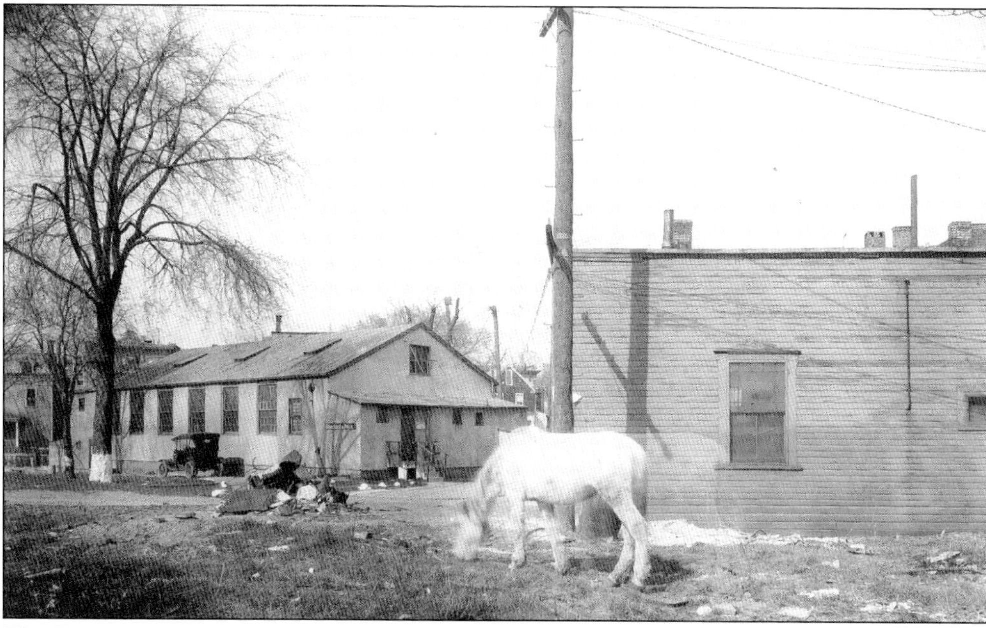

The Town Improvement Association took photographs of scenes of which it disapproved, and this one behind the station on Glenwood Avenue was on its list. The date is pre-1912, after which the area changed drastically with the electrification of the railroad and the creation of Lackawanna Plaza. The building in the left background was the home of the Libman Infants Wear Company. The grazing horse adds a bucolic note.

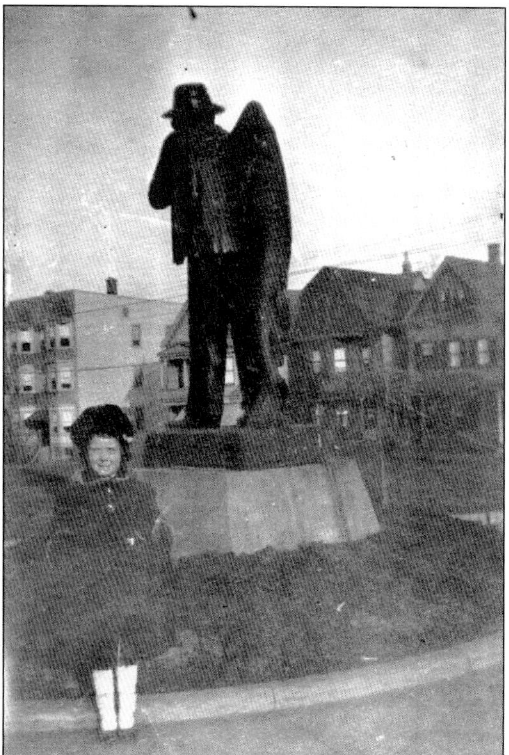

MGM had its Leo, Borden's had Elsie, and Scott and Bowne had its old fisherman carrying a huge codfish on his back. Alverta Brotherhood poses smilingly by the life-sized statue in front of the Scott and Bowne building on Orange Street. The company processed and refined cod liver oil to produce its own product, Scott's Emulsion, and advertised it worldwide.

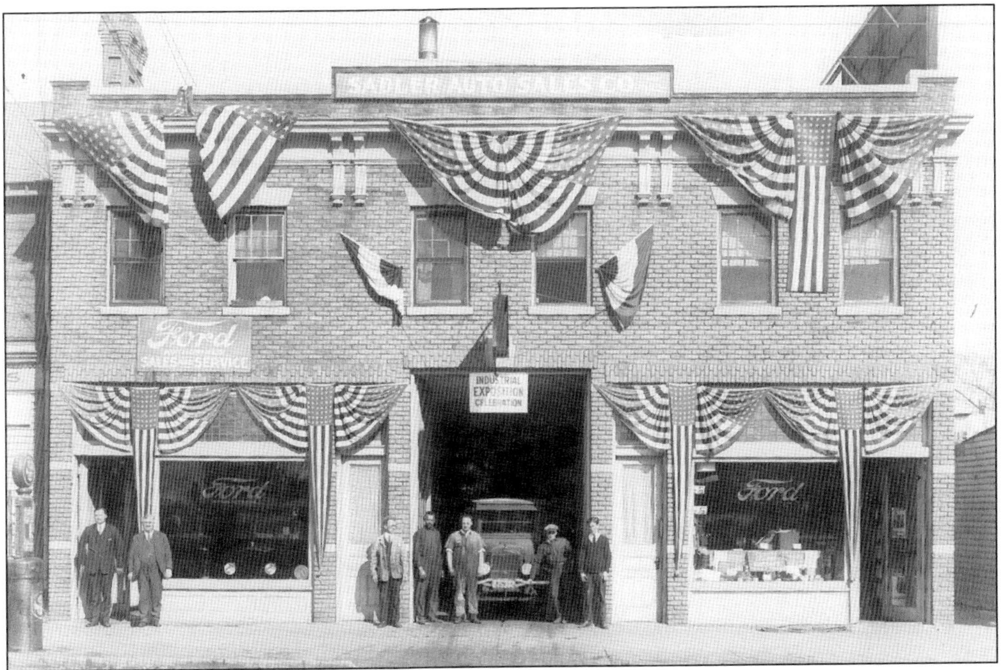

Fred Sadler (later mayor) stands proudly, second from the left, in the doorway of his Ford Sadler Automobile Sales Company that he founded in 1914 at 610 Bloomfield Avenue. This larger garage was built across the street four years later and was so successful that two adjacent lots were bought for a possible future expansion. The yellow brick structure still stands opposite the west end of Liberty Street.

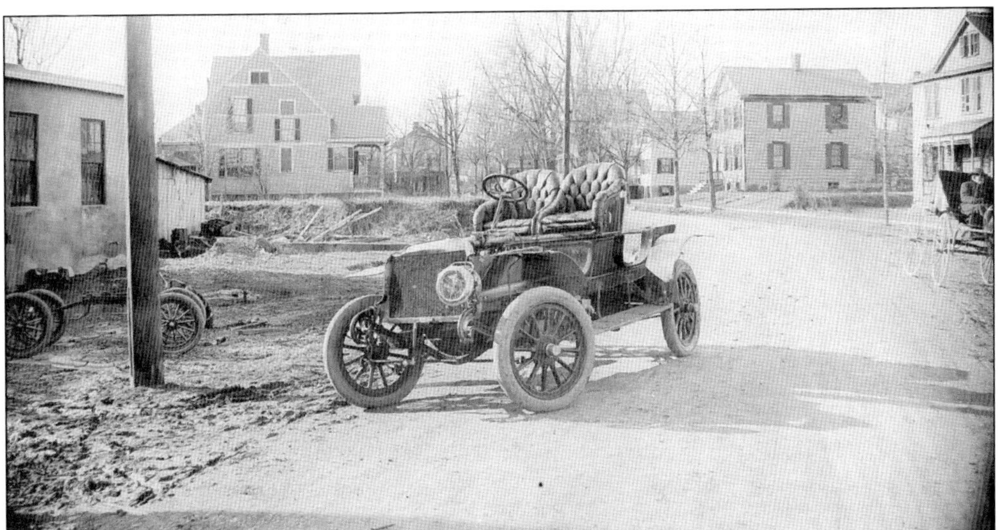

It looks as though somebody made an illegal turn on red in the days before there were traffic lights. The bumper has been salvaged, and the motorist has come to the right address for repairs: Glenwood Avenue and Henry Street, the automobile repair shop of Albert Loppacker. Except for the two nearest the camera, almost all of the now century-old homes in the photograph are still standing.

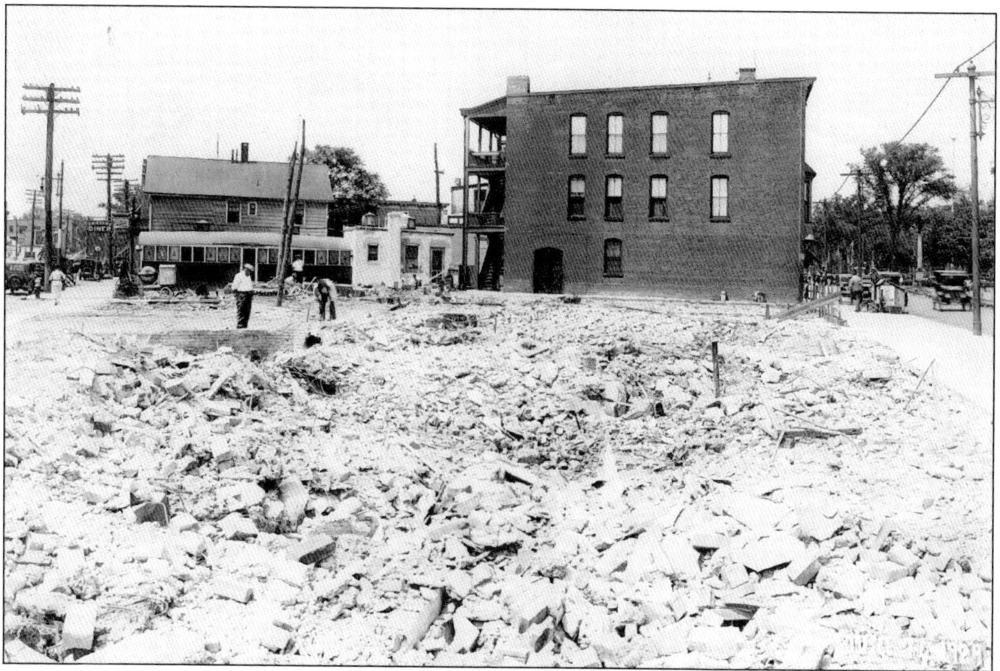

The old First National Bank, a Bloomfield landmark for only 30 years, was reduced to rubble by June 11, 1929, the date written on this photograph of the site. The old Ericson's Diner has been replaced by a new one. The 1889 building housing Ruvo's Confectionery still stands on the right next to the site of the new Bank and Trust structure.

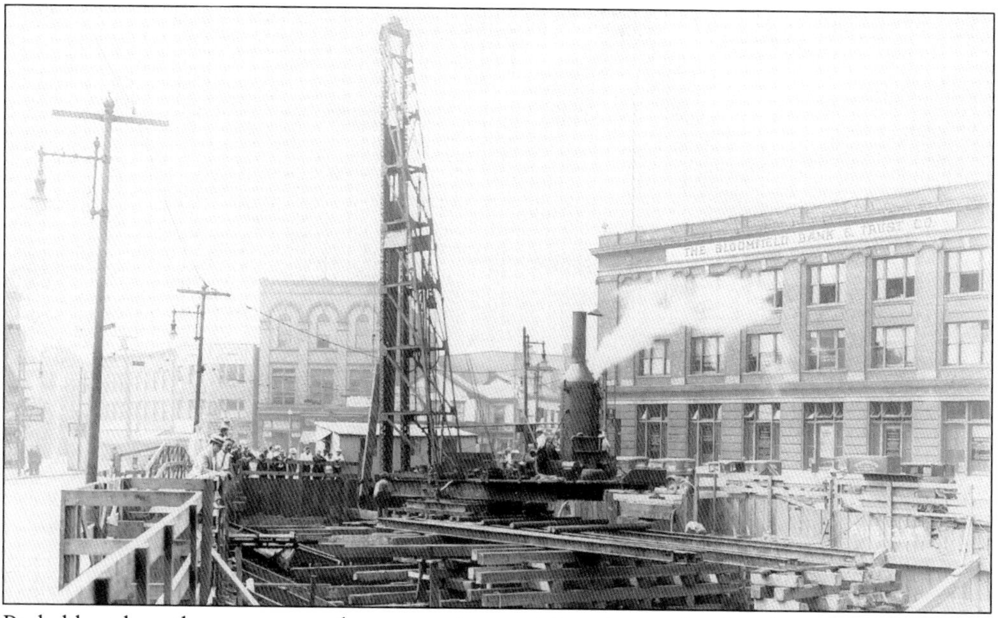

Probably taken the next year, the excavation and foundation for the skyscraper are almost completed as this steam-driven pile driver begins the underpinnings for a new steel framed building. Across Bloomfield Avenue to the right can be seen the old Bloomfield Trust Company, which had merged with the bank to form the new company. All of the trust company's first floor has since been replaced by small individual shops.

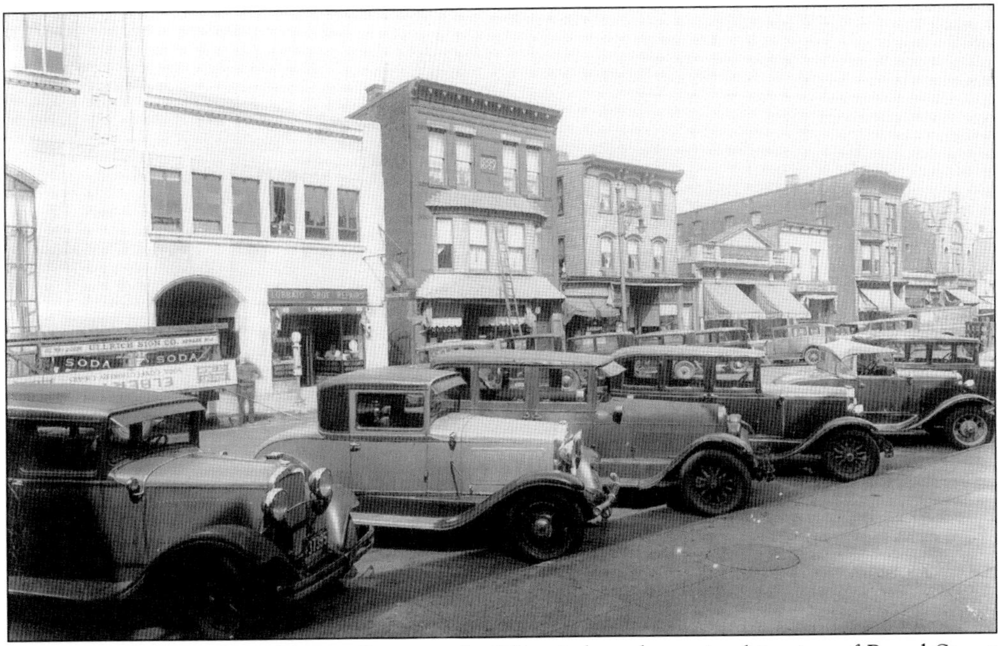

The Bloomfield Bank and Trust Company building is brand-new in this view of Broad Street around 1932–1933, and some of the offices in the bank building are still unoccupied. The 1889 brick structure still stands next to the bank, and there are other holdovers from the 19th century that remain standing today. Moran's store at No. 28, with its interesting facade, was drastically modernized in the 1930s.

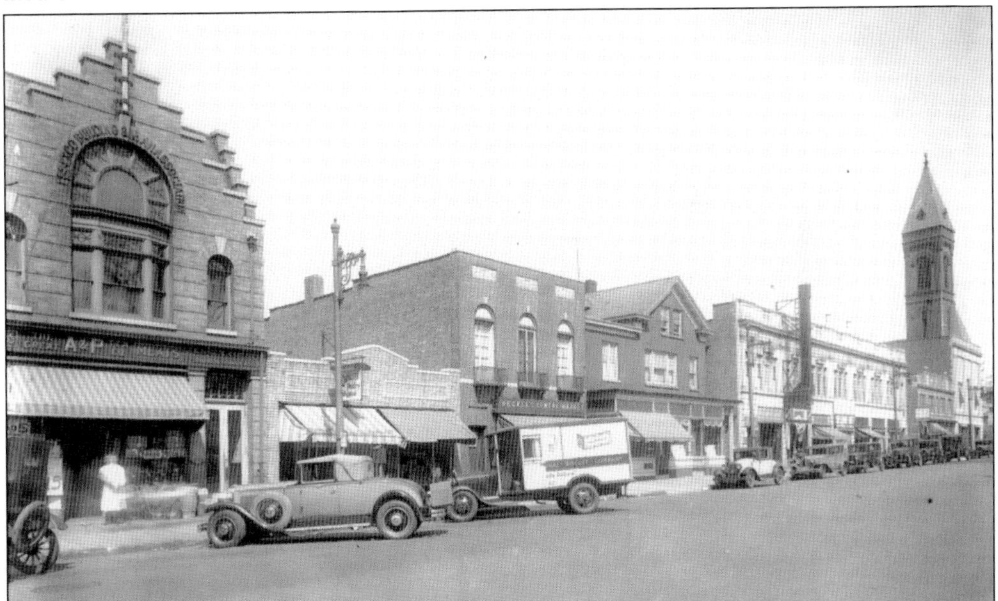

Farther north on Broad Street from the old 1880s savings and loan building, most buildings have remained for the past 70 years, although occupied by different businesses. The Geib Bakery, just right of center, was demolished in the mid-1950s when it had become the home of Bishop-Phillips Florist. The large white Park Building near Sacred Heart Church was the site of the Gardner mansion until 1925.

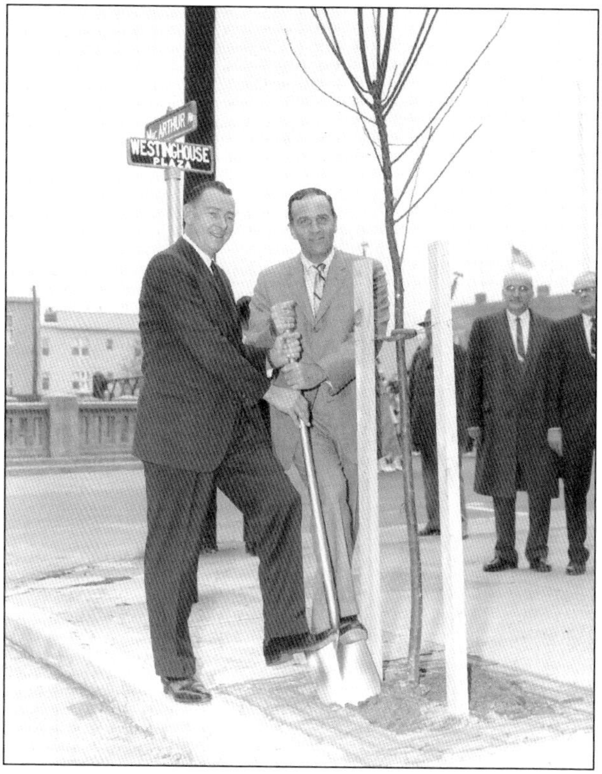

Mayor Walter Davis (right) helped plant a shade tree on the newly named Westinghouse Plaza, originally the northern end of Moulter Place. MacArthur Avenue, shown on an early map as Clearview, was renamed during World War II. One of the largest industries in Bloomfield (after Westinghouse) was General Electric, which produced air conditioners and industrial controls. During World War II, it employed almost 2,000 people in vital war work.

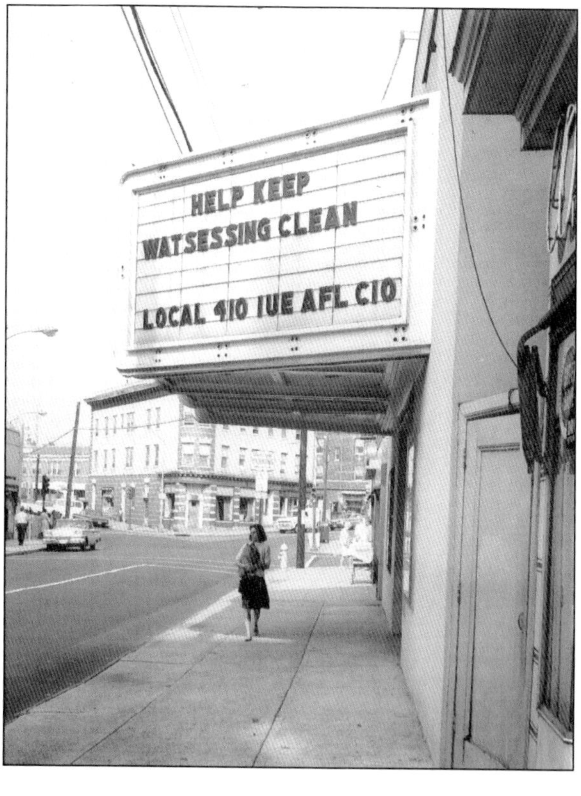

A third-run house with the lowest admission price in New Jersey was the Savoy (pronounced SAV-oy) Theater in Watsessing Center. By the late 1950s, it had stopped showing films and, after standing vacant for three years, became the home of the International Electrical Workers Union. It changed hands again, becoming a shop for the sale of magic goods. It has since been drastically remodeled with an entirely new front.

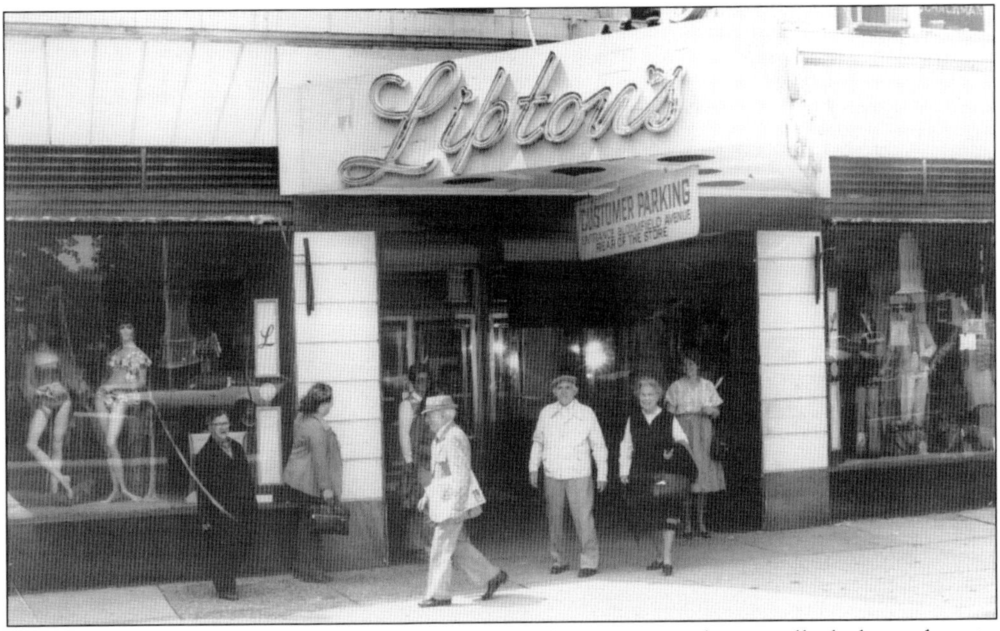

For 72 years, there was a Lipton's store in town, beginning with a small clothing shop in Watsessing in 1909. Twenty years later, Abraham Lipton saw to the construction of a building in the business district accommodating seven shops and 14 offices. Lipton's store, bearing his name, became the cornerstone merchandiser in Bloomfield Center and flourished as its reputation grew. Lipton retired at age 91 in 1982.

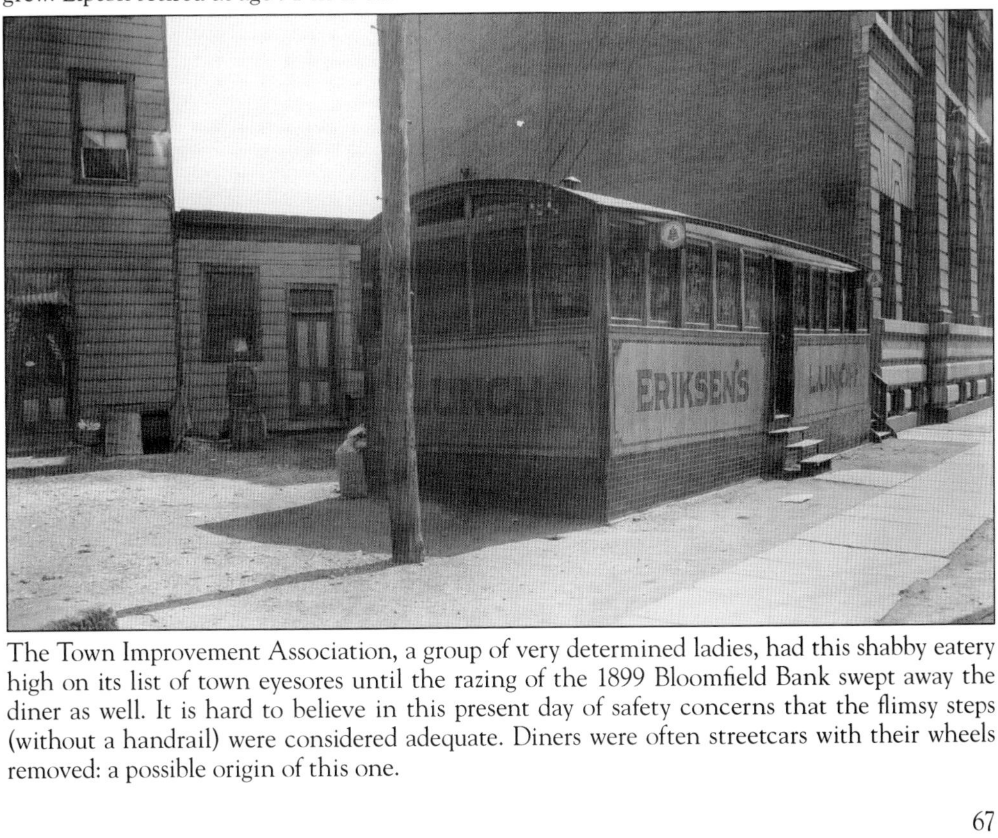

The Town Improvement Association, a group of very determined ladies, had this shabby eatery high on its list of town eyesores until the razing of the 1899 Bloomfield Bank swept away the diner as well. It is hard to believe in this present day of safety concerns that the flimsy steps (without a handrail) were considered adequate. Diners were often streetcars with their wheels removed: a possible origin of this one.

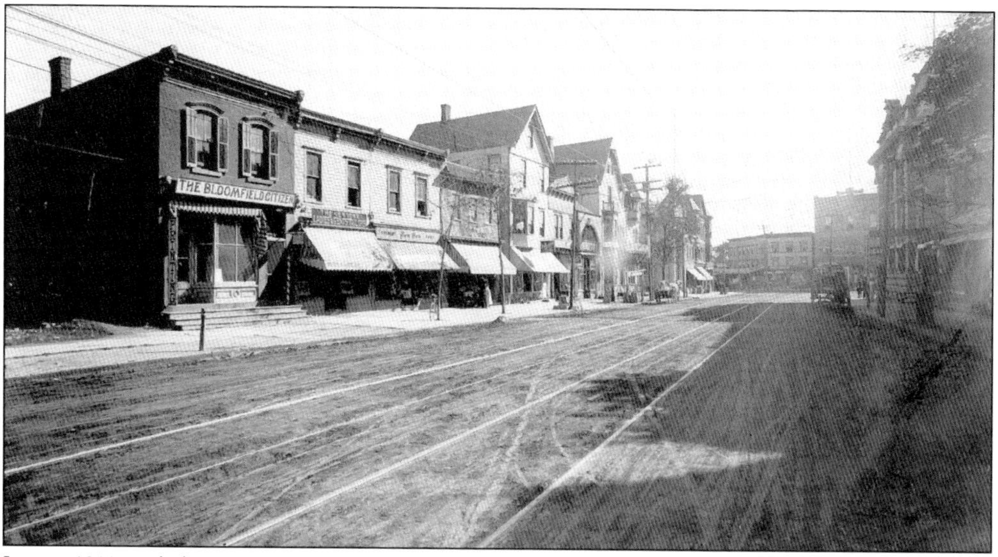

It was 1911 and the town kept up-to-date by reading the *Bloomfield Citzen*. Next door was the Moses and Gottleib Tailor Shop, and a few doors down, Bon Ton Millinery. Hollweg's Confection, over Frank Fisher's Shoe Store, was just a few steps down on Broad Street from the *Bloomfield Citizen*'s office. The newspaper was founded in 1883 and was the town's second paper, following the *Bloomfield Gazette*.

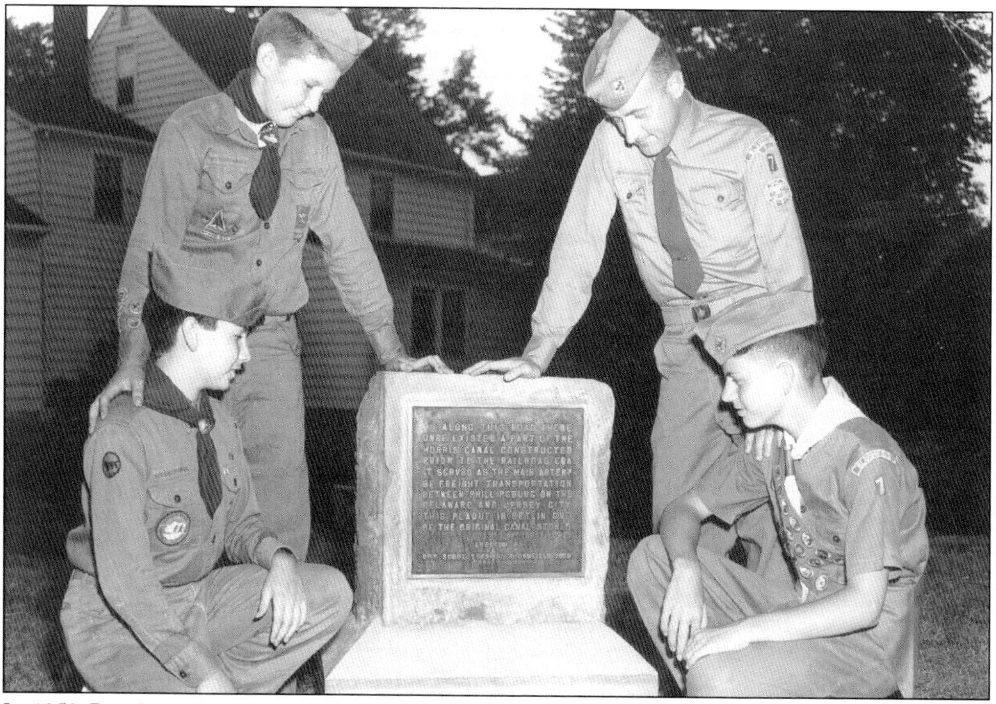

In 1959, Boy Scout Troop No. 7 dug out one of the original Morris Canal stones and transported it to town. One year later, in June 1960, the original canal stone was set in a four-foot-square cement foundation and the bronze tablet, its history authenticated by the New Jersey Historical Society, inserted by the scouts. Their excellent work commemorated the passing of an era in American commercial transportation.

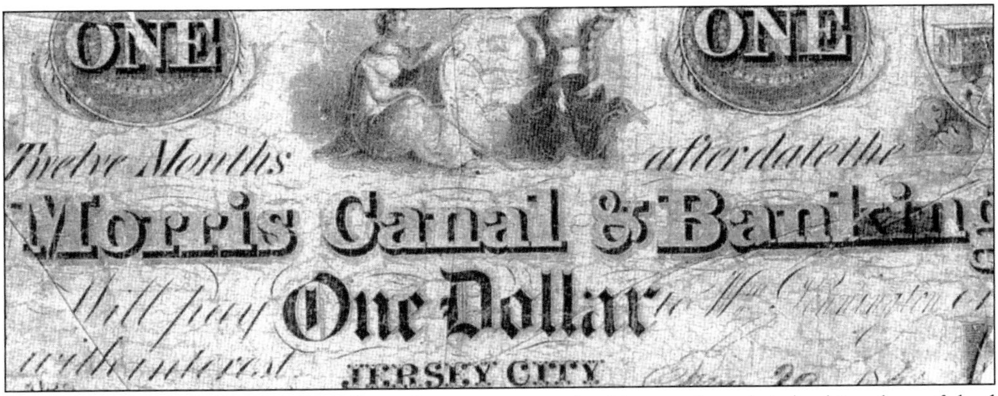

A tattered Morris Canal and Banking Company note, looking as though it had just been fished out of the canal at low water, was found in an antiques shop in Jersey City. The handwritten date appears to be June 29, 1862, although the canal company failed to pay a mortgage taken out in Holland in 1830. Having indulged in numerous financial shenanigans, the company found itself insolvent.

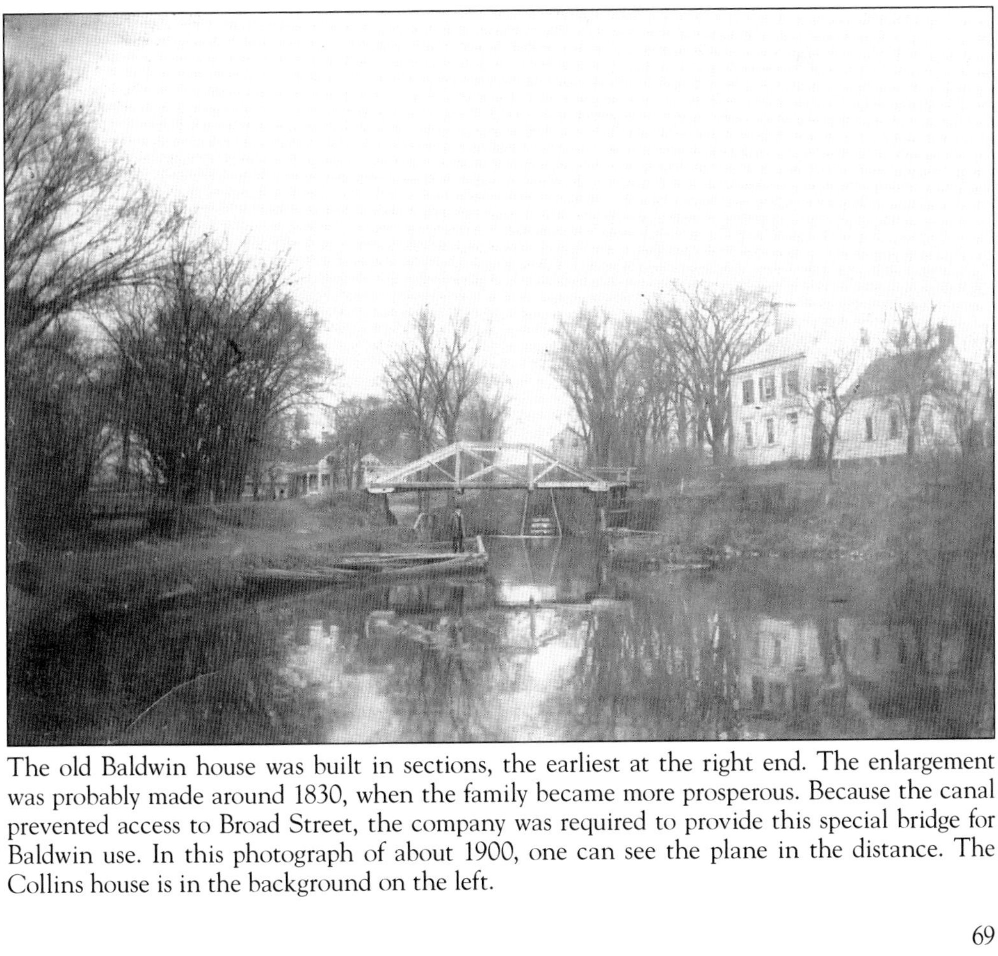

The old Baldwin house was built in sections, the earliest at the right end. The enlargement was probably made around 1830, when the family became more prosperous. Because the canal prevented access to Broad Street, the company was required to provide this special bridge for Baldwin use. In this photograph of about 1900, one can see the plane in the distance. The Collins house is in the background on the left.

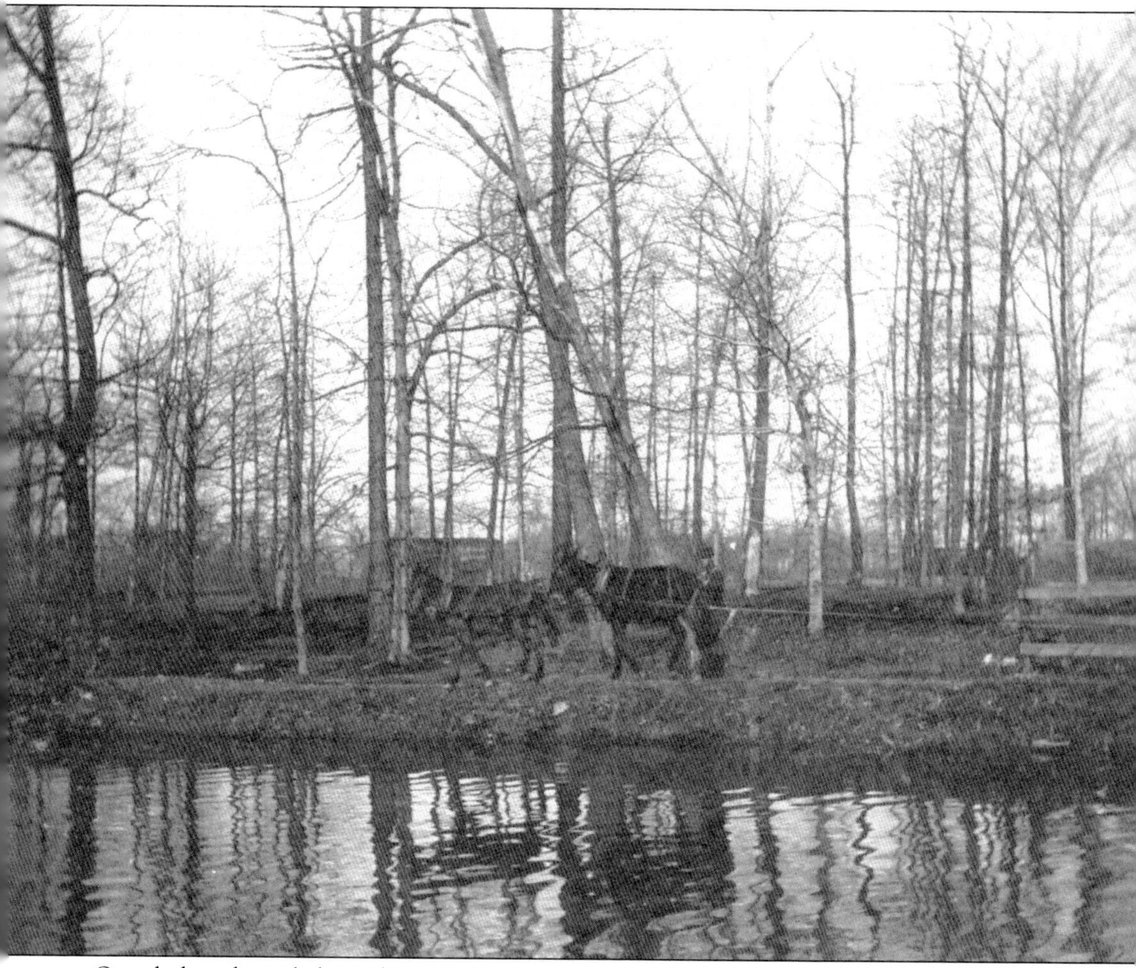

One dark and one light mule were, for some reason, called a Jersey team. This straight stretch of water and the obviously rural setting point to a location somewhere in Brookdale, but the photograph has no written indication of either location or date.

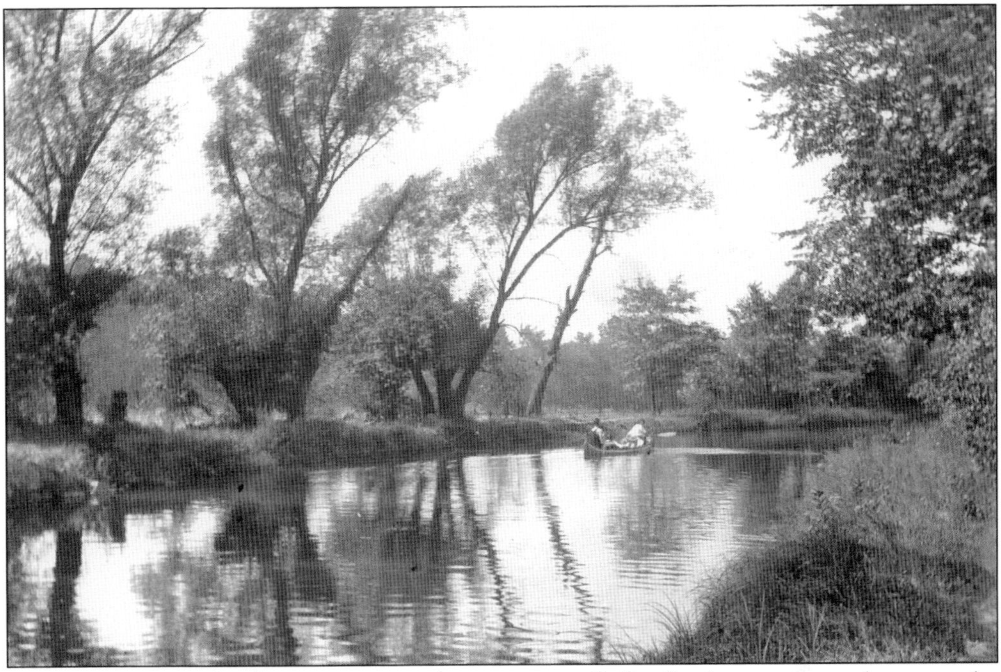

David and Jean Oakes kept a canoe at their estate on Belleville Avenue, located next to the canal, in which they used to paddle from the lock at Montgomery Street to the incline plane on Sundays when the canal was not in operation. A proposal to preserve a section of this picturesque waterway for boating and swimming resulted in nothing being done.

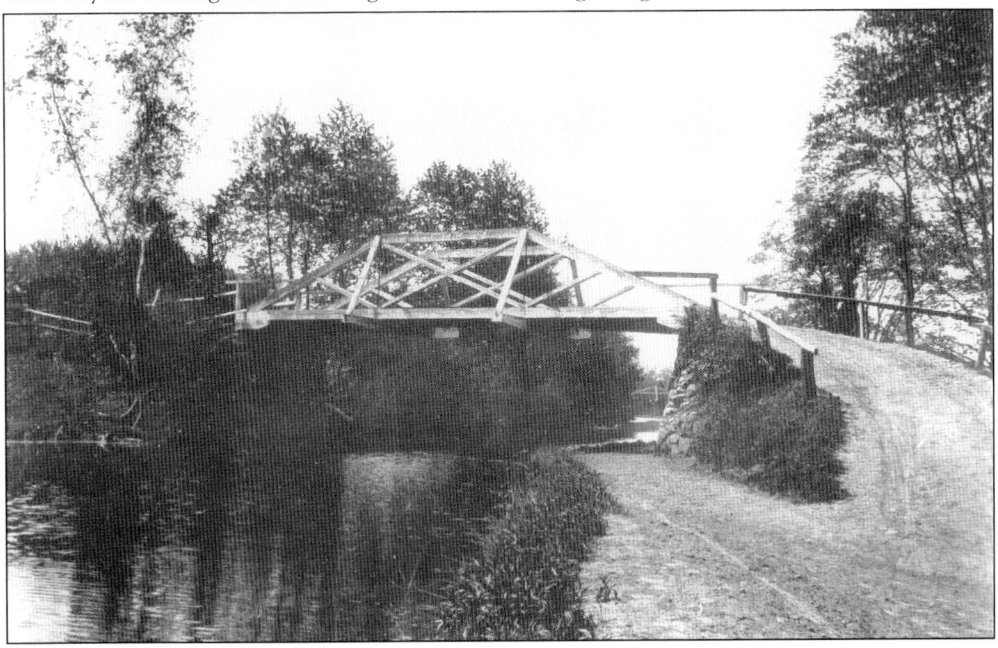

"Change bridges" were used where the towpath changed from one side of the canal to the other. When a traveling boat reached a change bridge, mules were unhitched, led over the bridge, down the other side, and hitched to the barges to continue the journey to the Delaware River. This is one such bridge at James Street.

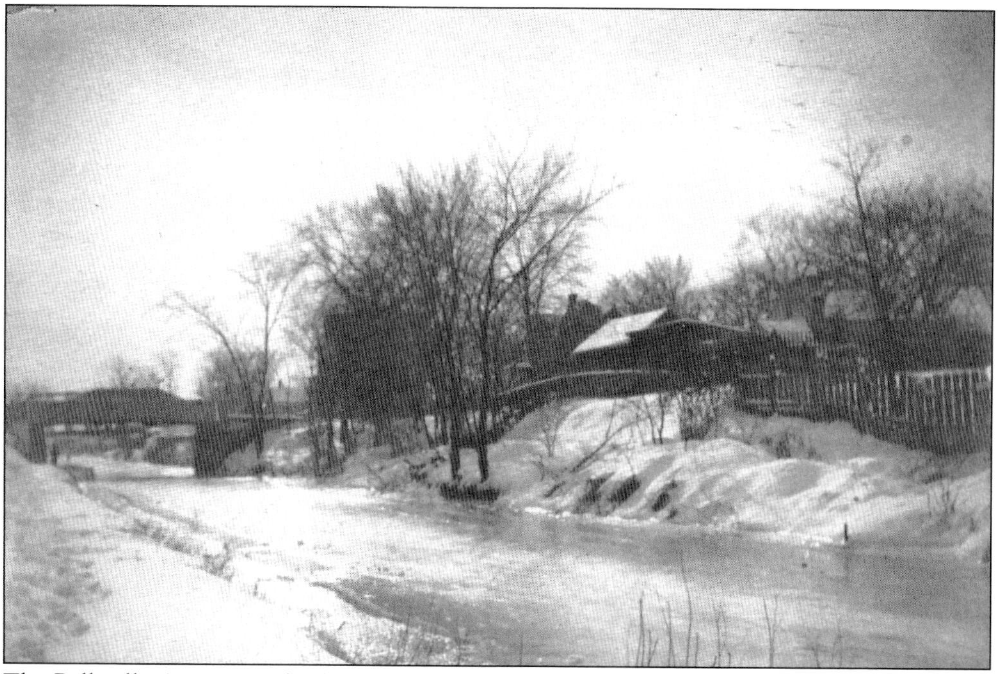

The Belleville Avenue Bridge had a distinctive appearance, being the only one in Bloomfield with its A-Frame covered with boards. Looking southwest, one can see the backs of the houses on Spruce Street to the right. The canal has been shut down for the winter, and the sound of the conch shell horn blown by the boatmen will not be heard again until March.

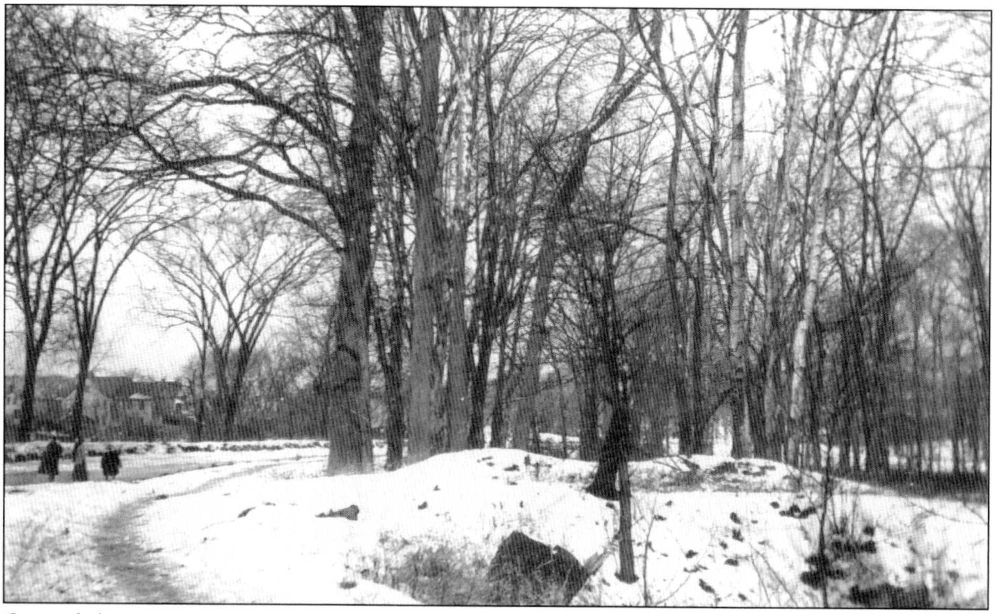

One of the most picturesque parts of the canal was in the area where it passed the Oakes Millpond. Located high above this artificial body of water fed by the Third River, the canal provided few benefits for the Oakes manufacturing operation except for supplying coal, which off-loaded at the point where the canal turned toward Belleville Avenue. After the canal was drained, coal was still stored at that spot.

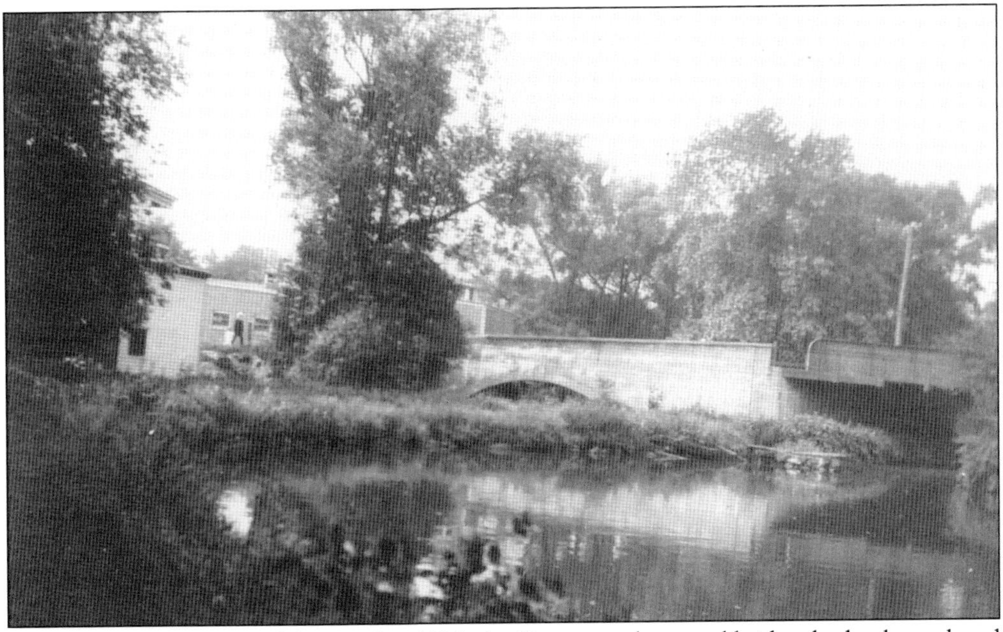

After the abandonment of the canal in 1924, the flimsy wooden canal bridges had to be replaced by new ones designed to carry heavy modern traffic. In this area, the Third River and the canal crossed, requiring some fancy engineering to keep them apart. The canal is on the right, under the iron bridge, and the river flows under the concrete arch to the left. Both bridges have since been replaced.

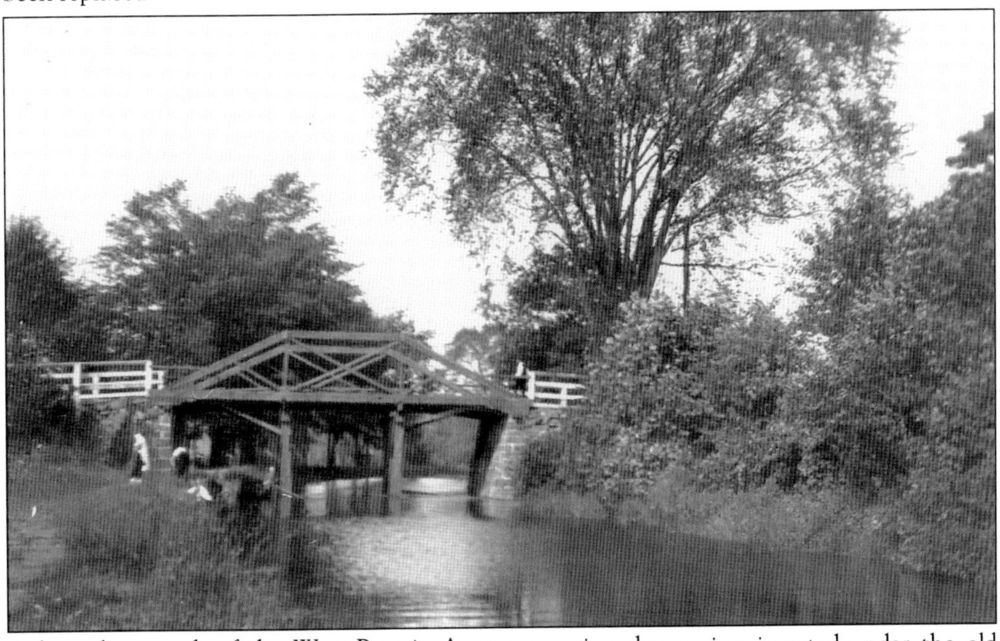

A late photograph of the West Passaic Avenue crossing shows piers inserted under the old wooden bridge to keep the increasing road traffic from crashing through the decaying structure. These piers would have been an impediment to canal traffic and seem to be an indication that the waterway has been abandoned. However, it was still in use as a source of waterpower for the nearby Marcal Paper Mill.

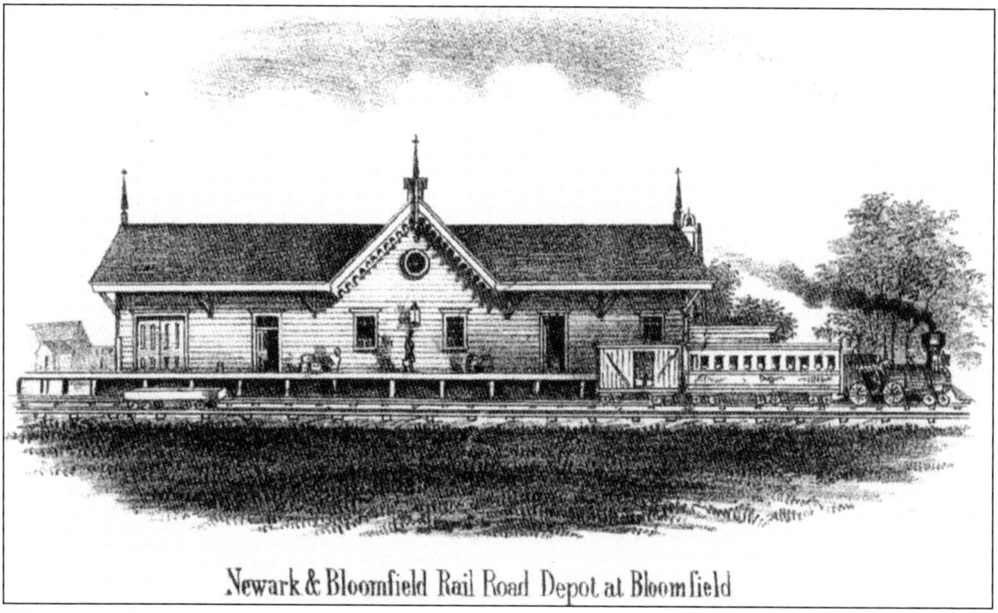

The original 1850s station was much smaller, as is shown by this lithograph from the 1865 map of Bloomfield. For some unknown reason, this was printed as a separate illustration that bears the handwritten notation "from A. J. Davis' scrapbook." Davis (1803–1892) was a noted American architect, but it is not know how or why he had an interest in this building, unless he was its designer.

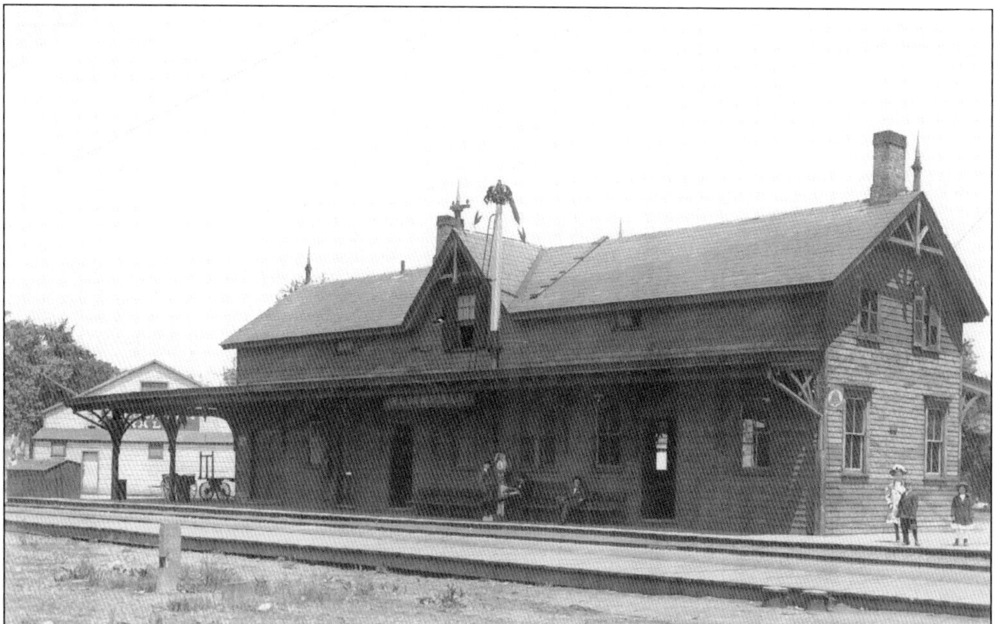

A photograph of the original Glenwood Avenue station of the Lackawanna Railroad dated June 6, 1909, shows the 1850s structure as remodeled and enlarged in 1884 when the platform was covered, a porte cochere added to the north end, and the building repainted. It was demolished in 1912 when the line was electrified, the tracks raised to their present location, and the original roadbed paved as Lackawanna Plaza.

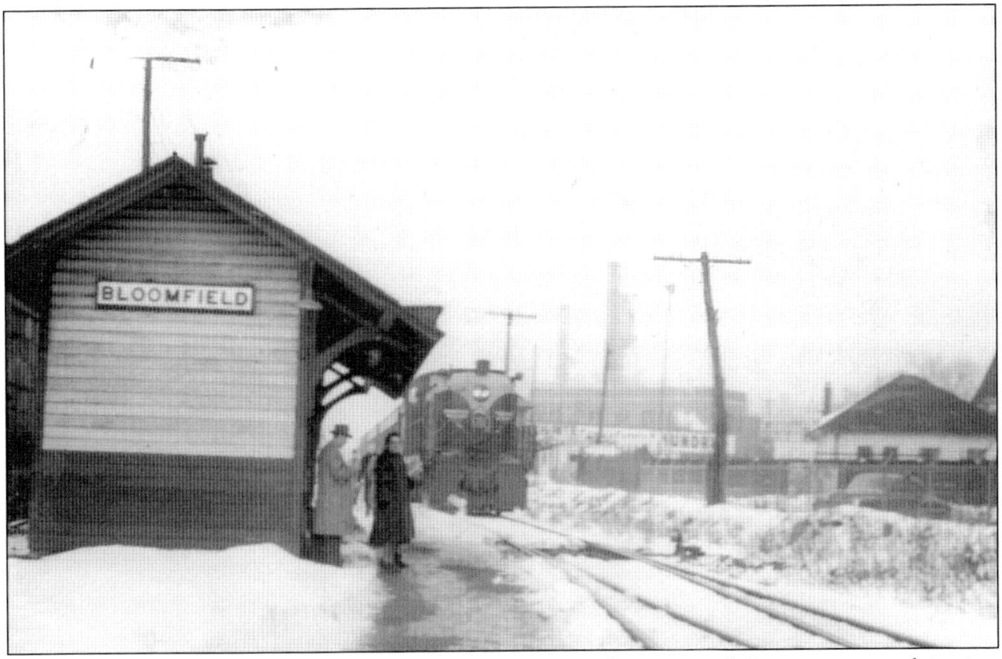

This 1955 photograph is labeled "Last train to stop at this station." Passengers are shivering outside of the inadequate shelter provided by Conrail as the Orange-bound locomotive lumbers into the station. In the background are the factory of Lehn and Fink (makers of Lysol) on Bloomfield Avenue and its water tower built in the shape of a bottle of its product.

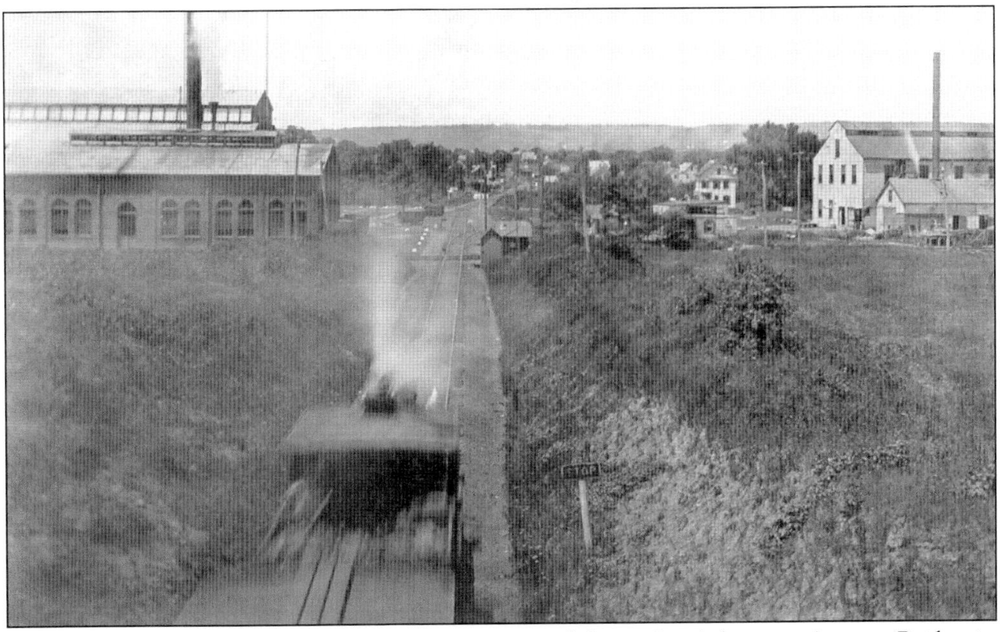

Seen here is a pre-1918 photograph taken westward from the Arlington Avenue Bridge in Watsessing, just as the steam locomotive passed underneath on its way to the Oranges. The building to the left is Sprague Electric, and to the right is the Wiggins Wall Covering Company. After Sprague was purchased by General Electric, the present six-story building was built on Lawrence Street behind Sprague on a remnant of the Noll Dairy Farm.

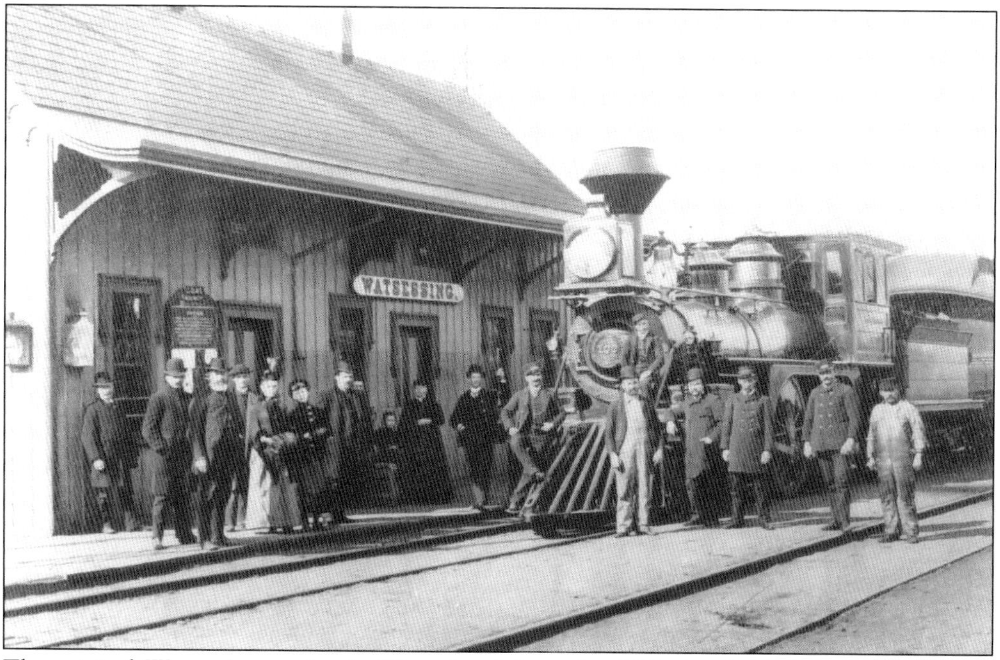

The original Watsessing station building dated from the 1870s but by 1883 was found to be inadequate. An addition of 14 by 16 feet was made for two new waiting rooms, a larger office, and an expanded platform to be covered by a roof. A second floor was also proposed at that time, but it is not known if this was carried out.

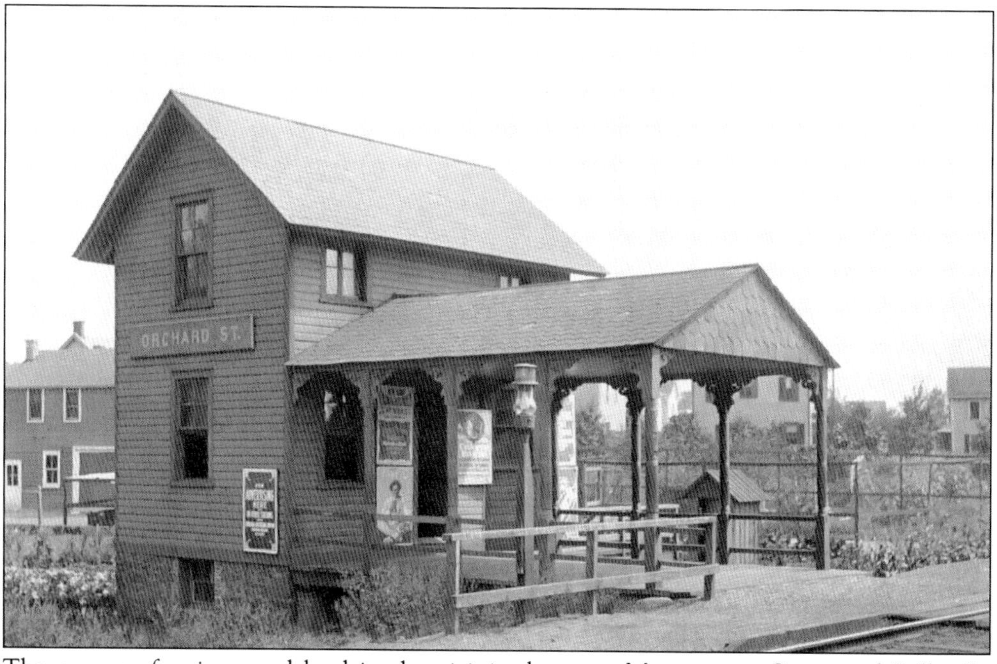

The owners of unimproved land in the vicinity between Montgomery Street and Belleville Avenue made the new Midland Railway of great interest. As early as 1867, the proposed route had been hinted at by two parallel lines on a map of the Bayliss farm. In 1909, the Orchard Street station had a total of 28 weekday and 14 Sunday trains stopping here.

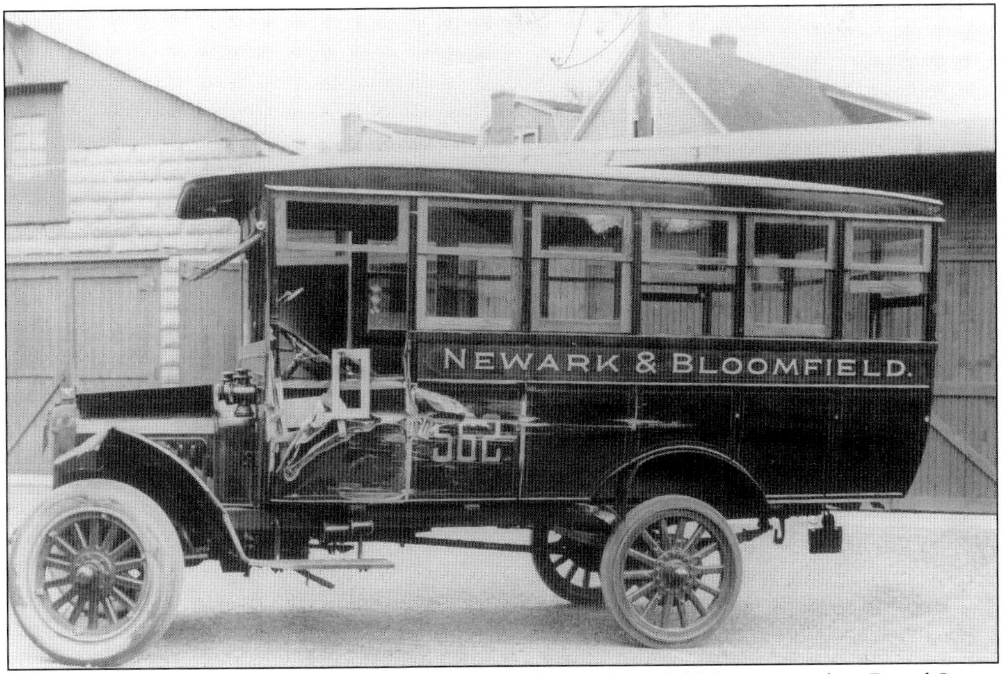

This is one of the privately owned jitneys that ran along Bloomfield Avenue and on Broad Street to Bay Avenue in the 1920s, before these competing vehicles were consolidated into the massive Public Service Corporation. The headlights were lit by kerosene; the Klaxon horn was made in Bloomfield. "Jitney" was 19th-century slang for a nickel, the price of a ride.

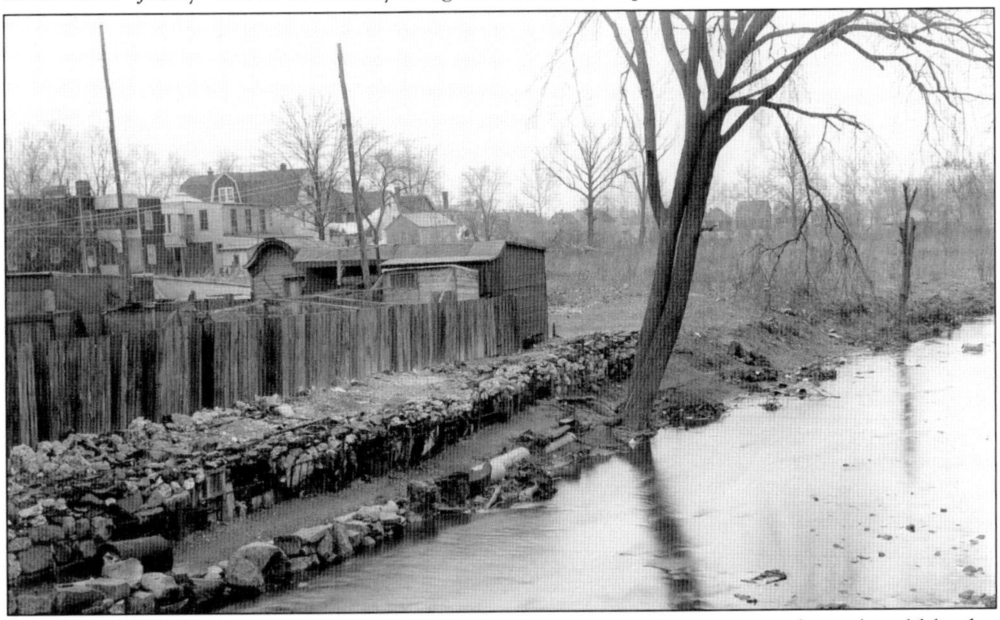

An early-1900s photograph taken by the Town Improvement Association from the old bridge was meant to show this town eyesore on Franklin Street and the Second River. Soon afterward, the river undermined the foundations and caused some of the houses to collapse. The south wall of the remaining structures was shored up by timbers until the construction of the parkway bridge in the early 1950s brought about their demolition.

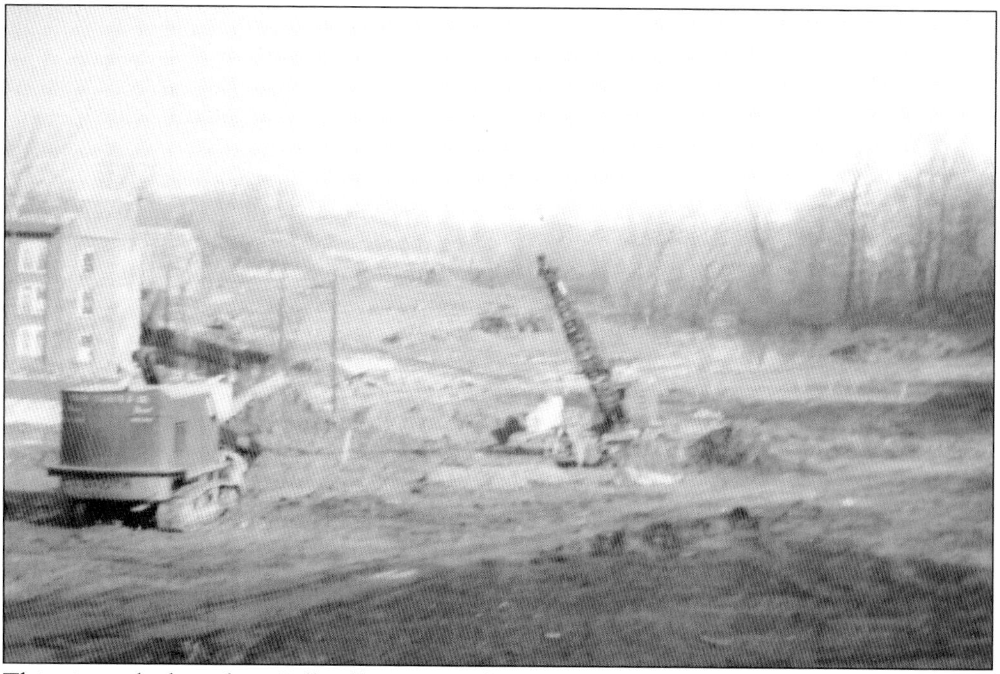

This view is looking from Belleville Avenue, through Oakes Woods, and over the Third River as the parkway heads to Brookdale. Demolition of a portion of the Oakes Mill began in 1954 as workmen laid the footings for the underpass at Belleville Avenue. The company provided employment for more than 100 years, ending in 1945. The historic mill buildings are now an industrial village used by a dozen small enterprises.

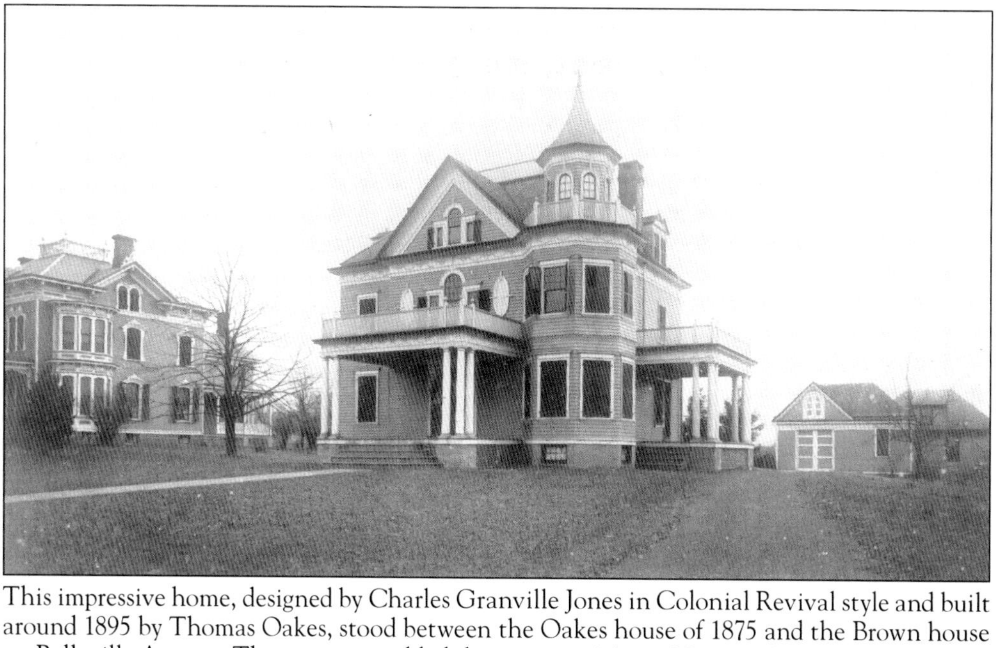

This impressive home, designed by Charles Granville Jones in Colonial Revival style and built around 1895 by Thomas Oakes, stood between the Oakes house of 1875 and the Brown house on Belleville Avenue. The tower resembled the tower on Mount Vernon, George Washington's home in Virginia. Barns can be seen in the rear of the property. The house was sacrificed to the parkway.

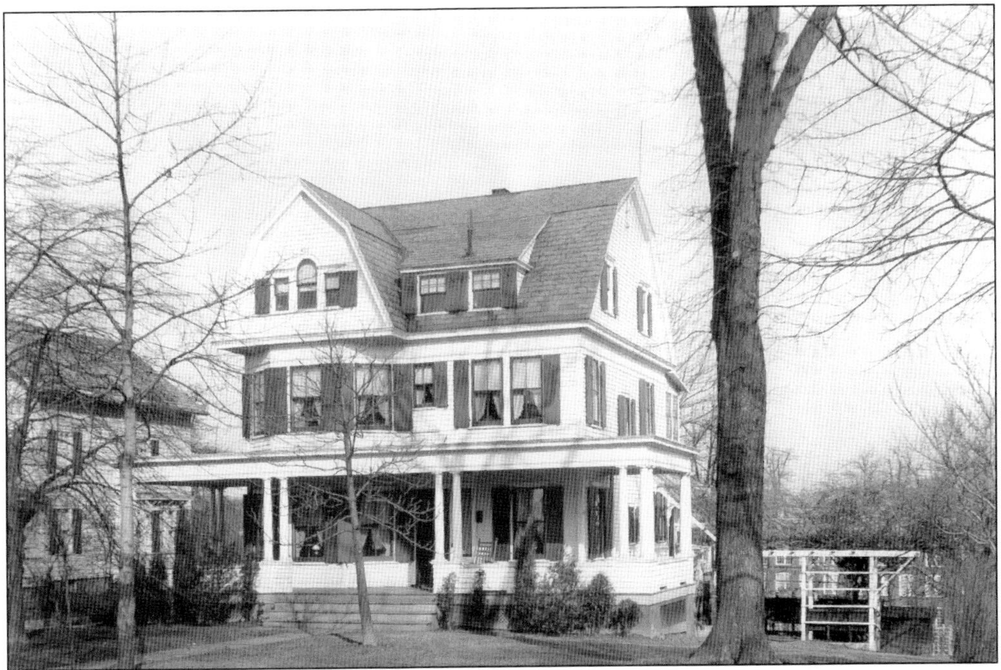

Built in 1890, 209 Belleville Avenue was the residence of Clarence Richards Schuyler. The Schuylers were lateral descendants of Maj. Gen. Phillip Schuyler of Revolutionary War fame. Through the trellised garden area on the right, one can see the Oakes Mill just beyond the Third River. Next door, on the left, is the 1870s Cockefair home. Both houses were demolished for the parkway.

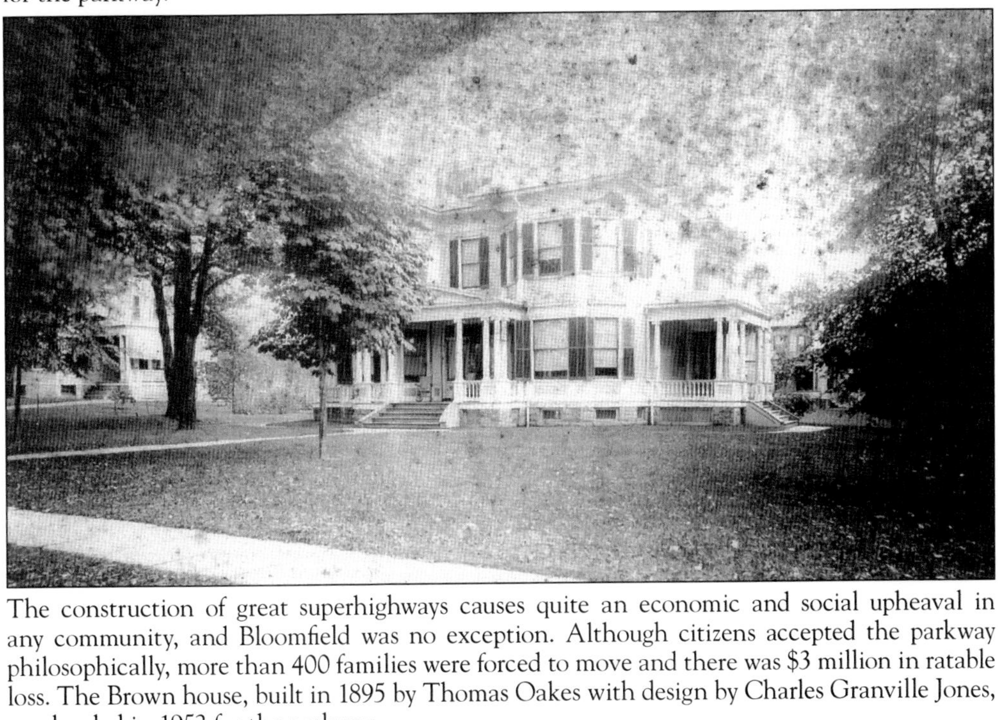

The construction of great superhighways causes quite an economic and social upheaval in any community, and Bloomfield was no exception. Although citizens accepted the parkway philosophically, more than 400 families were forced to move and there was $3 million in ratable loss. The Brown house, built in 1895 by Thomas Oakes with design by Charles Granville Jones, was leveled in 1952 for the parkway.

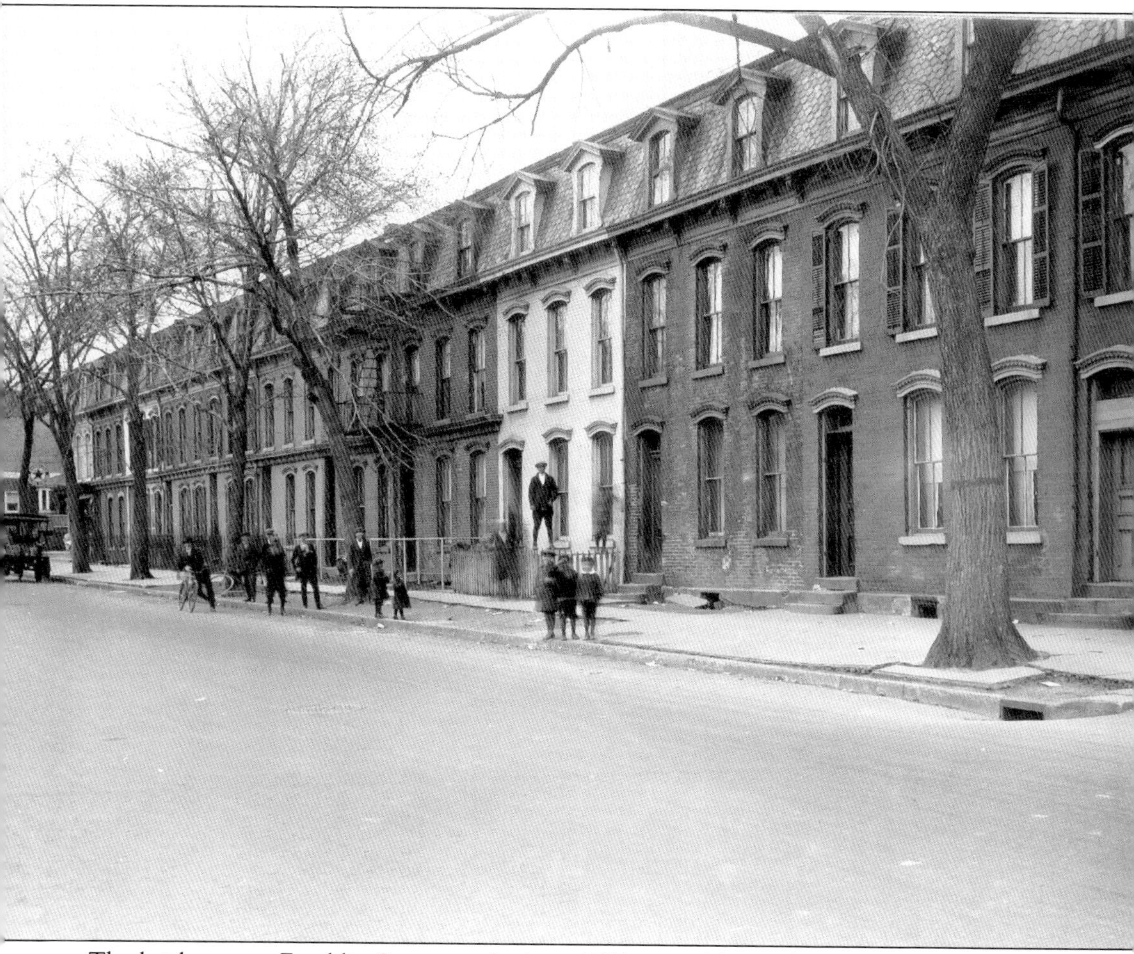

The brick row on Franklin Street was built in 1875, one of five such rows in Bloomfield. More of these row houses had been planned, but the panic of 1876 brought an end to building. The property was allowed to deteriorate until two of the houses on the edge of the Second River collapsed, probably due to flooding. On the far left is a view of the Dodd house.

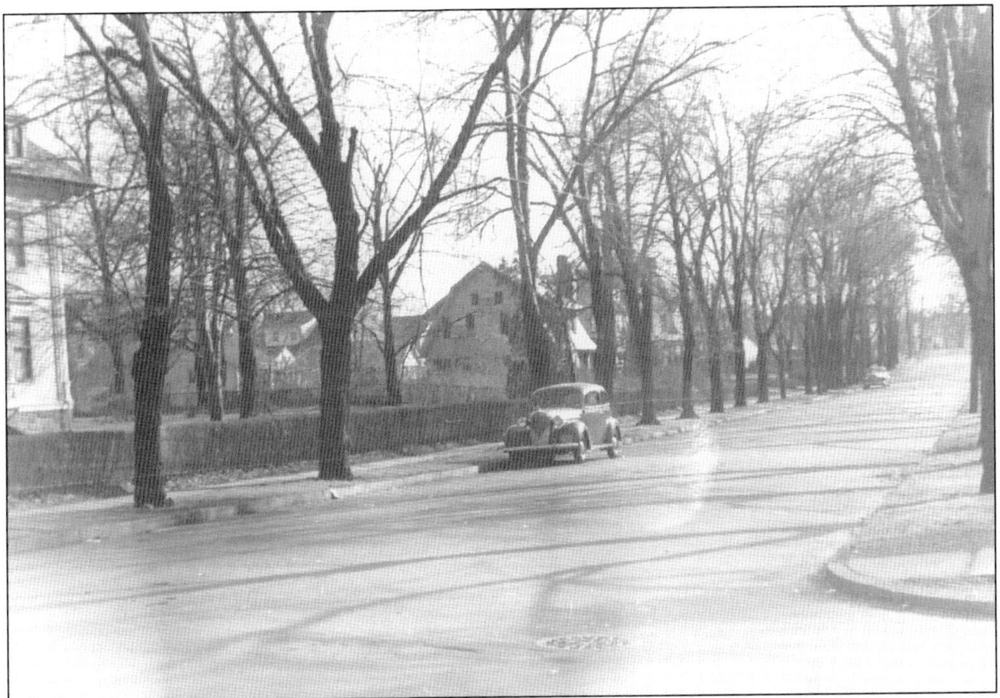

This photograph shows a view of Walnut Street about 1948, looking south. Nothing in the picture is there today, including the street itself. The parkway took the entire block in 1952. However, the Dutch Colonial house in the center was moved to the corner of Beach and Spruce Streets, where it still stands today. In 1939, the street was considered one of the most beautiful in town.

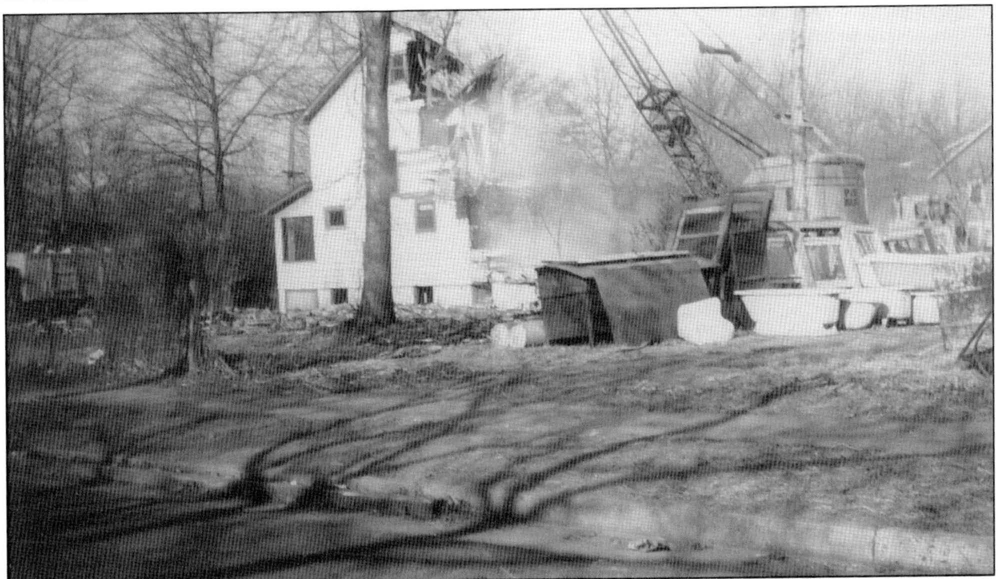

The new superhighway was projected to take an estimated $3 million in ratable loss and 400 properties, including 15 industrial buildings, 11 stores, and a convalescent home. In 1953, teams of inspectors began checking homes along the parkway route. Pictured here is the demolition in progress of a private home with salvaged hot water tanks and bathtubs on the ground.

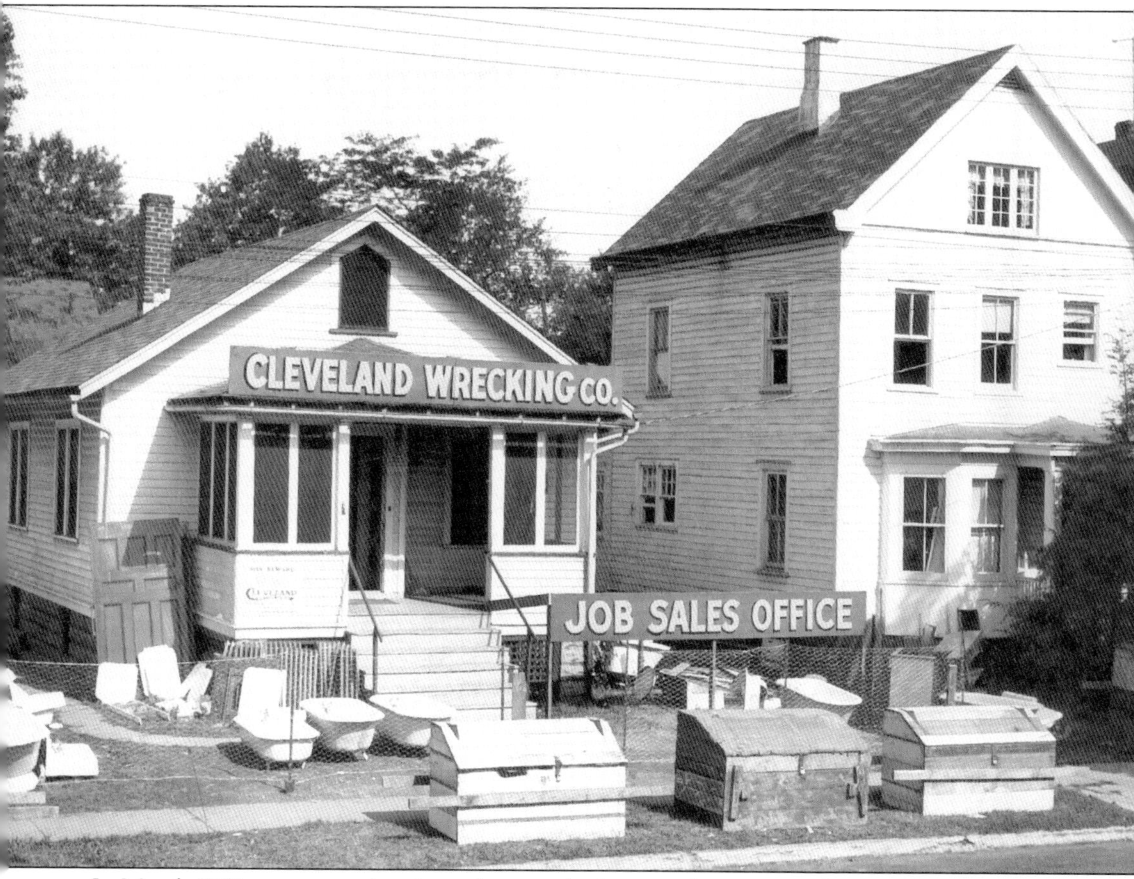

In March 1953, representatives from the state highway authority agreed to appear at Watsessing School to provide specific facts for a public struggling to plan the future for their families. Many Bloomfield owners and tenants were expected to move by June 1, 1953. The Cleveland Wrecking Company had the contract, and here they go to work salvaging bathtubs, windows, and anything else of value.

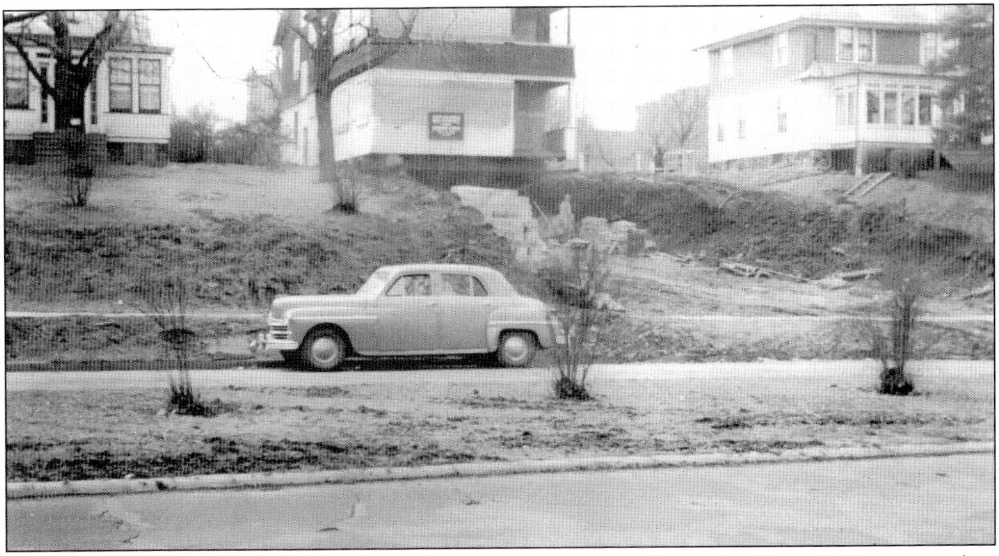

Ever since the early days, when the parkway was known as Route 4, Bloomfield more or less supported the highway as a good idea. Of all the big towns affected, Bloomfield offered fewer objections and more cooperation than any other. This house (center) at 132 Newark Avenue was moved to escape demolition. The state offered houses for sale at low cost, if the buyers provided for removal to a new location.

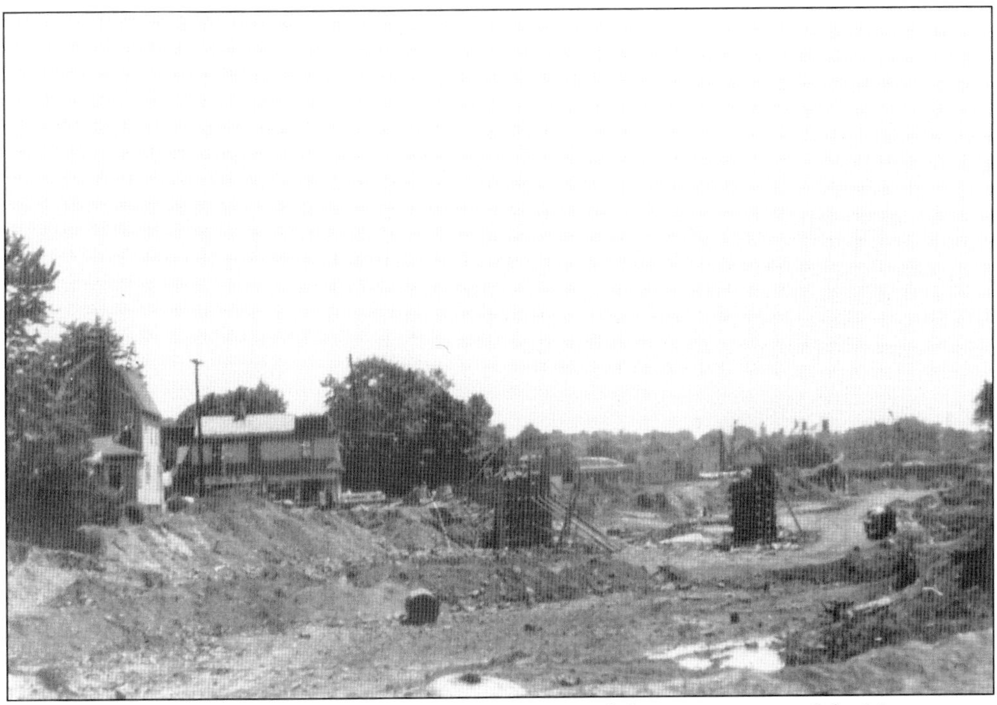

The camera caught the shirttail of Montgomery Street and the construction of the Montgomery Street Bridge. The stores and the houses on the left are still there. In the far distant background are the chimneys of Berkeley School on Bloomfield Avenue.

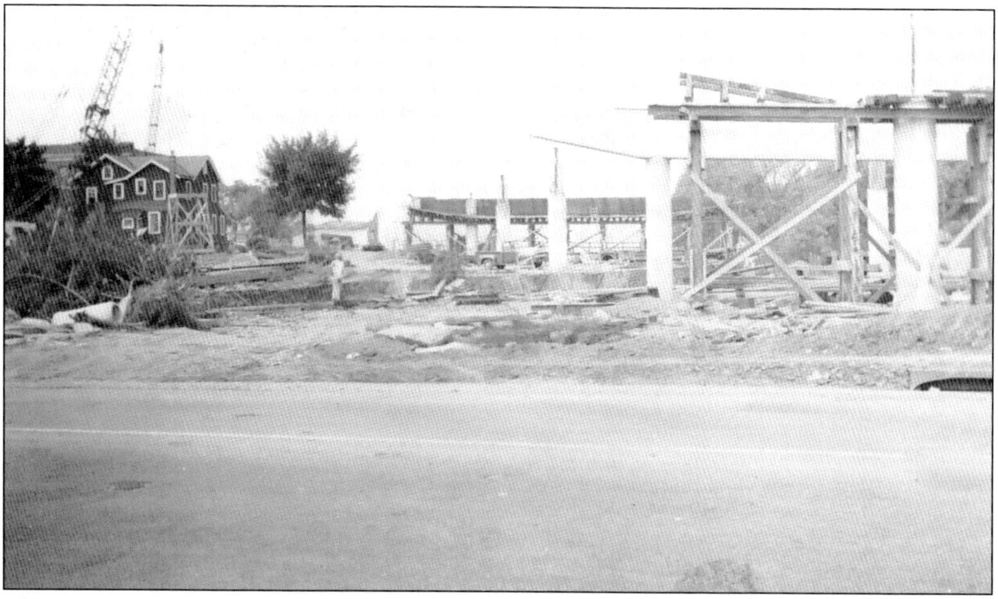

This view is west from the corner of Race Street. The house on the left on Bloomfield Avenue has since been replaced by a parking lot. The Second River crosses between Franklin Street and Bloomfield Avenue. Bridge and entrance and exit ramp construction replaced houses and other buildings in this area.

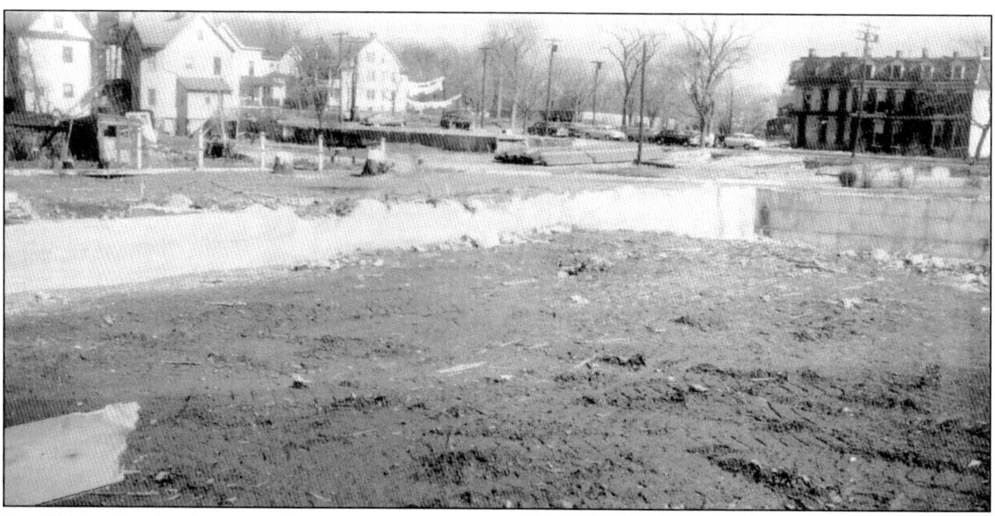

In 1964, the highway authority reported that Interchange 148 construction would be a multimillion dollar undertaking. The authority acquired four homes and one small factory on Myrtle and Willow Streets for construction of the northbound exit and the southern entrance to the parkway from Bloomfield Avenue. The view is toward Franklin Street, showing the partly demolished brick row and the 1719 Dodd house and Metz Hotel gone.

Four

MEMORY BOX

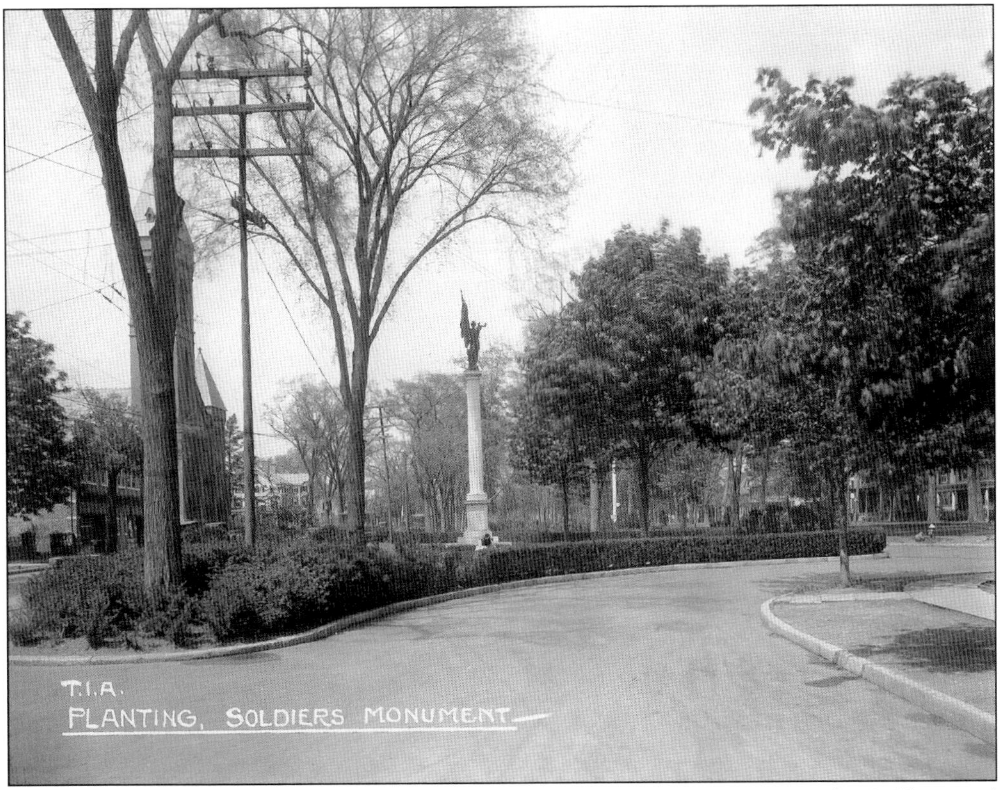

Located in the center of Bloomfield and at one of its busiest intersections, the Soldiers and Sailors Monument was unveiled during the week of the town's centennial celebration in June 1912. The statue, a lasting memorial to honor the soldiers and sailors who served in the country's wars from the Revolution on, was designed and sculpted by Sally James Farnham.

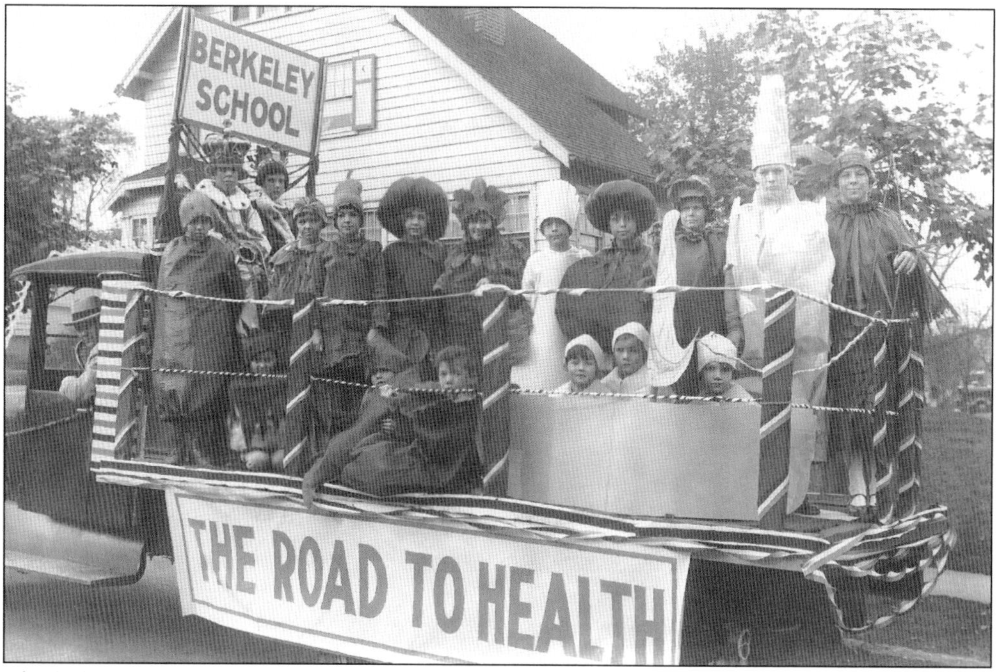

The kids are all dressed up as various healthful veggies on this 1928 float, all ready to parade up Broad Street to the dedication ceremonies on Municipal Plaza. The town was justifiably proud of the impressive structure that had replaced the makeshift town offices located at various temporary locations for more than a century. The scene was photographed on Vernon Terrace.

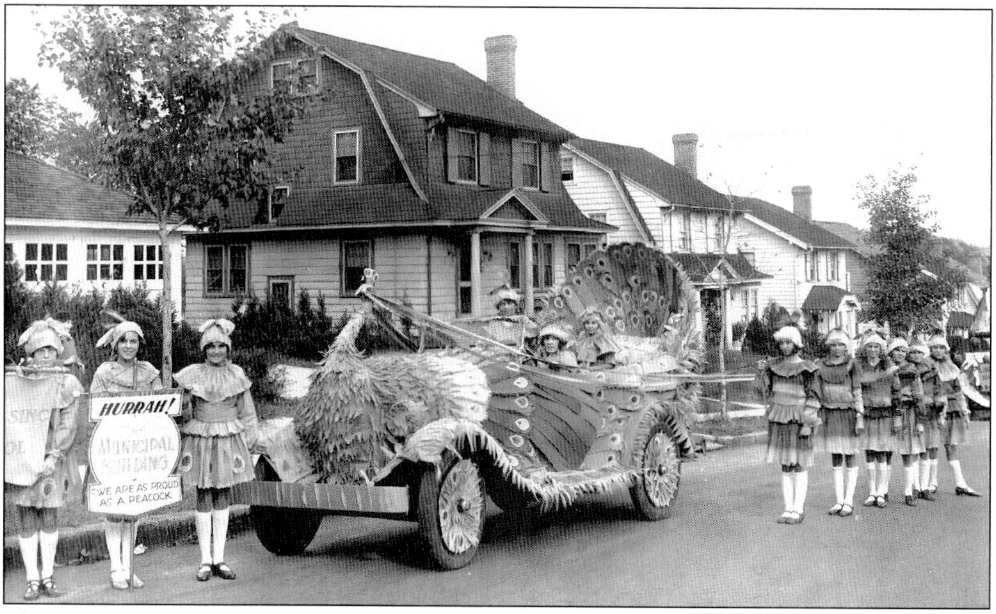

This 1920s touring car has practically disappeared under the artistic efforts of what seems to be Watsessing School's contribution to the festivities. Just out of sight to the right, the Liberty School contingent is getting ready to step off in a parade down Broad Street that none of these kids would ever forget. The photograph was taken on Vernon Terrace, which has remained almost unchanged for more than 75 years.

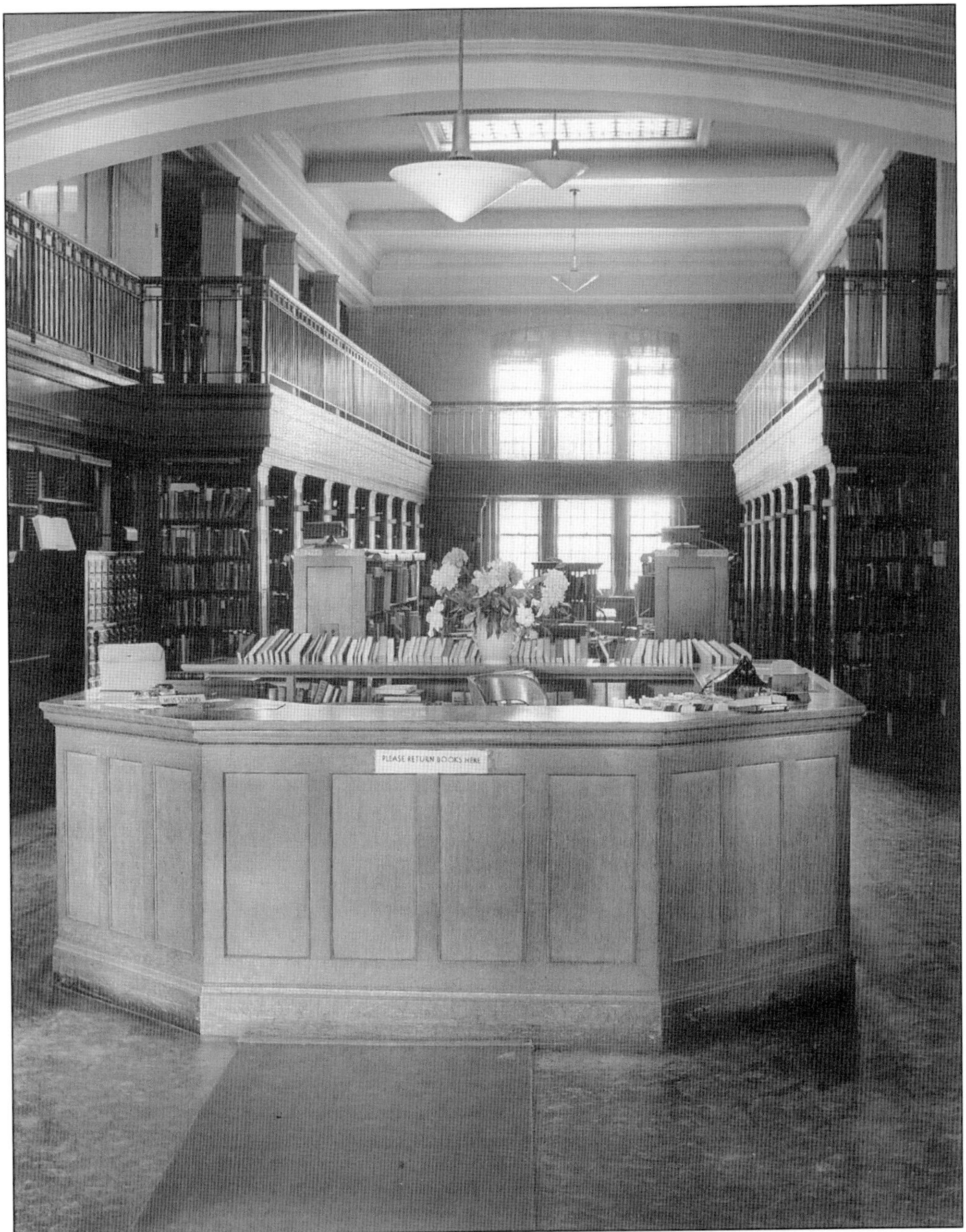

Looking pretty much as it did when the 1925 public library opened, the main desk was photographed about 10 years later by H. D. Sheldon of West Caldwell. The original lighting fixtures and furniture were still in place, including a rather quaint revolving bookcase in the center background. The western sun shines through the large window, which overlooks the Amzi Dodd barn on State Street.

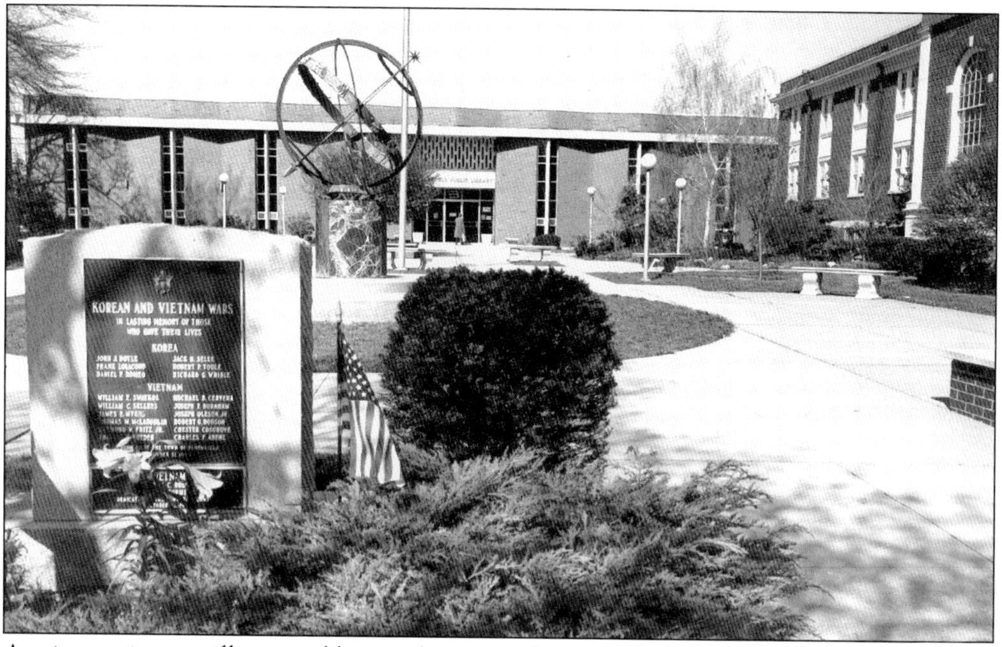

An impressive armillary on library plaza was donated in 1962 by public and parochial schoolchildren, who gave it to the town on the 150th anniversary of its founding. Kenneth Lynch, a Bloomfield artisan who began as a blacksmith's apprentice, designed and executed the metalwork. In solemn ceremony 11 years later, the granite monument honoring fallen heroes in the Korean and Vietnam Wars was dedicated.

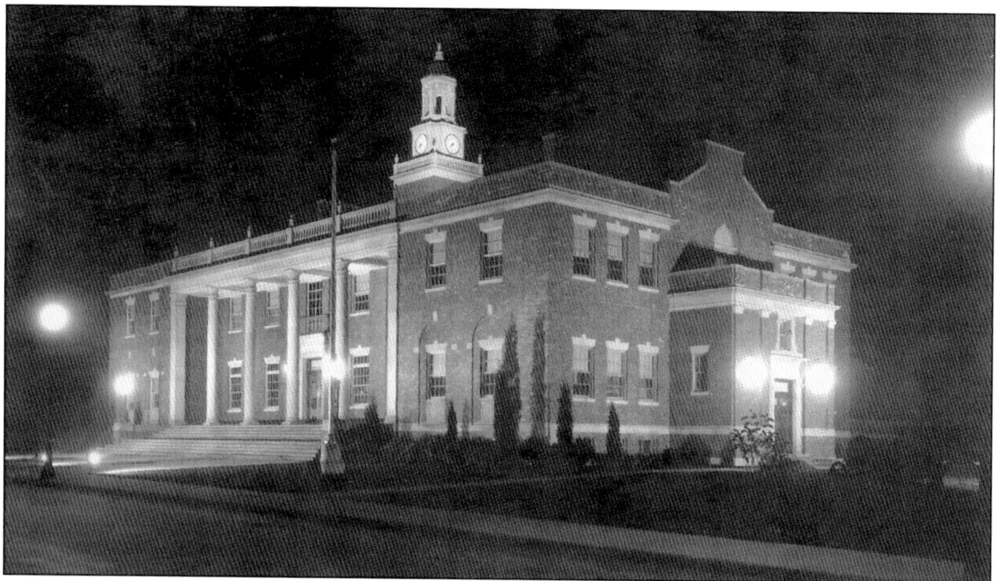

Seen here is a 1928 nighttime view of Bloomfield's pride, the floodlit municipal building, which was erected on a brand-new street, Municipal Plaza. The street was constructed on a section of land that cut through the G. Lee Stout estate from Montgomery Street to Bloomfield Avenue. Space was preserved for a new federal post office across the street, a goal that was realized when the present building opened in 1933. It replaced a series of several other inadequate buildings in various locations.

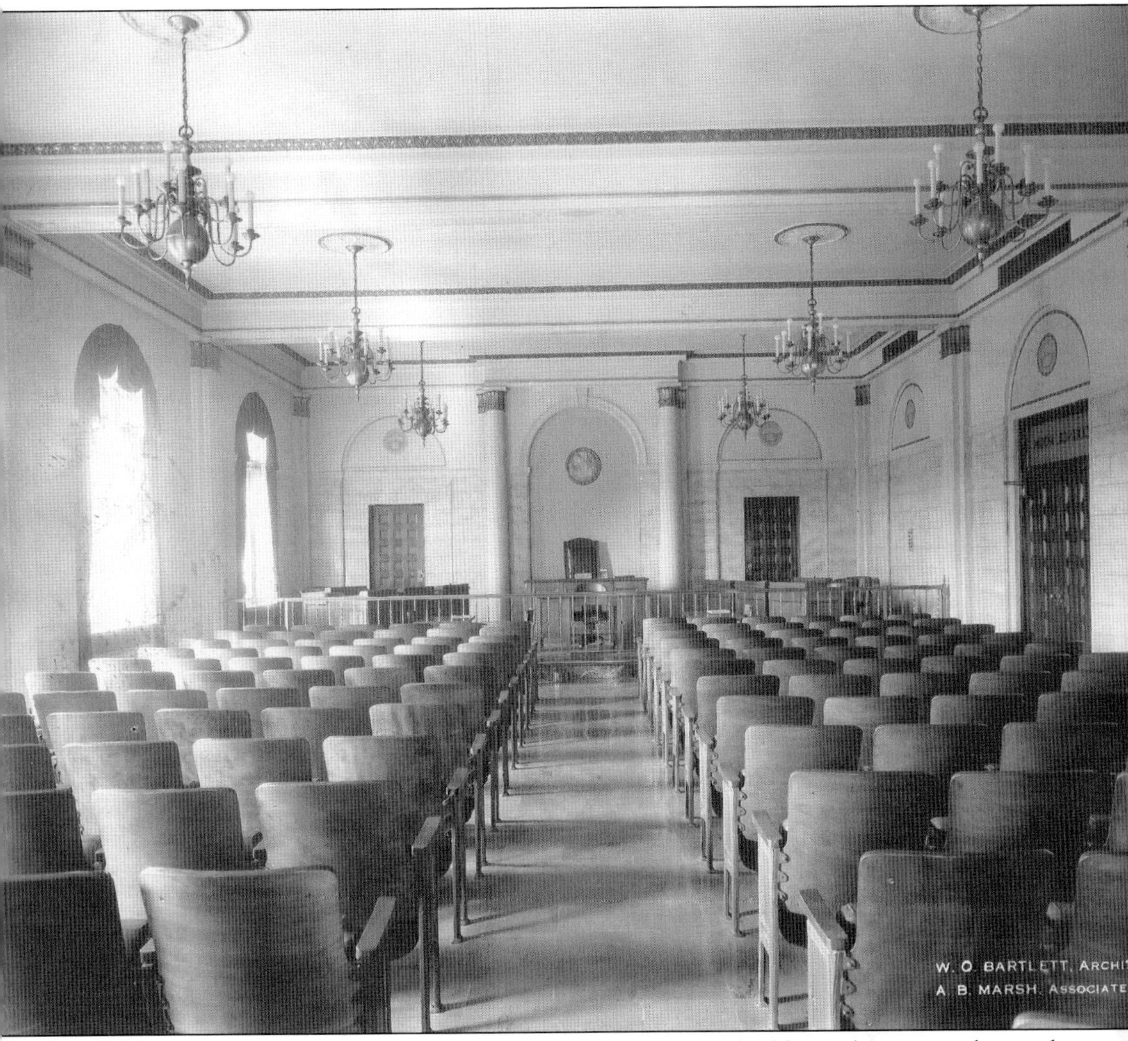

Bartlett and Marsh, the architects of Bloomfield's new municipal building, who were justly proud of its Georgian Revival architecture, took this 1927 photograph. Subsequent redecorating and the accumulated clutter of 80 years has somewhat altered its simplicity.

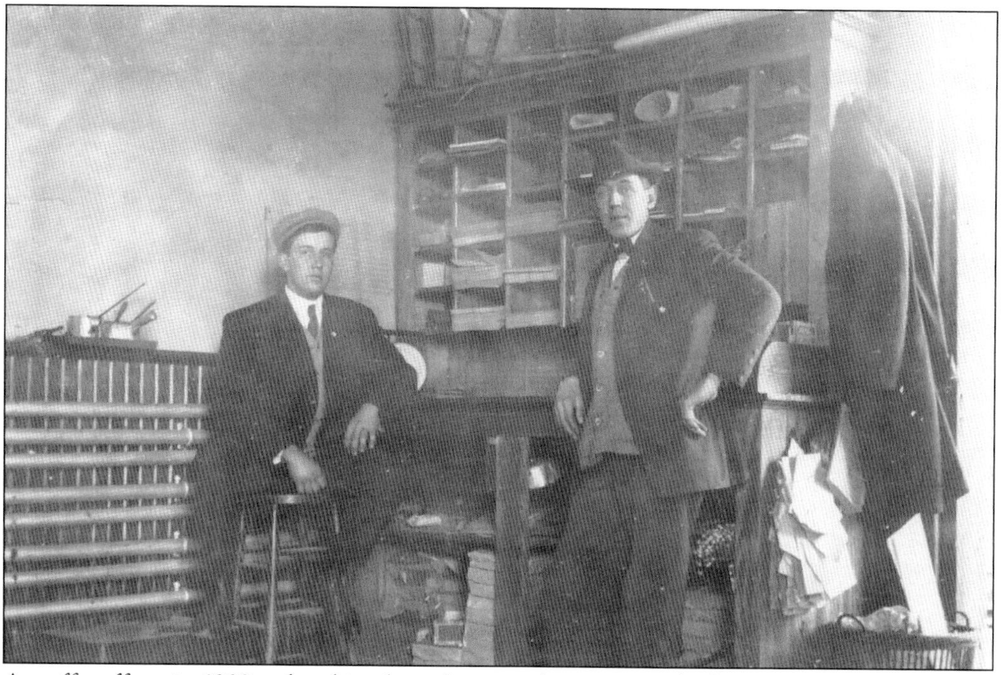

A traffic officer in 1909 rode a bicycle with a speedometer attached to it, and his duty was to catch speeders. Two years later, the foot-powered bicycle gave way to a motorcycle. Uniformed policemen did all the work of investigating, tracking down, and apprehending lawbreakers. The detective bureau was created about 1927 with only two plainclothesmen. Later two more were added. Today it stands at eight detectives.

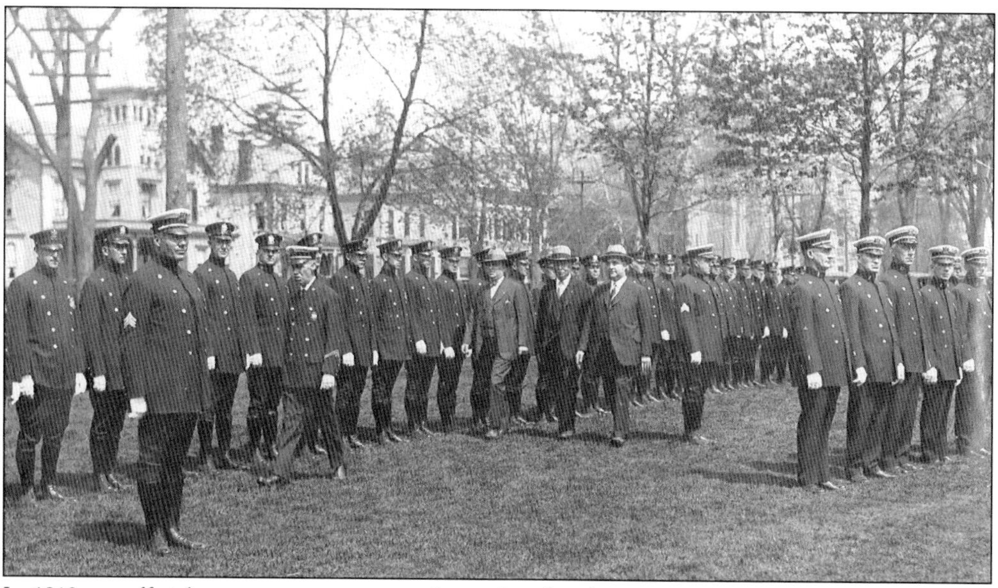

In 1812, an official town government was formed and with it came Bloomfield's first law officers. The early appointments of constables and justices of the peace served as the nucleus of the present-day department, which consists of 128 officers. Plenty of brass and gold was evident when white-gloved officers stood at attention on the green in 1927, under the leadership of Chief Joseph Huddy.

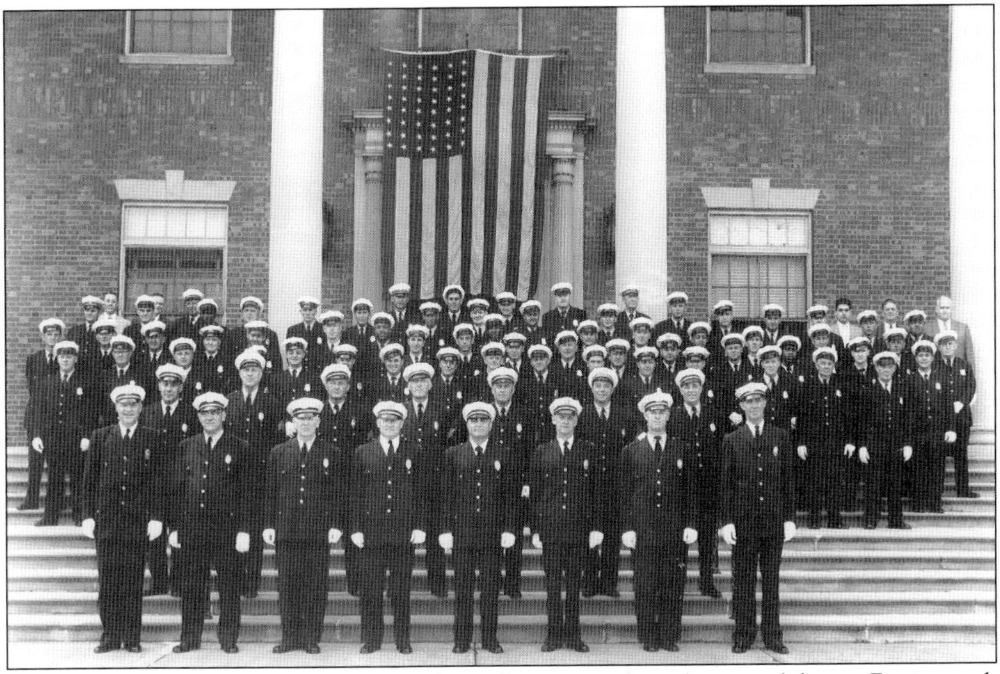

During World War II, 15 Bloomfield police officers served in the armed forces. For its work in war bond drives and the assistance given town organizations, the department received commendations from the Treasury Department and the Red Cross for meritorious service. When this 1956 photograph of Bloomfield's finest was taken, police headquarters were located on the first floor of town hall. The current Law Enforcement Building was completed in 1970.

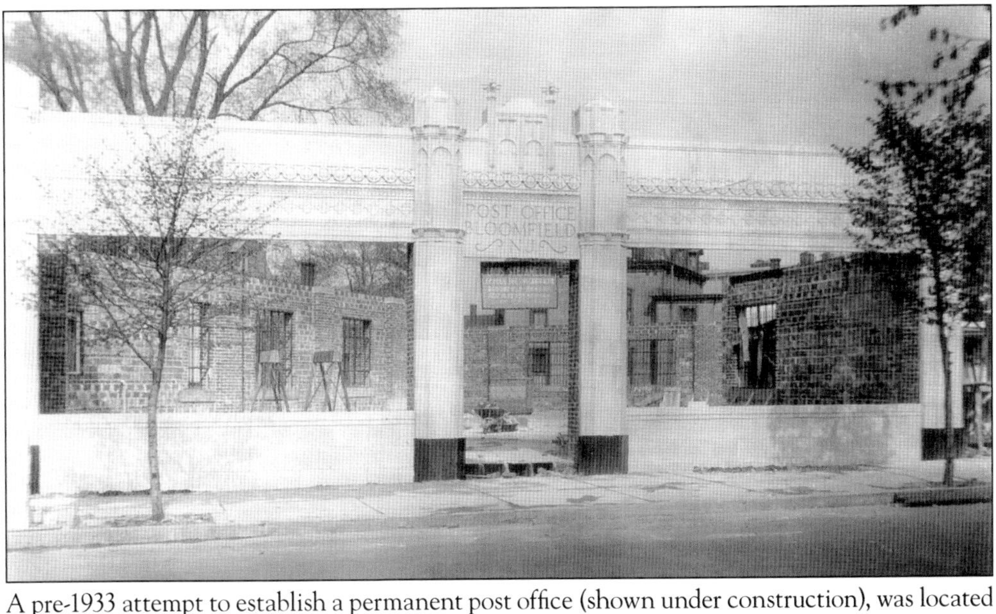

A pre-1933 attempt to establish a permanent post office (shown under construction), was located on Lackawanna Plaza in 1926. Six years later, this inadequate structure was abandoned, then used by various businesses, becoming the Anderson Candy Factory in the 1950s. It was recently demolished as part of the Washington Triangle renewal scheme. (Courtesy of the New Jersey Historical Society.)

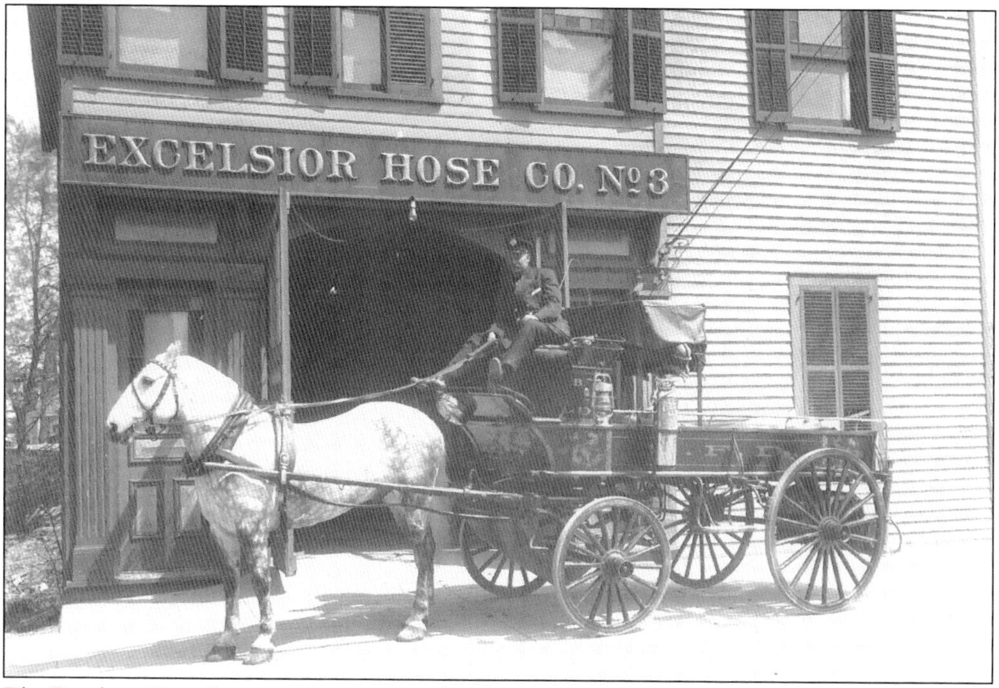

The Excelsior Hose Company was organized at the Bickler Paper Box Factory at 32 Maple Street in 1883. The hose carriage moved to the barn at the rear of 22 Maple Street one year later. From 1883 to 1924, the fire department used horse-drawn wagons equipped with hoses and ladders. In 1924, the Bloomfield Fire Association raised money to purchase its first modern fire truck, a Ford.

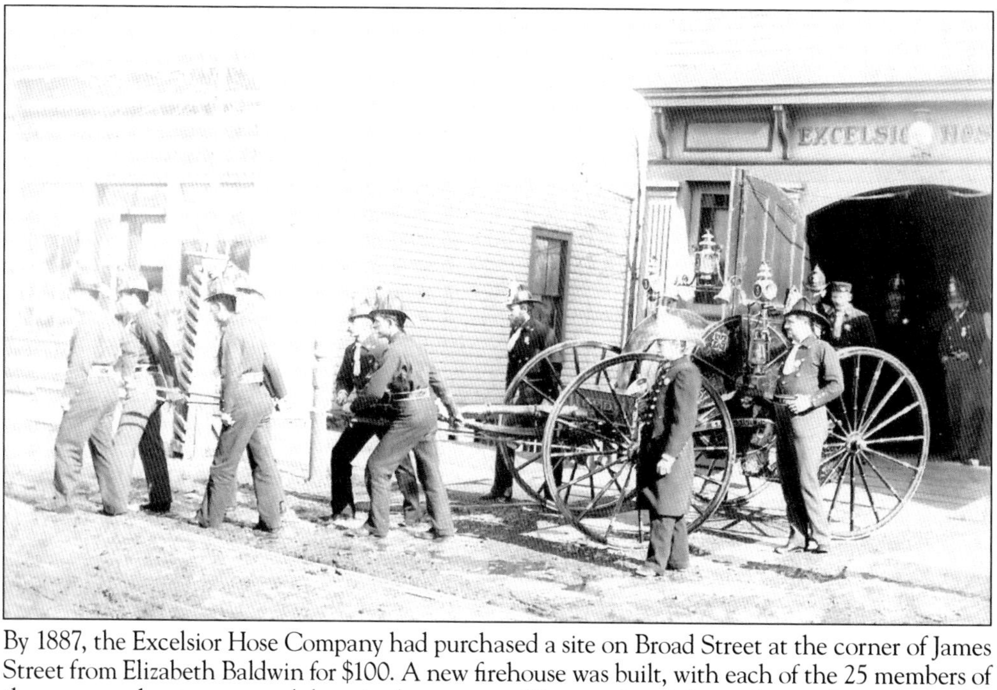

By 1887, the Excelsior Hose Company had purchased a site on Broad Street at the corner of James Street from Elizabeth Baldwin for $100. A new firehouse was built, with each of the 25 members of the company having an equal share in the property. They equipped themselves with regulation fire hat, belt, and red shirt. In 1902, a hose wagon built in Bloomfield was put into service.

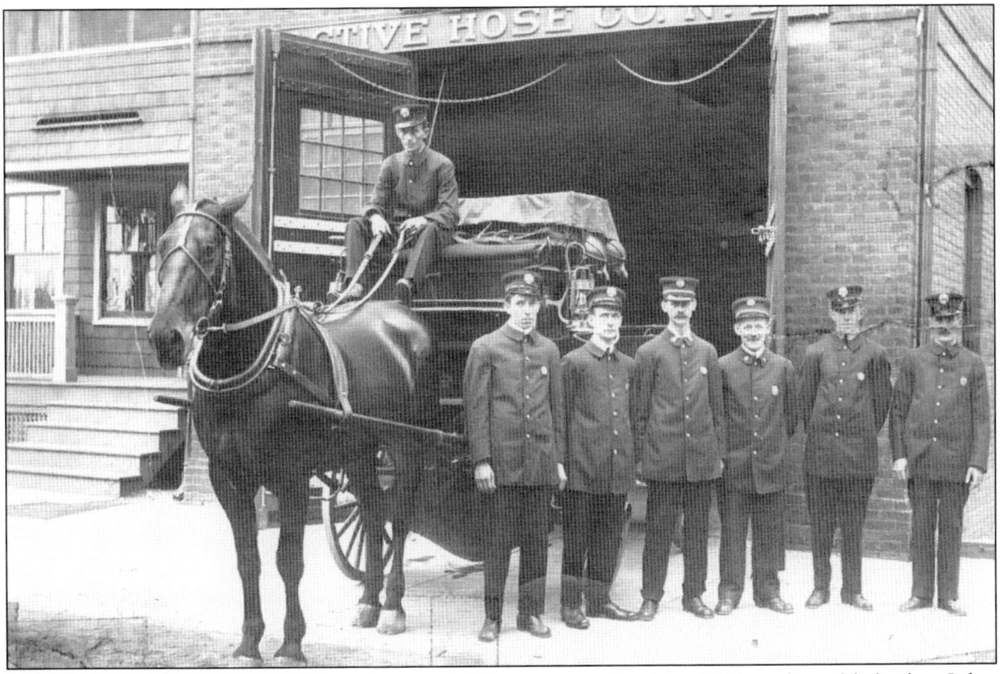

The Active Hose Company, seen here in 1907, was organized in 1885 and established at John Wild's carpenter shop on Myrtle Street. In 1887, now on Willow Street, the hose company had a four-wheeled jumper, better known as a Spider. The equipment was rugged; fires in Bloomfield Center could be answered by taking a shortcut along the Lackawanna tracks, bumping the horse cart and pumper along the railroad ties.

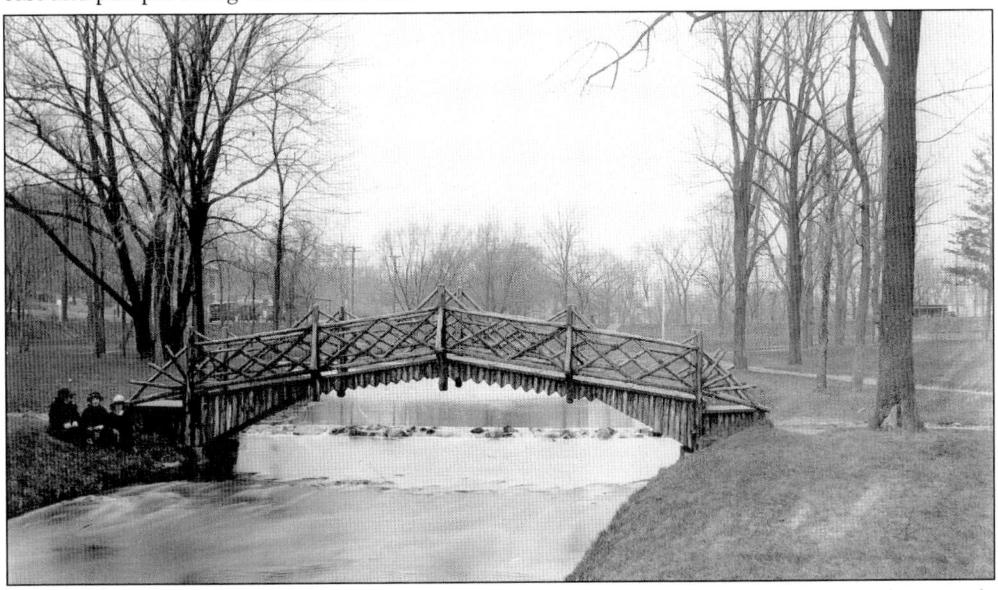

An attractive bridge in the rustic style spans the Third River in Brookside Park. Unfortunately numerous floods, the latest in 1999, have washed away several bridges since this one disappeared. The area was once industrial, the site of a pond belonging to the old Morris Mill and several millraces running through the property. Parts of the Morris Canal incline planes were made in this mill in 1825.

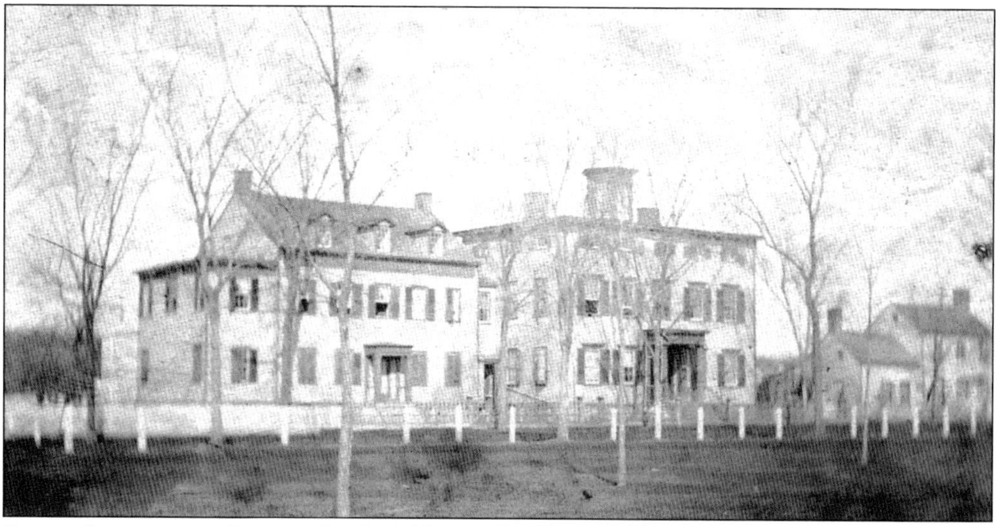

Facing the green, on the site of today's library, the Bloomfield Female Seminary began in 1836 and lasted 18 years. Well-educated and deeply pious, Harriet B. Cooke came to town to be its principal. Madame Cooke's School, as it became known, was a center of significant intellectual and religious influence. Many young women came a long distance to attend the prestigious school as students or boarders.

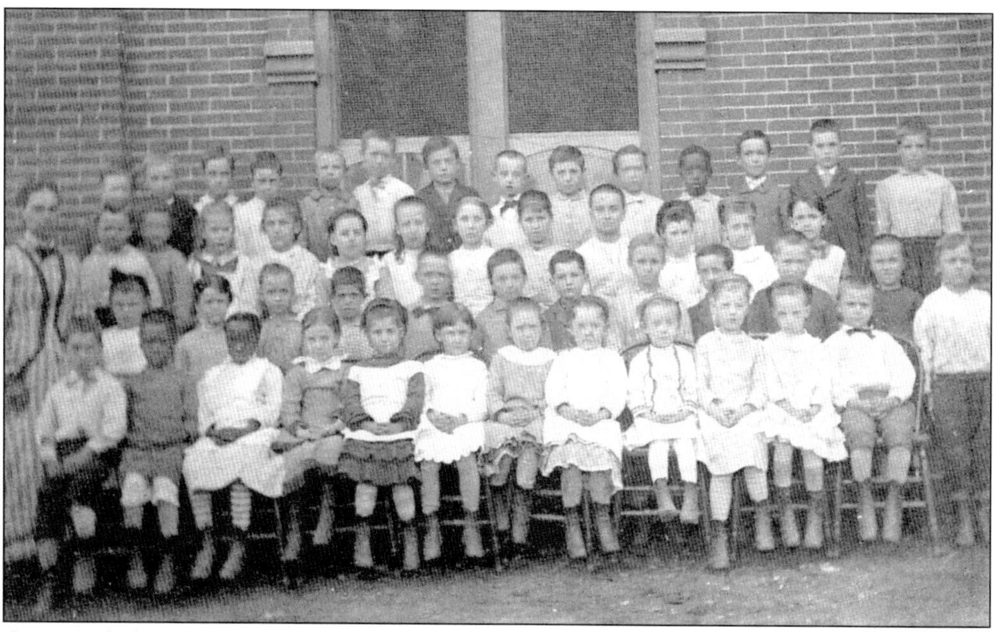

One year before these children posed by their Center Primary School in 1880, people gathered on the sidewalks and cheered as fire horses pulled the hose carriage purchased by the newly formed Phoenix Hose Company. One year after they posed, the Watsessing Free Public Library was organized in Van Giesen's store at the corner of Dodd Street and Watsessing Avenue. By 1900, a building with a reading room was erected.

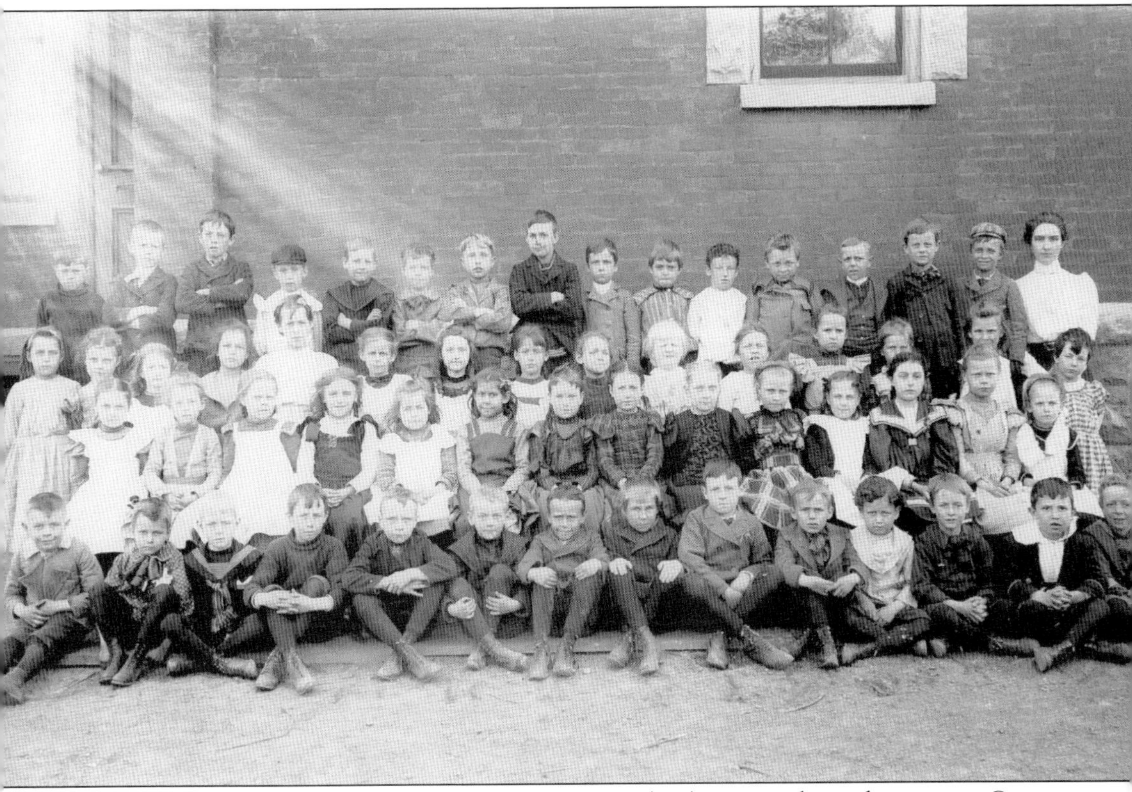

The town was growing steadily and eager to approve school projects deemed necessary. Center Primary School on Liberty Street, pictured above, appeared on the public school horizon in 1883. By 1900, it had been enlarged twice. Free public lectures were given each winter in the assembly hall beginning in 1903. Miss Taney and her class pose for their photograph that same year.

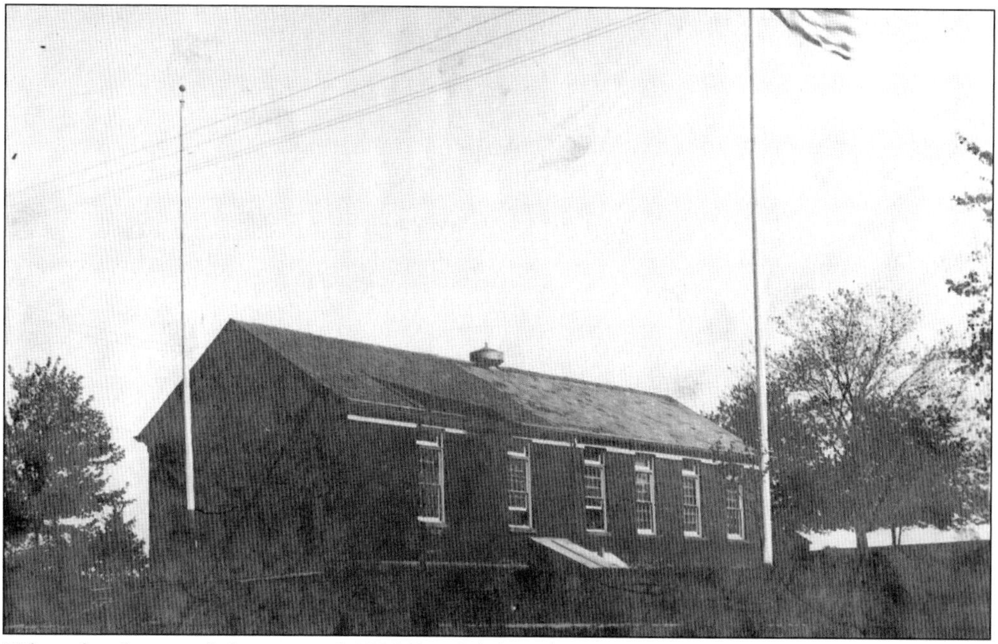

When fire destroyed the original 1785 Brookdale School near Yantecaw Avenue, a new frame structure was built at a more centralized location, where the Brookdale Firehouse is today. Used as a pay school until 1849, it became a free school; a new brick building went up in 1857. In 1909, the present Brookdale School was erected across the street and the old Brookdale School was converted into a firehouse.

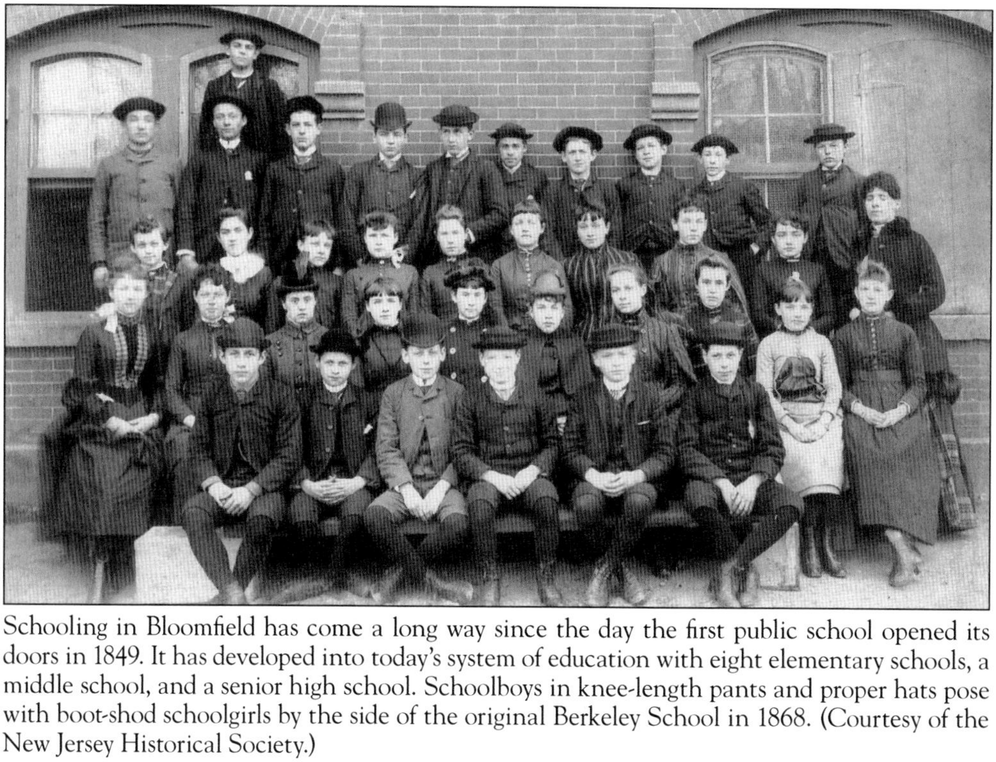

Schooling in Bloomfield has come a long way since the day the first public school opened its doors in 1849. It has developed into today's system of education with eight elementary schools, a middle school, and a senior high school. Schoolboys in knee-length pants and proper hats pose with boot-shod schoolgirls by the side of the original Berkeley School in 1868. (Courtesy of the New Jersey Historical Society.)

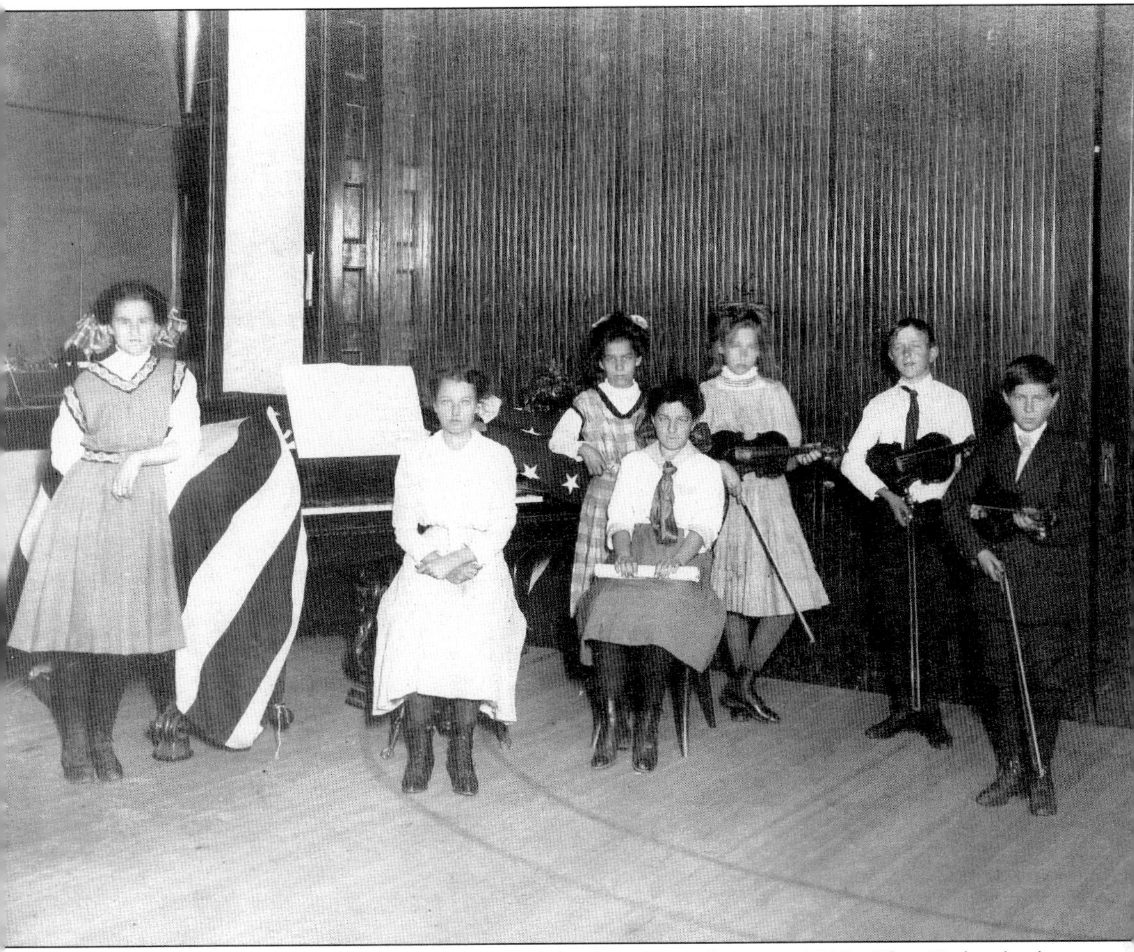

Scholars in town classrooms were few and far between when, in 1895, Glen Ridge broke away from Bloomfield and took several hundred schoolchildren. But the public was all for education—enough to build three new school houses in 1898. A March 1902 concert in Watsessing School was very successful. The proceeds were used to complete the privet hedge around the school and add books to the library.

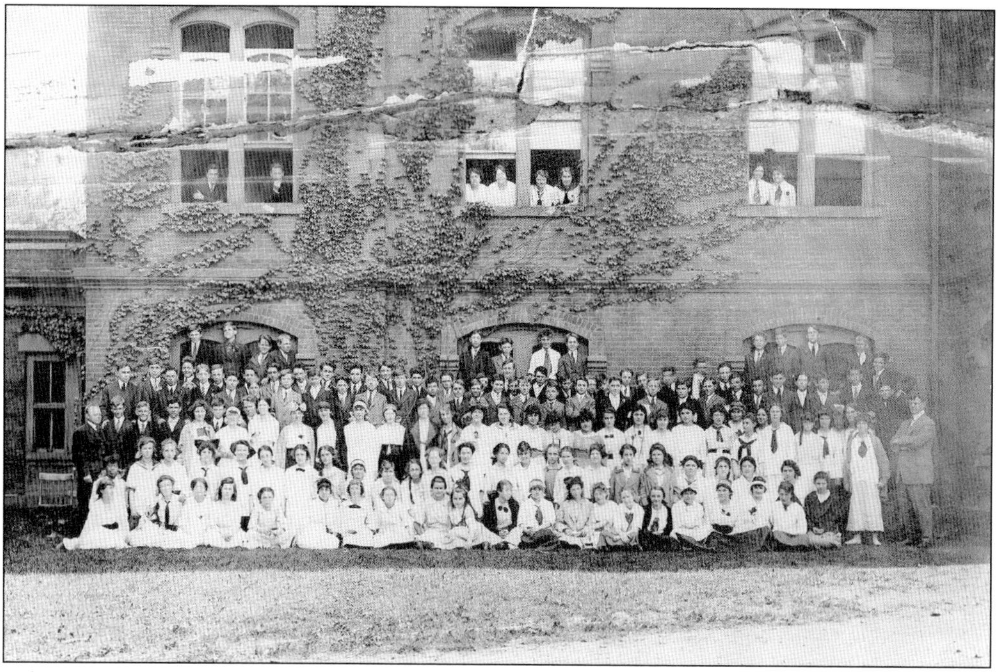

When the present Bloomfield High School opened its doors in 1913, the original high school at Broad Street and Belleville Avenue became Park Grammar School. The eighth-grade graduating class poses here in front of the old red brick building in 1915. The students received their diplomas and then crossed the street to begin their studies in the new high school. The remodeled 1871 high school now houses school administration offices.

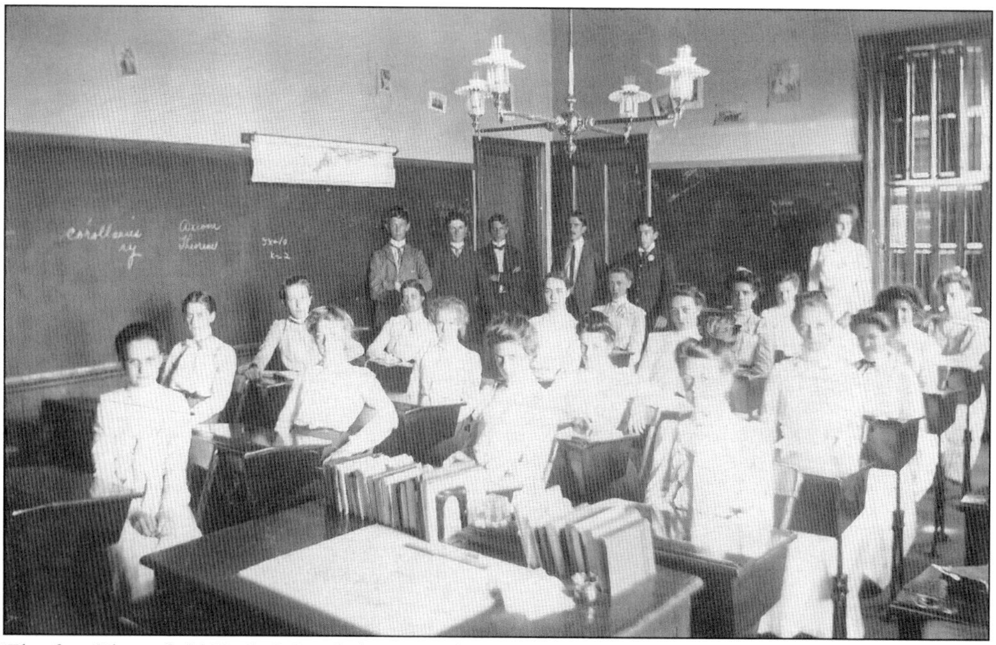

The first Bloomfield High School class, numbering 22, began its studies in the red brick building on Broad Street and Belleville Avenue in January 1873. The math class of 1900 sat under gas lamps in the original high school, still searching for the meaning of the elusive *x*.

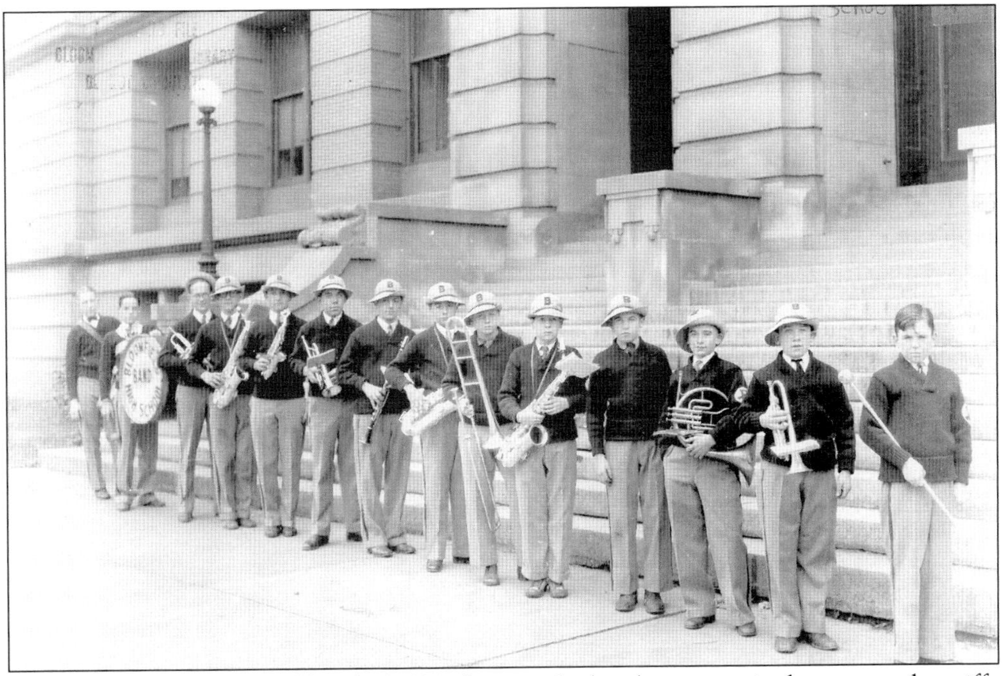

The boys in the high school band of 1924, the year the band was organized, were not the spiffy spit-and-polish group of today. Foley Field did not exist until the early 1930s, when it was built as a project by the Works Progress Administration on the site of the northern end of Oakes Pond. It is possible that football games may have been played in Watsessing Park until then.

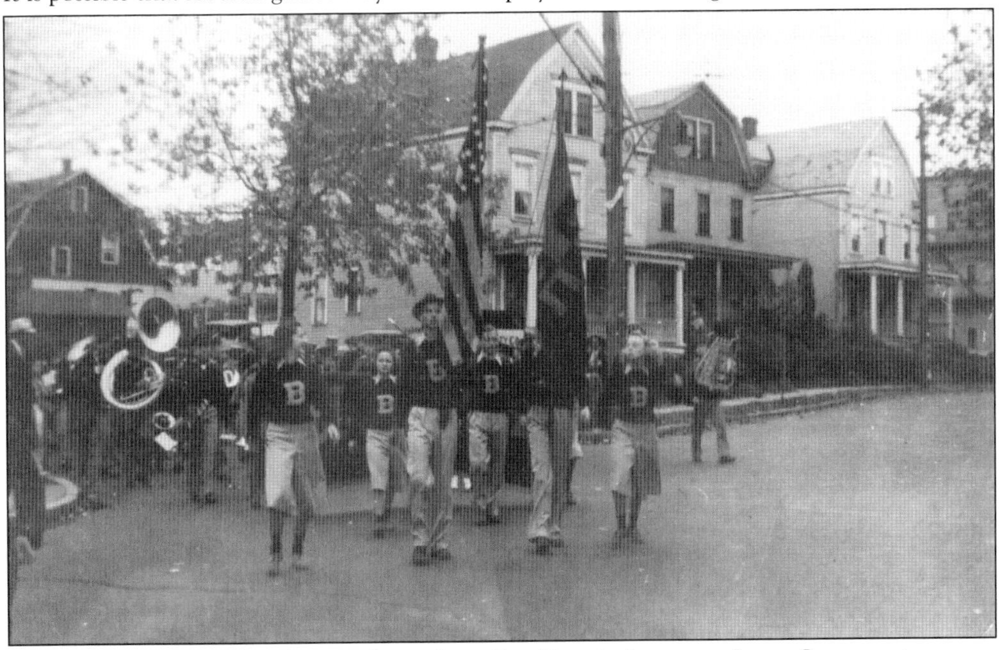

The 1940 high school band is marching along East Passaic Avenue at James Street on its way to Foley Field via the Morris Canal towpath that was used as a convenient pedestrian shortcut and bridle path before being paved over by Kennedy Drive in the 1950s. The scene remains pretty much the same today, although a new house stands on the corner in the left background.

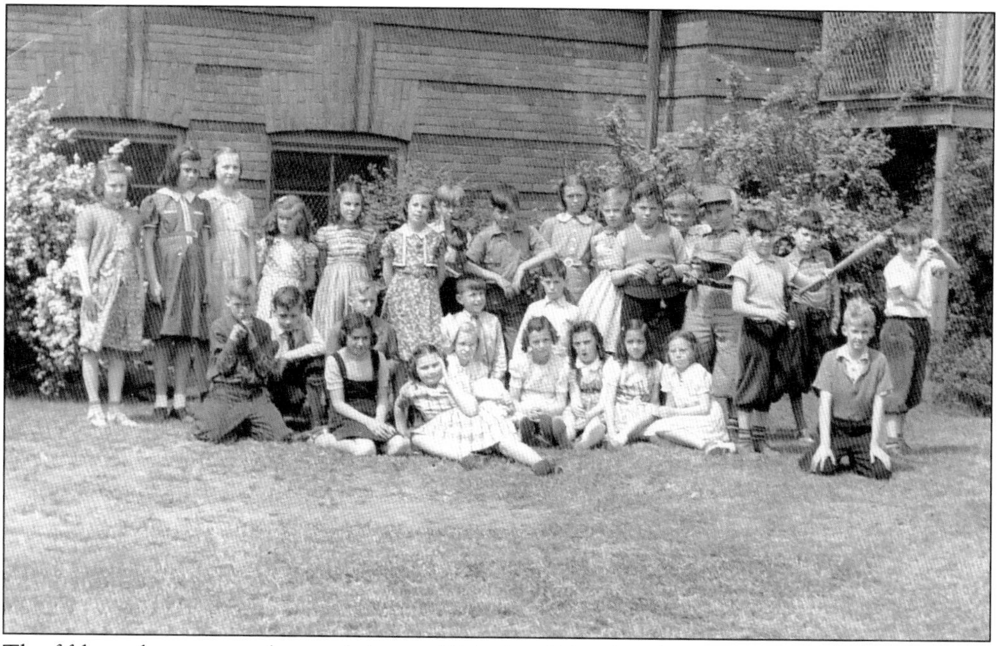

The fifth grade poses on the south lawn of Fairview School with sport equipment popular with kids at that time. The New York World's Fair ("The World of Tomorrow") had just opened, marking the last year of uneasy peace between World Wars I and II. These kids would not see army service at that time, but some of them would later be caught up in the Korean War.

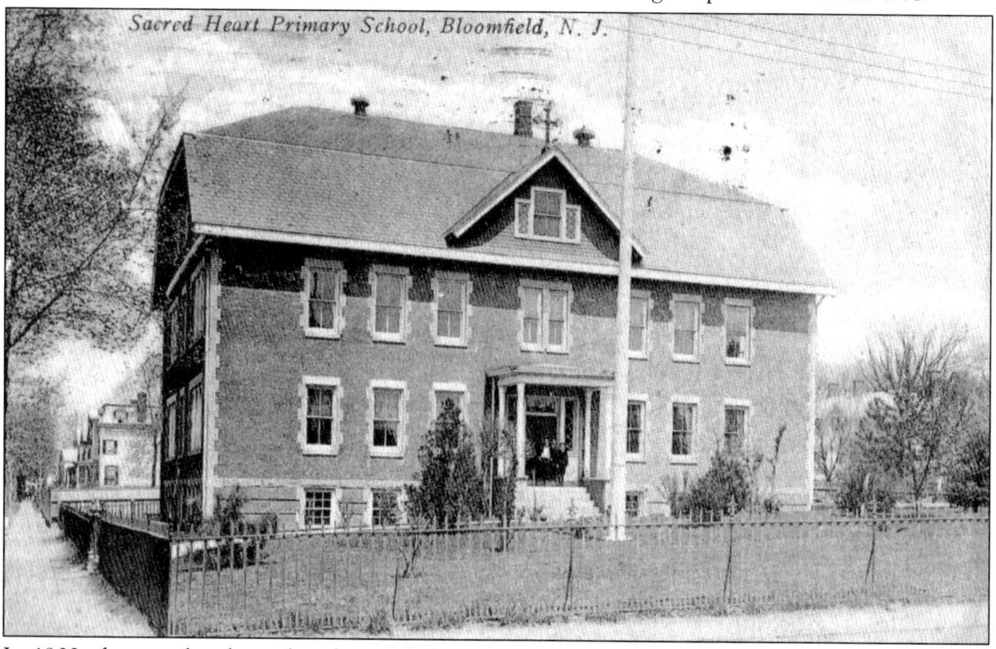

In 1902, the greatly admired and remarkable Rev. Joseph Nardiello saw the need for more space for the young children attending Sacred Heart Primary School and made plans for a new building on Liberty Street in the rear of the church. In order to build, several old houses that stood on the property had to be removed. The grounds were enclosed by an iron railing and beautified by numerous plantings.

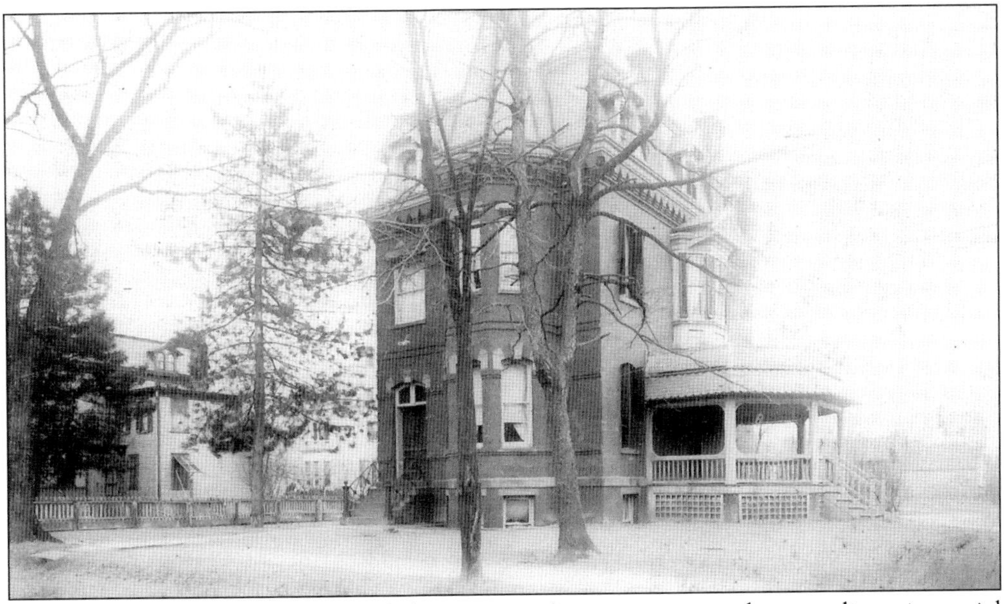

One year after the Civil War ended, a group of young men sought to enliven its social entertainment by forming the Mabel Sociable Club. This handsome building on Liberty Street with its octagonal tower, handsome chandeliers, billiards parlor, library, and dining room provided the Mabel Sociables with the setting for many a congenial evening. The structure later became part of the public school system, the George Morris School.

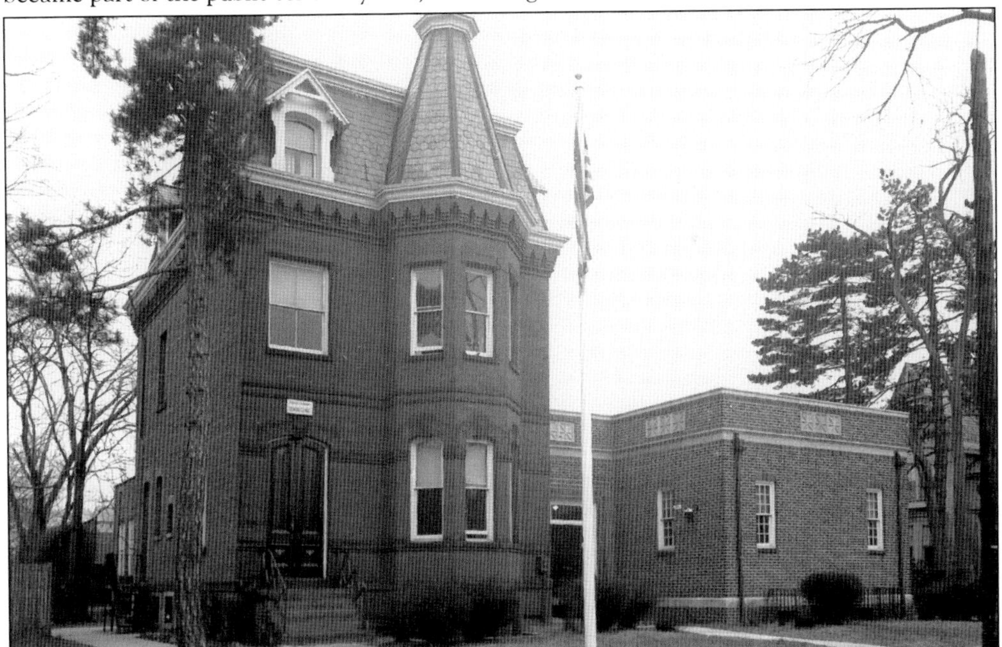

The Mabel Sociable Club occupied this fashionable brick building (left) on Liberty Street in 1889. George Morris School, the 1925 structure on the right, was used to educate special education children. When this photograph was taken, the second floor of the old club building was used by the board of education as a free dental clinic for Depression-era children. The building is now part of Bloomfield College.

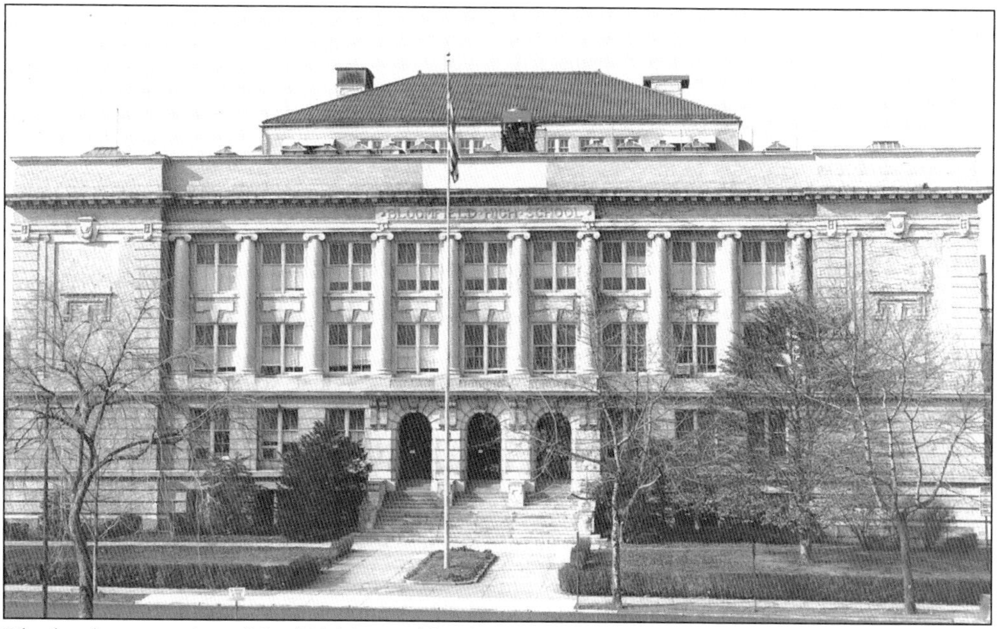

The land was purchased for $16,000, and by the time the building was completed, the total cost of the 1913 high school came to $250,000. The faculty, including the principal, numbered 17. In 1923, the Belleville Avenue wing was added. The constantly rising increase in enrollment by 1929 necessitated further expansion. With the enormously transforming additions undertaken recently, this beautiful 1970s photograph may stir a memory or two.

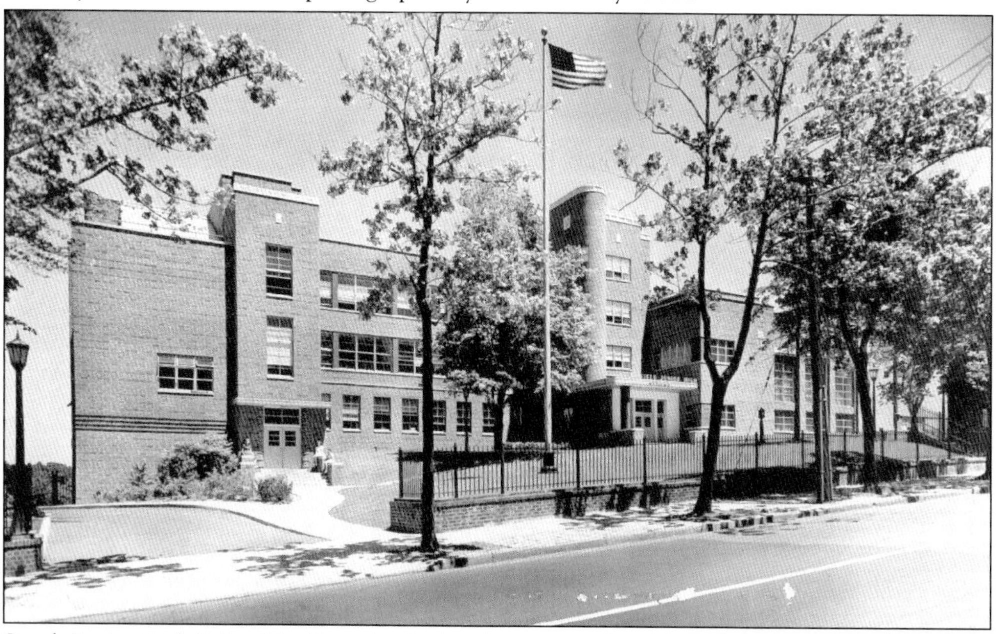

South Junior High School, built on the Richards estate on Franklin Street at a cost of $1,258,028 with $566,113 coming from a Works Progress Administration grant, opened its doors in 1940. The school won wide acclaim for its notable architecture, modern equipment, and teaching methods. Marble walls and blue tile floors in the entrance made for a memorable first impression. It was very nearly new when this photograph was taken.

After playing shortstop in Watsessing School, Alec Ferguson tried pitching when the Bloomfield Lyceum team of 1915 was formed. The New York Yankees signed him late in the 1916 season and then began the training that was to take him to the top. Ferguson reached the pinnacle of success in his sport when he pitched two games in the World Series of 1925 between his Washington club and Pittsburgh.

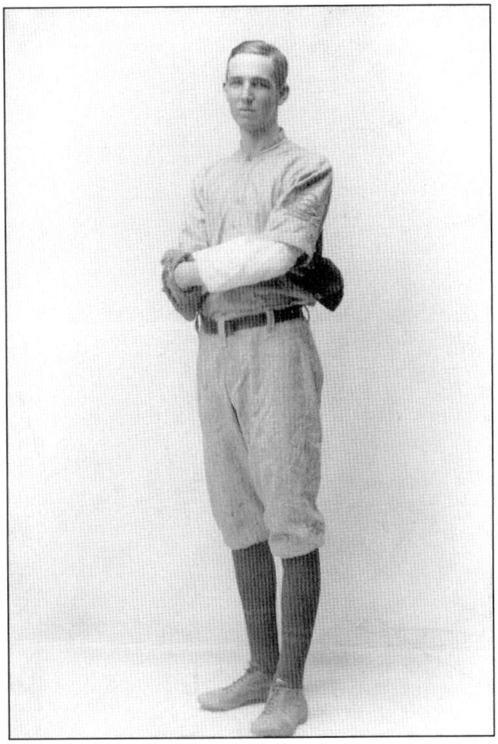

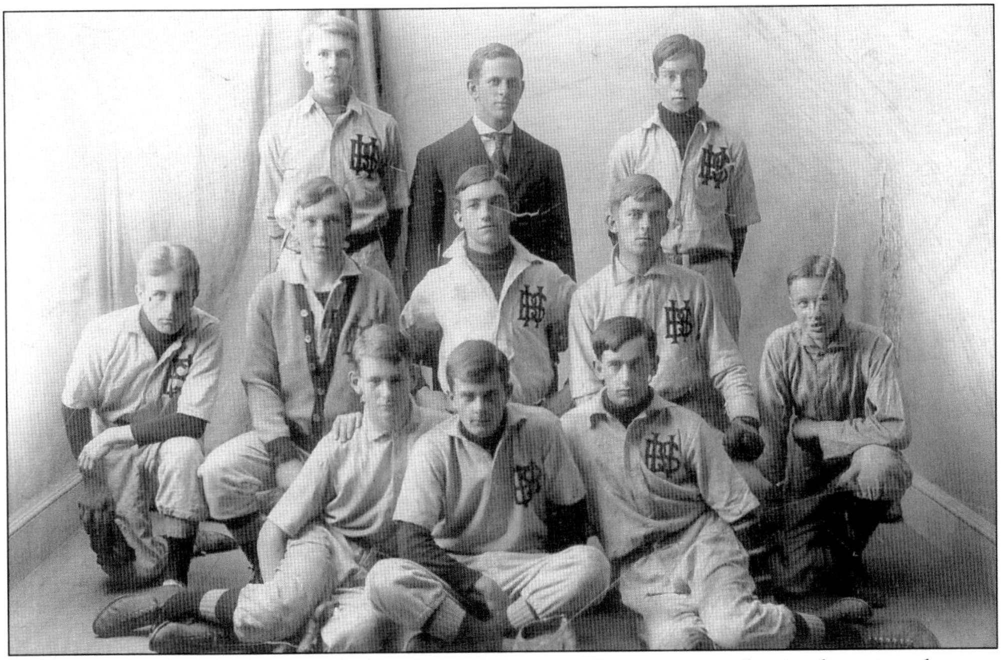

The lineup of players who excelled on Bengal teams and went on to play in the minor leagues included Bill Hassell, Ernie Hambacher, Ted Mazur, and Bob Miller. Hank Borowy, class of 1935, played for the New York Yankees. The 1908 team of Lou Jennin, Bill Rawson, Harrison Gahs, Morrell Hinkle, Fred Storm, Myrrin Edwards, Mahlon Milliken, Pier Cady, Bill Martin, and Bob Betts pose for the yearbook photograph.

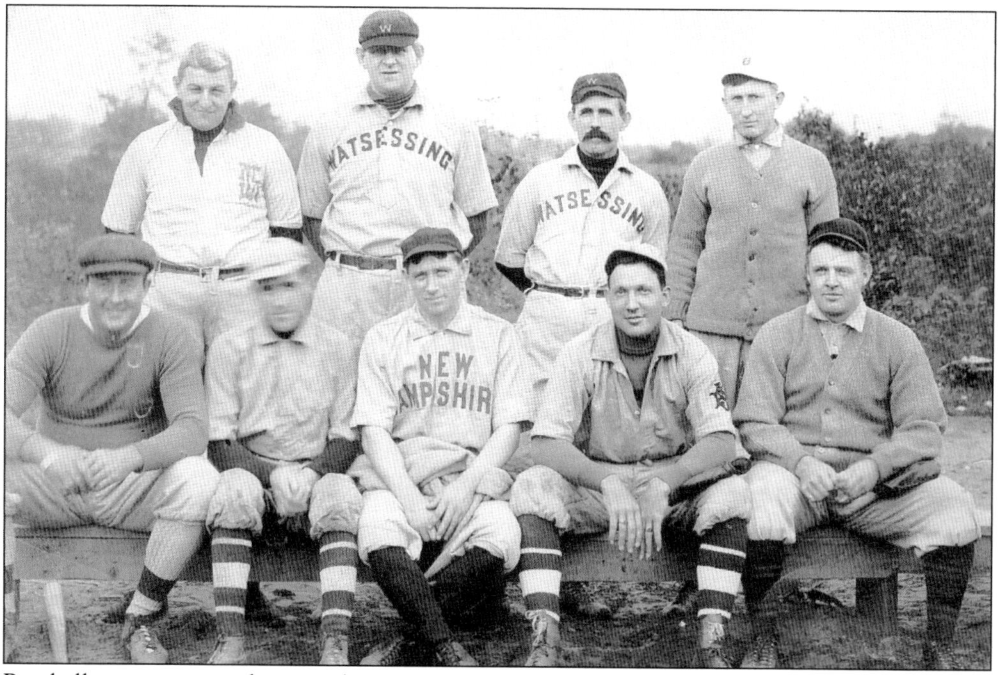

Baseball was at its ascendancy in the 1900s in Bloomfield with the Watsessing games commanding popular attention. The Watsessing baseball team of 1903 was considered one of the best amateur nines around. Arch rivals of Bloomfield, the team had three semiprofessional players who later became professionals: Larry Hesterfer, Herbert Fay, and Otto Hambacher. The club played on Charles Street, later on Arlington Avenue, and still later on Locust Avenue.

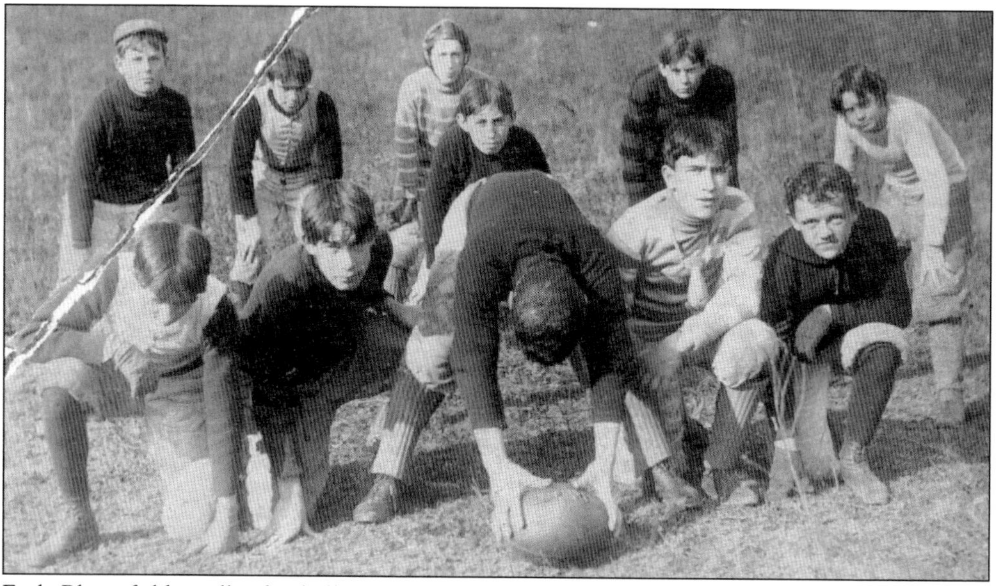

Early Bloomfield sandlot football was enthusiastically played in the neighborhoods: no pads, no helmets, and no expensive footgear. Joseph Garrabrant, second from left in the first row, went on to play on the Bloomfield football club captained by Sam Breadon. Breadon lived in town from 1898 to 1904 on Montgomery Street and later became owner of the St. Louis Cardinals and a flock of farm clubs.

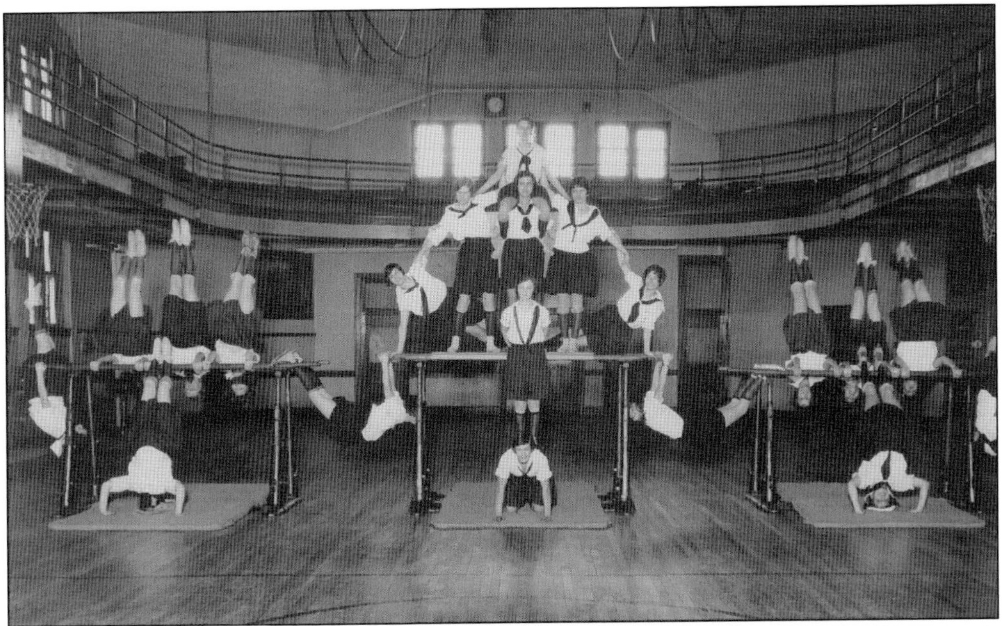

Wearing pleated blue or black serge bloomers, topped by heavy white duck middy blouses with broad black bow ties, black cotton stockings and white sneakers, the 1929 high school girls' gymnastics team performed in the old gymnasium. On one occasion, the girls rolled their stockings below the knee. The result was a sharp rebuke from the board of education. The black stockings were to remain in place.

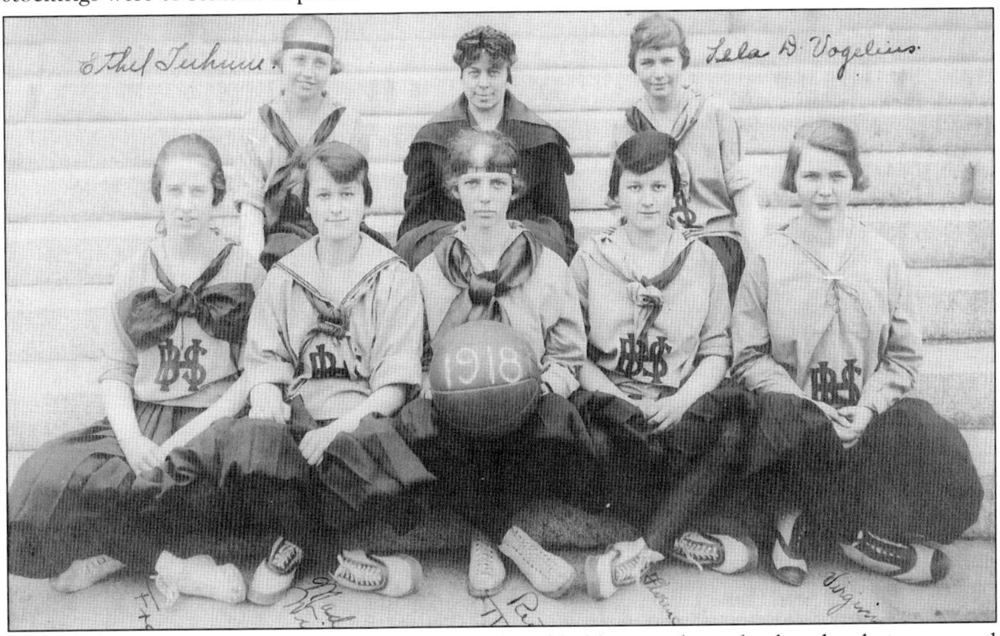

Playing in their regulation 32-pleated skirts and middy blouses, the girls played only intramural games during the basketball season of 1918. The seniors, here with their coach Edith Russell played the sophomores, each team having previously won all its games. The sophomores triumphed 33-20, ending the season. Three years before, the girls' team played two of its games using boys' rules and won both games.

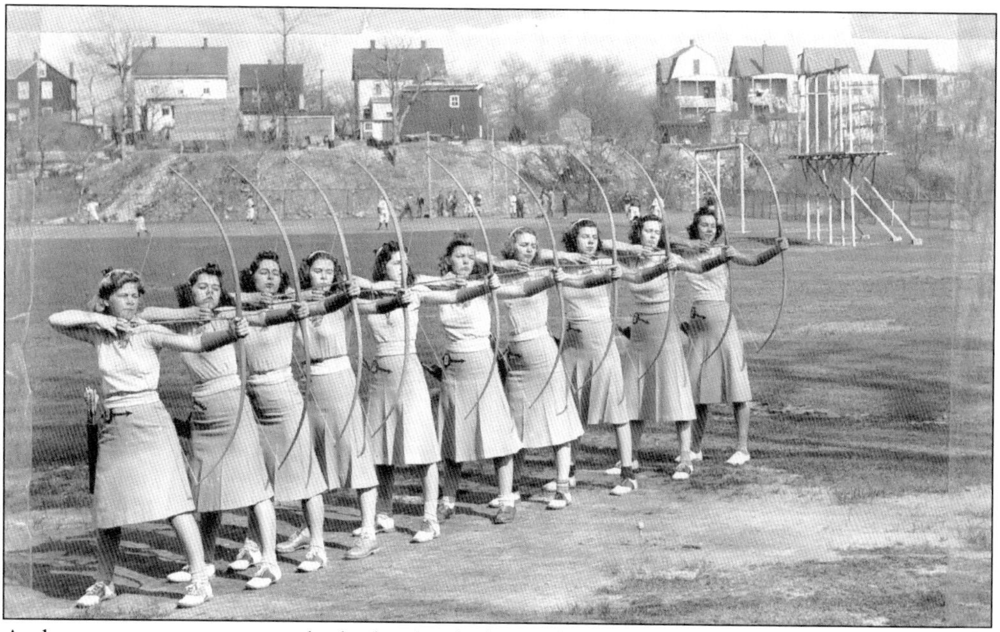

Archery was a new sport in the high school when Edith Russell began coaching it. This team of Bengal archers were winners of the 1940 National Archery Association Interscholastic Tournament. The team topped the country when they repeated the feat in 1941. In 1942, three teams were entered in the national competition and took first, second and fourth place, missing third place by just 21 points.

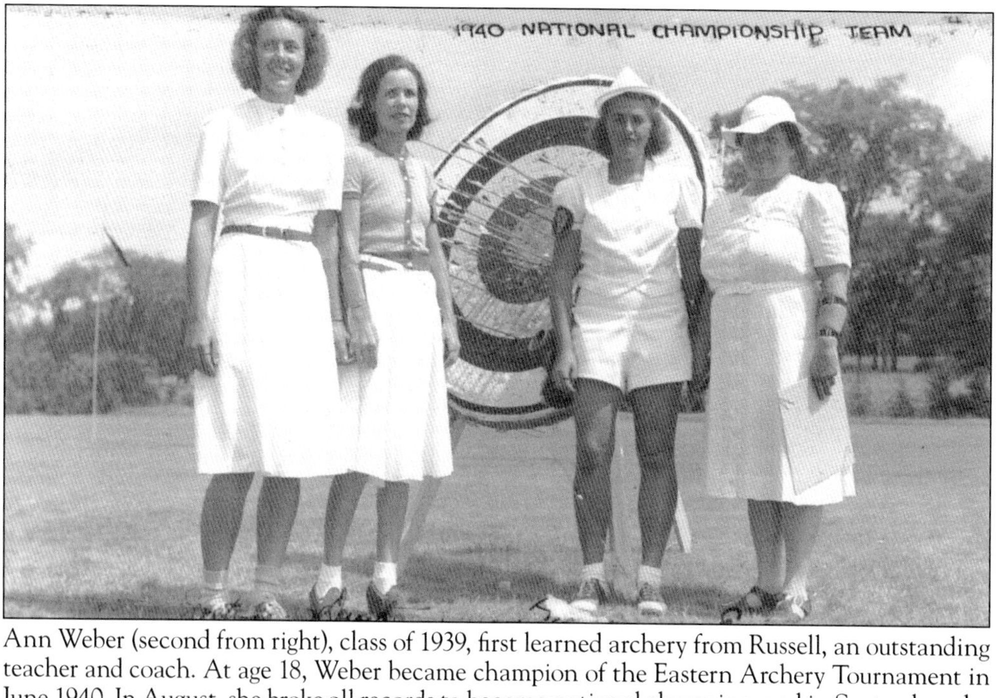

Ann Weber (second from right), class of 1939, first learned archery from Russell, an outstanding teacher and coach. At age 18, Weber became champion of the Eastern Archery Tournament in June 1940. In August, she broke all records to become national champion, and in September, she became New Jersey state champion. Following a meteoric rise to national prominence setting new records, Weber was the leading woman archer in the country.

Five

Parades and Patriotism

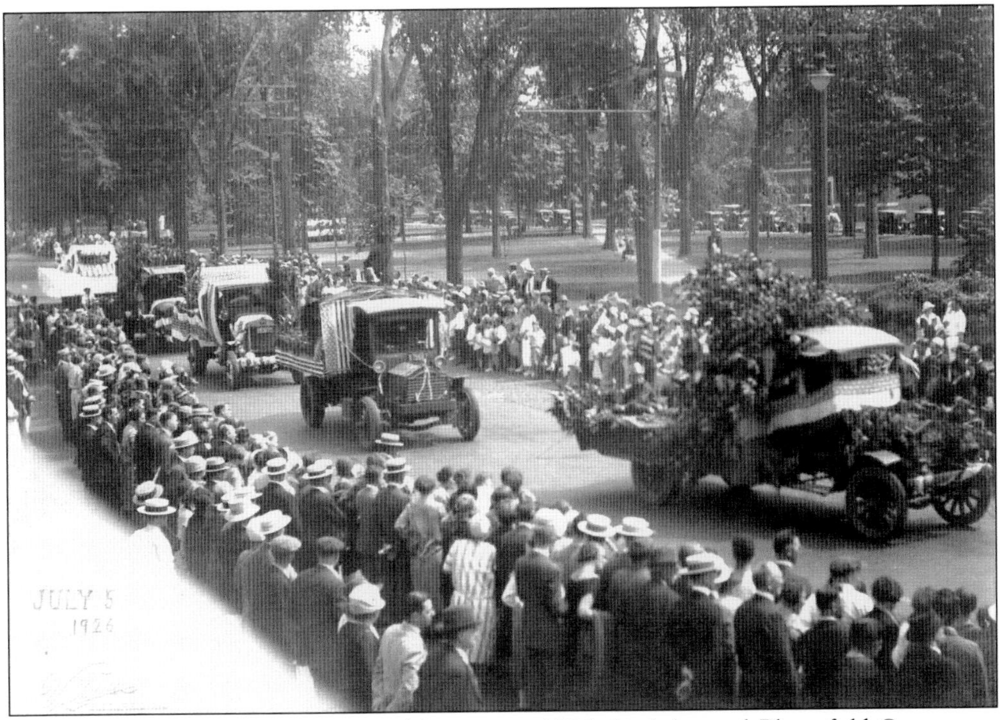

It was a special day. America was celebrating its 150th birthday and Bloomfield Center was proudly patriotic on July 4, 1926. One year later, trolleys of the Broad Street line were discarded, on their way to becoming a nostalgic memory. The Bloomfield Avenue trolleys continued their schedules from Montclair to Newark until 1952 when that line came to an end as well and Bloomfield Avenue was resurfaced.

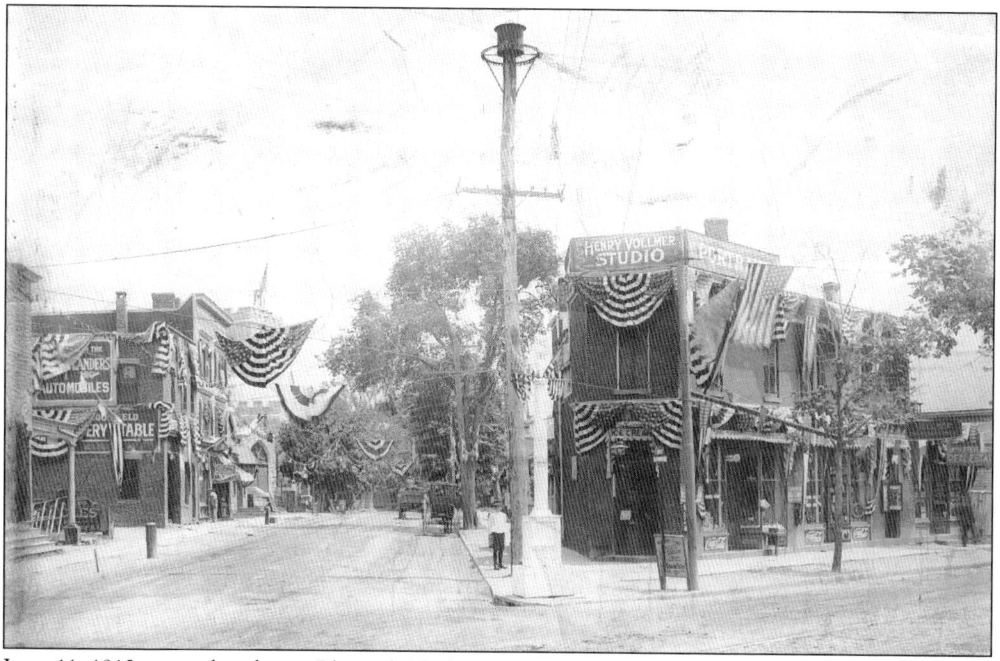

June 11, 1912, was a big day in Bloomfield: the town turned 100 years old. Everybody has broken out the bunting, including the livery stable on the left and the confectionery store on the right, with Henry Vollmer's studio one flight up. The electric car tracks from Newark are visible on Bloomfield Avenue, but there is nary an automobile in sight. The object on the top of the telephone pole may be an arc light.

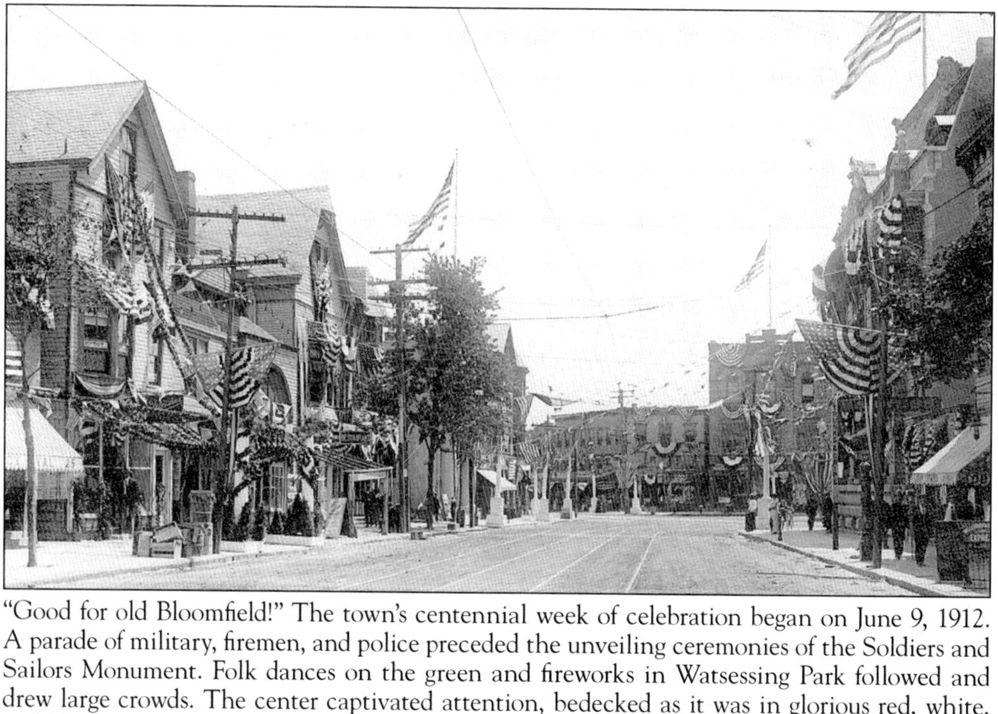

"Good for old Bloomfield!" The town's centennial week of celebration began on June 9, 1912. A parade of military, firemen, and police preceded the unveiling ceremonies of the Soldiers and Sailors Monument. Folk dances on the green and fireworks in Watsessing Park followed and drew large crowds. The center captivated attention, bedecked as it was in glorious red, white, and blue.

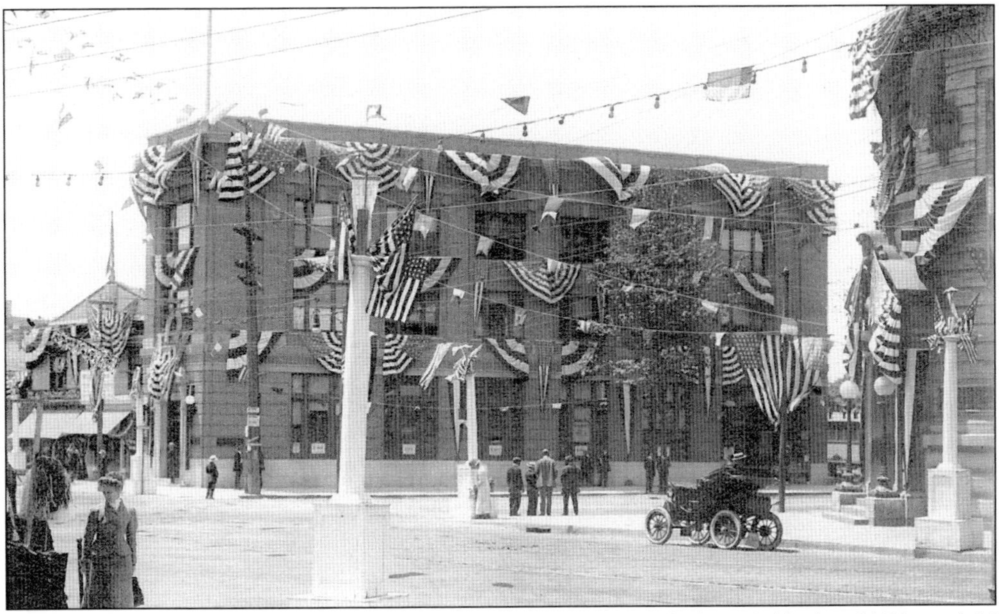

Shown decorated with flags to celebrate the 1912 centennial of Bloomfield, the old Bloomfield Trust Company, which merged with the Bloomfield National Bank in 1929, still stands at the corner of Bloomfield and Glenwood Avenues. The large banking room on the ground floor has since been remodeled into individual shops, but the structure looks pretty much the same today. Cohane's store on the left, however, is long gone.

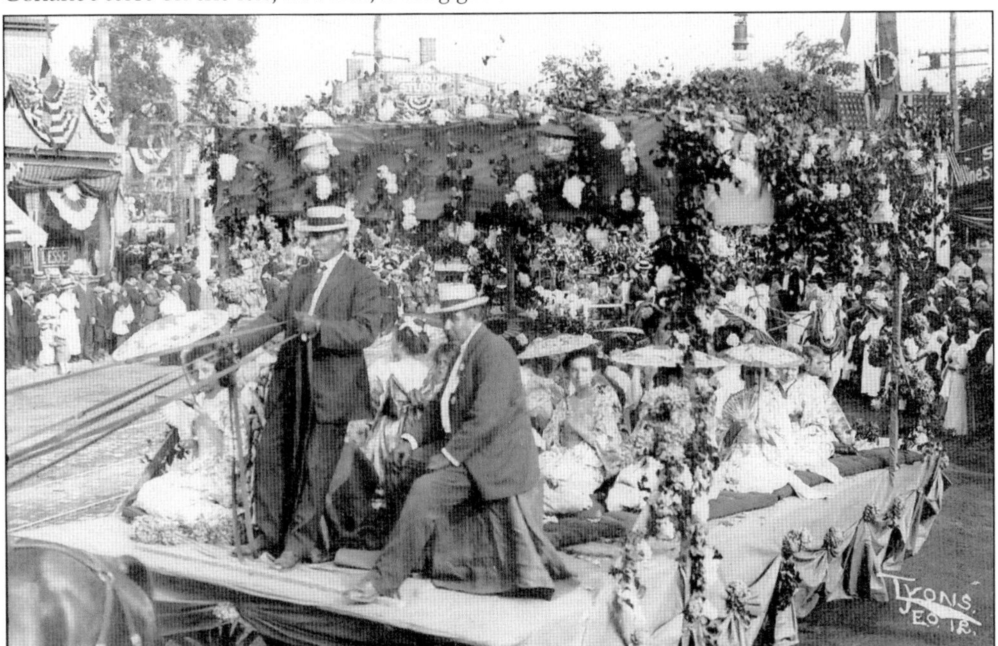

A centennial parade of 3,000 costumed children in 1912 began at Montgomery Street, passed the reviewing stand on Franklin Street, and made its way to the green. Brookdale School contributed three floats, each decorated in a Japanese motif. Fred Brokaw, who farmed in the Brookdale area, is at the reins of a horse-drawn garden float.

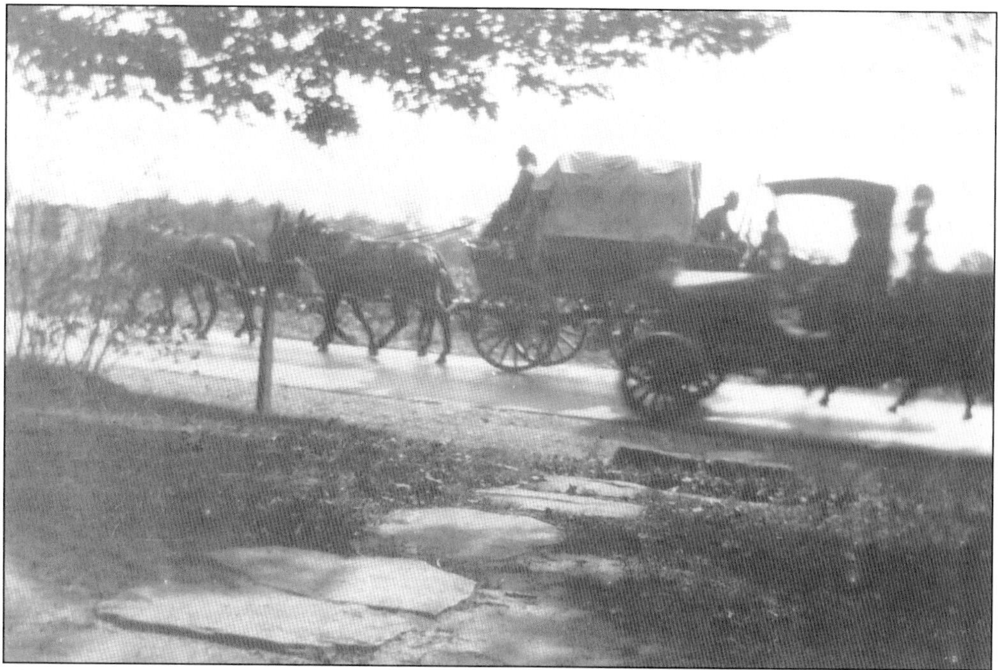

Bloomfield's earliest history dates from 1666 farms, and up until 1924, Brookdale was mainly farmland. In this World War I photograph, local farmers travel on Broad Street, north of Watchung Avenue. Poultry was judged at the community house and Brookdale schoolchildren enjoyed agricultural projects. In the years to come, shows, demonstrations, and competitions with farm animals and produce were popular town activities.

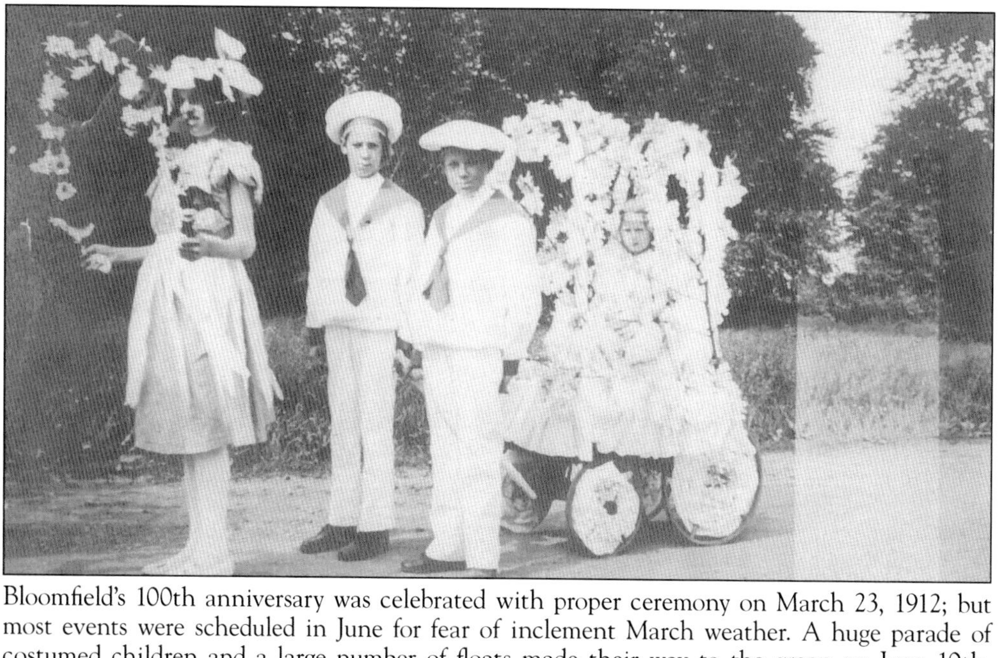

Bloomfield's 100th anniversary was celebrated with proper ceremony on March 23, 1912; but most events were scheduled in June for fear of inclement March weather. A huge parade of costumed children and a large number of floats made their way to the green on June 10th. Watsessing schoolgirls created their costumes of daisies, butterflies, and bumblebees. Pictured here in the cart is Lisa Johnson of Myrtle Street.

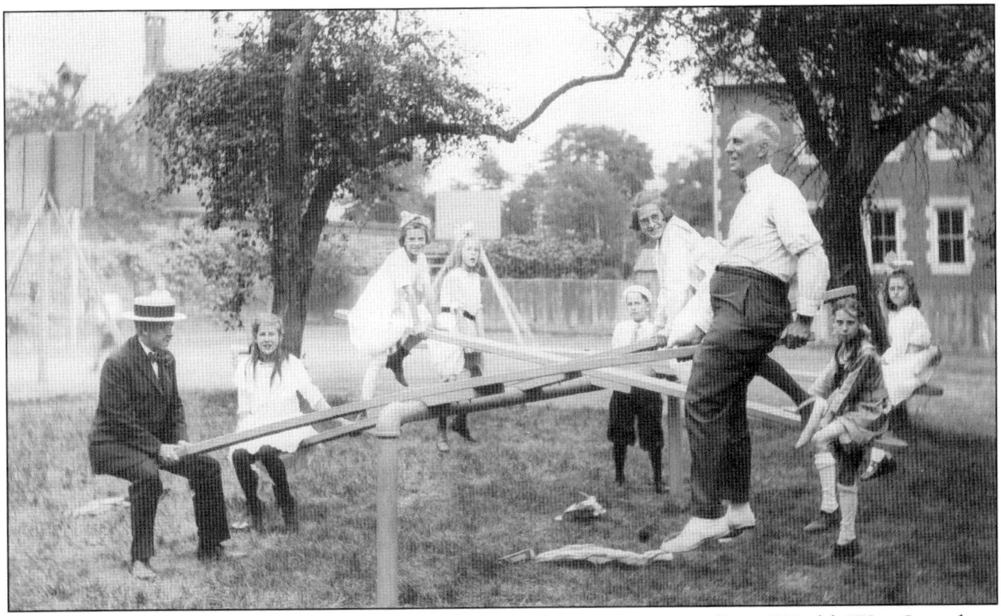

The town chose a special memorial to honor those who served in World War I and to commemorate those who died in the cause of democracy. The Community House was organized with the purchase of the Amzi Dodd residence on Broad Street in 1919. The plans were completed in 1924 when a spectacular opening day was celebrated. Enjoying some fun time with the children is Mayor Fred Sadler (left).

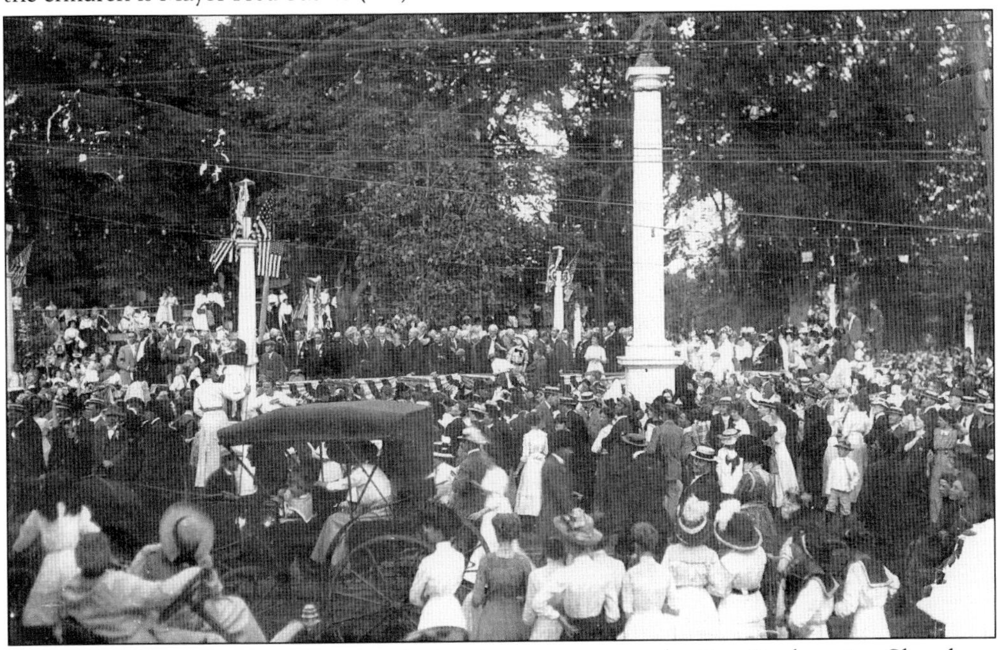

The town's actual centennial was marked with a ceremony at the First Presbyterian Church on March 23, 1912. John Franklin Fort, former governor of New Jersey, was the speaker. Fearing inclement March weather, further festivities were planned for June. One of the highlights was the unveiling of the Soldiers and Sailors Monument, which today stands at the end of the green. This scene is its dedication on June 11, 1912.

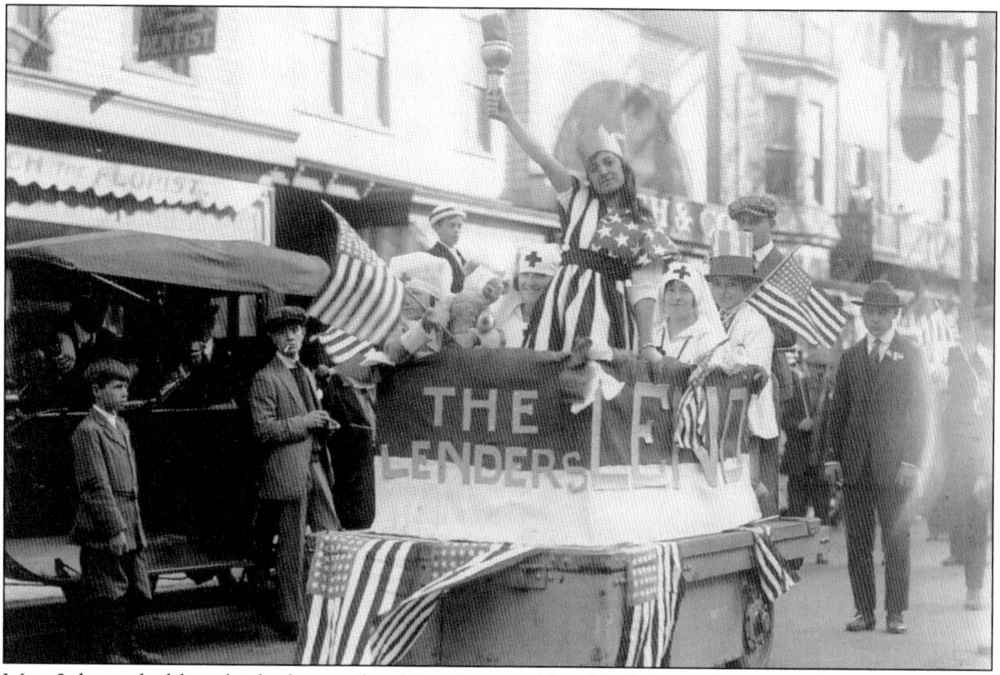

Miss Liberty holding high the torch of freedom and her Red Cross driver pitch in to make the 1918 parade memorable. Children responded to fund-raising by buying war stamps. A bronze tablet bearing the name of 39 patriots was paid for by schoolchildren. It reads, "to honor the residents who served in the war and to commemorate the names of those who died in the cause of democracy."

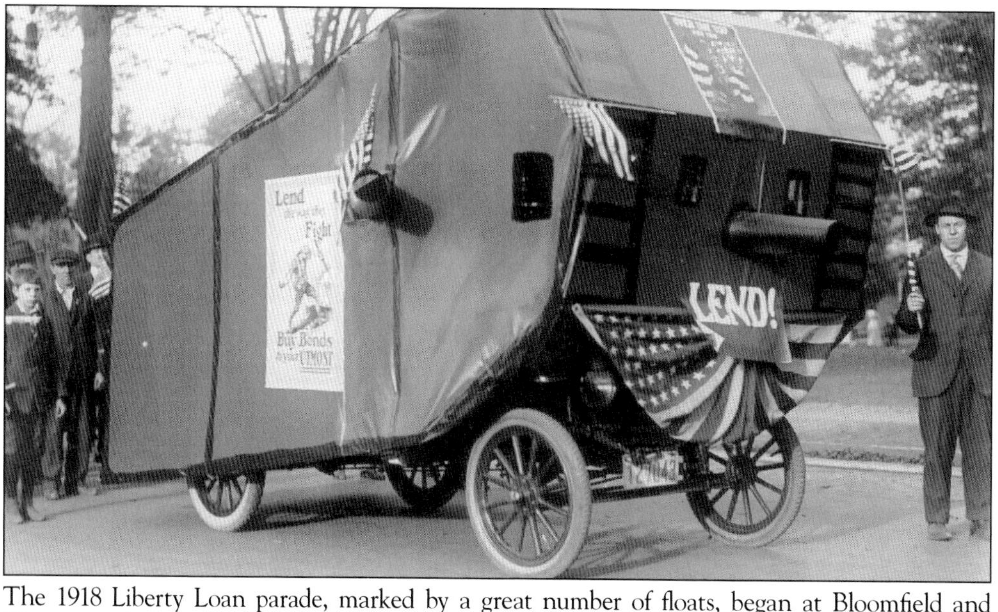

The 1918 Liberty Loan parade, marked by a great number of floats, began at Bloomfield and Watsessing Avenues and made its way to the high school. Mayor Fred Sadler issued a proclamation requesting a display of national colors and Red Cross insignia. Bloomfield's percentage of participation in World War I exceeded the national average for a town of its size. Some 1,200 men and 15 nurses found their way to active duty.

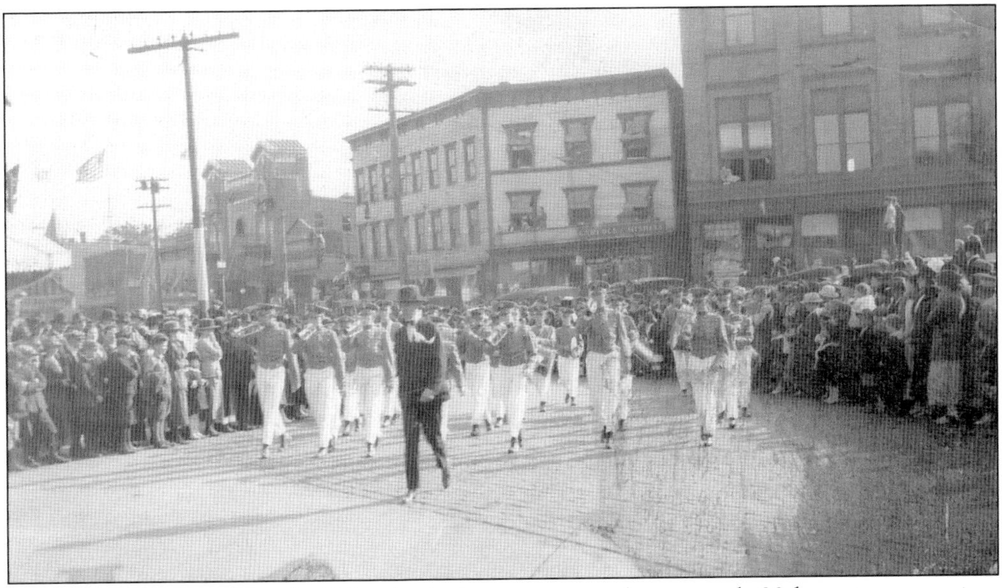

John H. Moran loved parades! Here he is shown on an unknown early-20th-century occasion, proudly turning the corner from Bloomfield Avenue onto Broad Street, just ahead of a brass band. He could very well be leading a contingent from Sacred Heart Church of which Moran was a devout member.

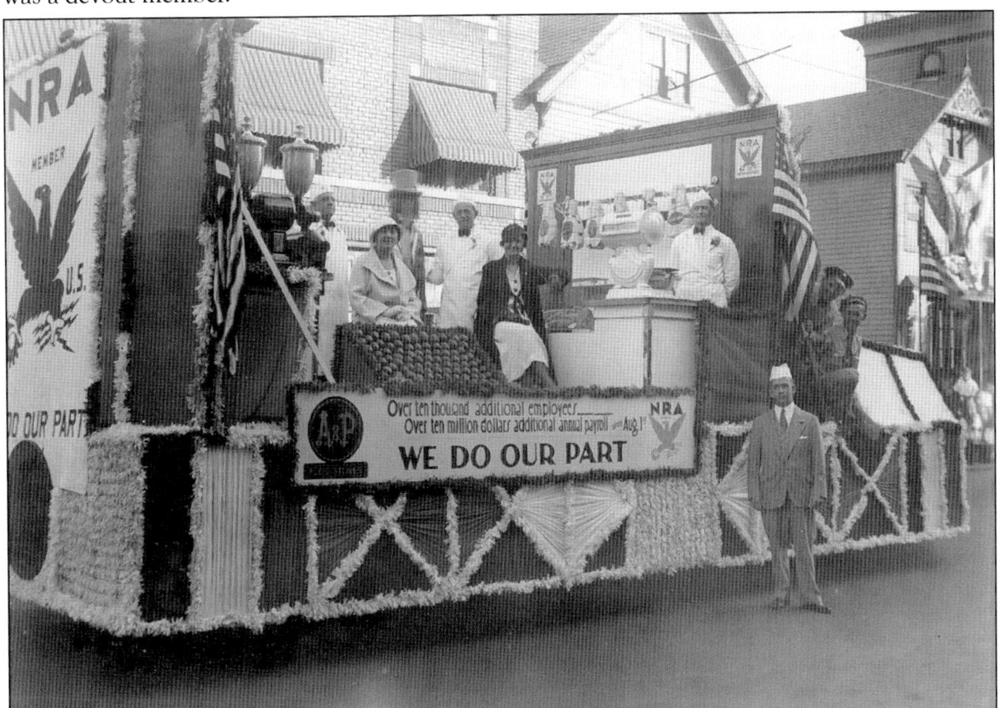

The A&P float in a National Recovery Act parade poses for a photograph in the North Center. The building at far right was the Excelsior Hose Company at the corner of James and Broad Streets. Its square tower was a landmark in the late 19th century. Its boxlike shape appears in the background of several photographs of the Morris Canal taken by Charles Warren Eaton.

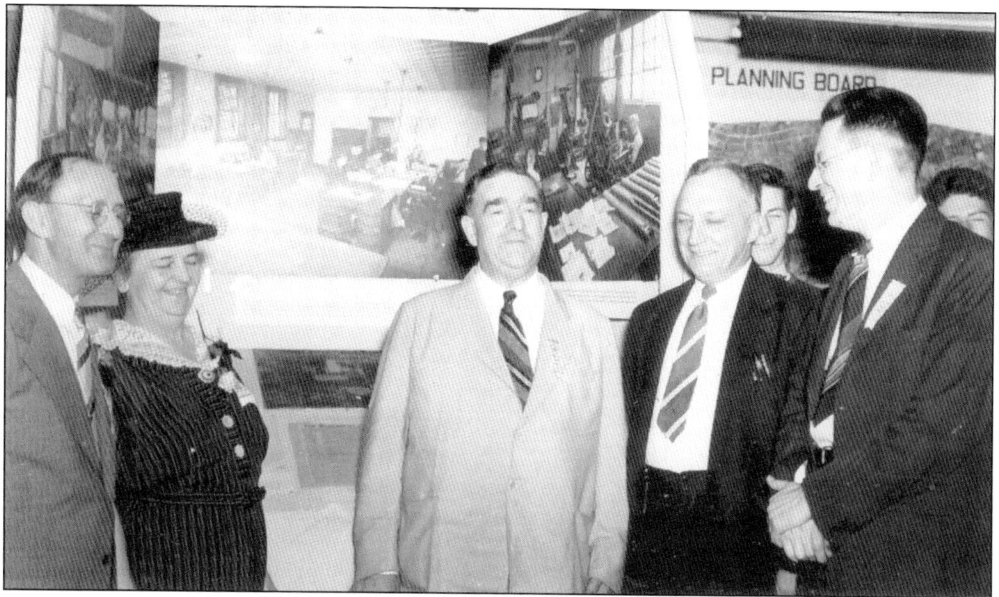

The occasion is the Know Your Town Exhibit of 1939, held in the gymnasium of the brand-new Bloomfield Junior High School on Franklin Street. Prominent in this photograph of the Independent Press display is former mayor Charles Demarest, standing center, and at the right is assistant principal of the high school Henry Hollingsworth. During Mayor Demarest's term of office, the elementary school that bears his name and the municipal building were constructed.

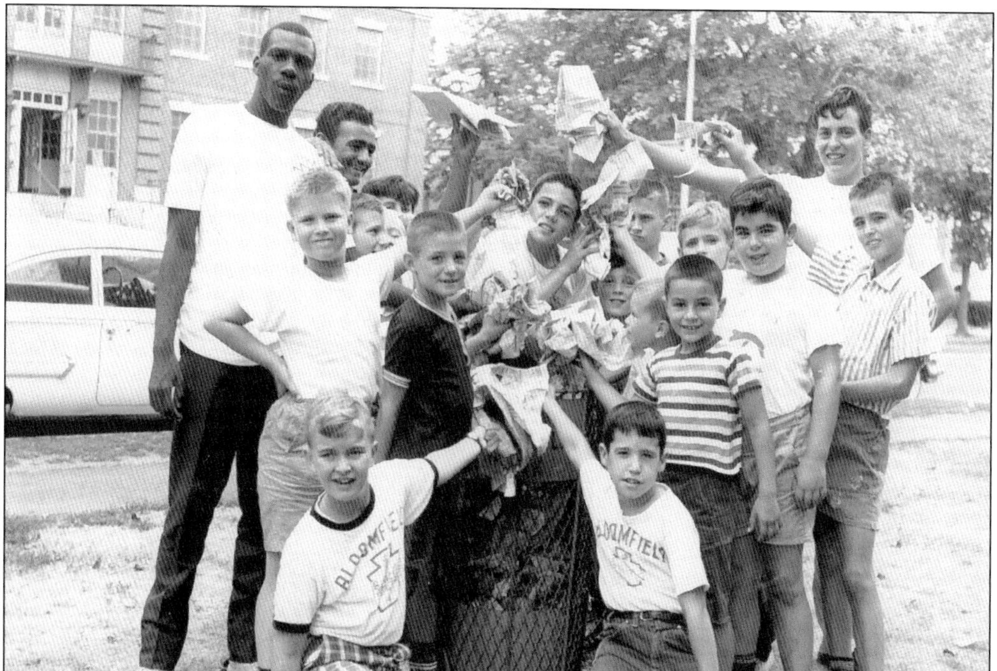

The Beautify Bloomfield campaign of 1966 got underway with the Boys Club doing its part to promote the worthwhile town project. The boys kicked off the self-improvement program by tackling the cleanup of the town green. The national effort to have towns and cities clean up and generally beautify their surroundings recalled the work of the Town Improvement Association (1907–1931).

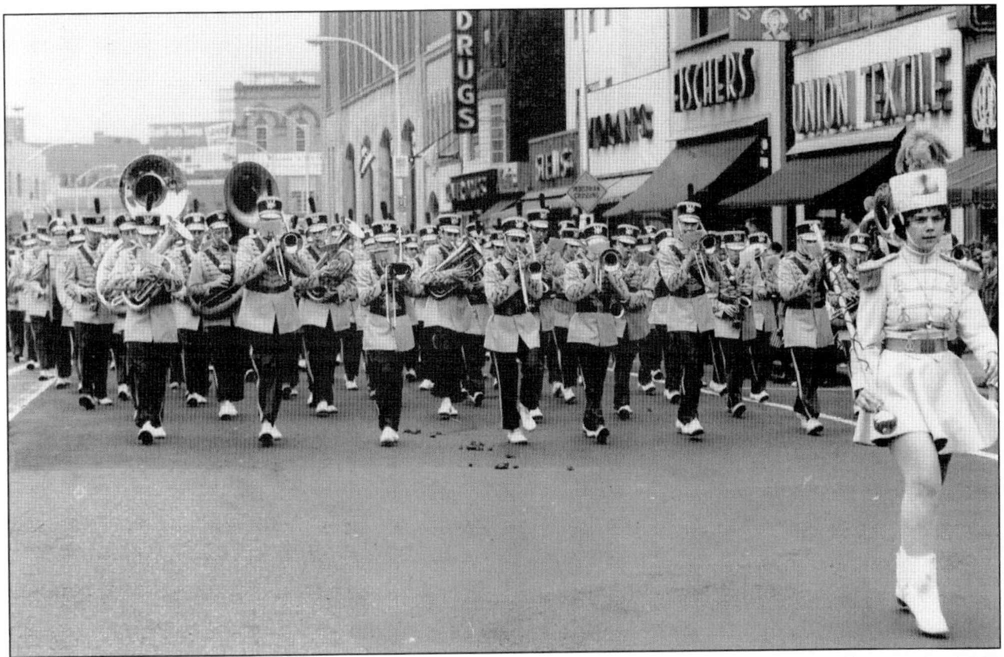

The Bloomfield High School Band steps proudly (and carefully) up Broad Street during the 1962 sesquicentennial celebrations. It had been preceded by horses along the way and the obstacle course it faced was a common one a half century before. Horses on the streets of town are a rarity today, but their manure was a serious problem in the 19th century.

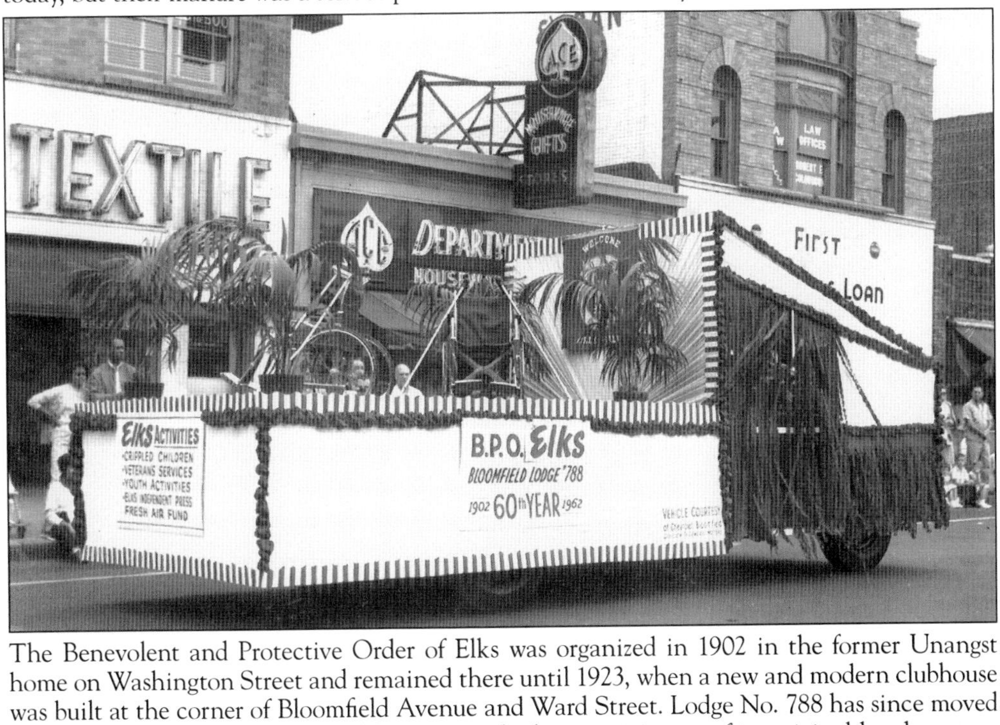

The Benevolent and Protective Order of Elks was organized in 1902 in the former Unangst home on Washington Street and remained there until 1923, when a new and modern clubhouse was built at the corner of Bloomfield Avenue and Ward Street. Lodge No. 788 has since moved to another home at 296 Bloomfield Avenue, which is reminiscent of its original headquarters. The organization recently celebrated its centennial.

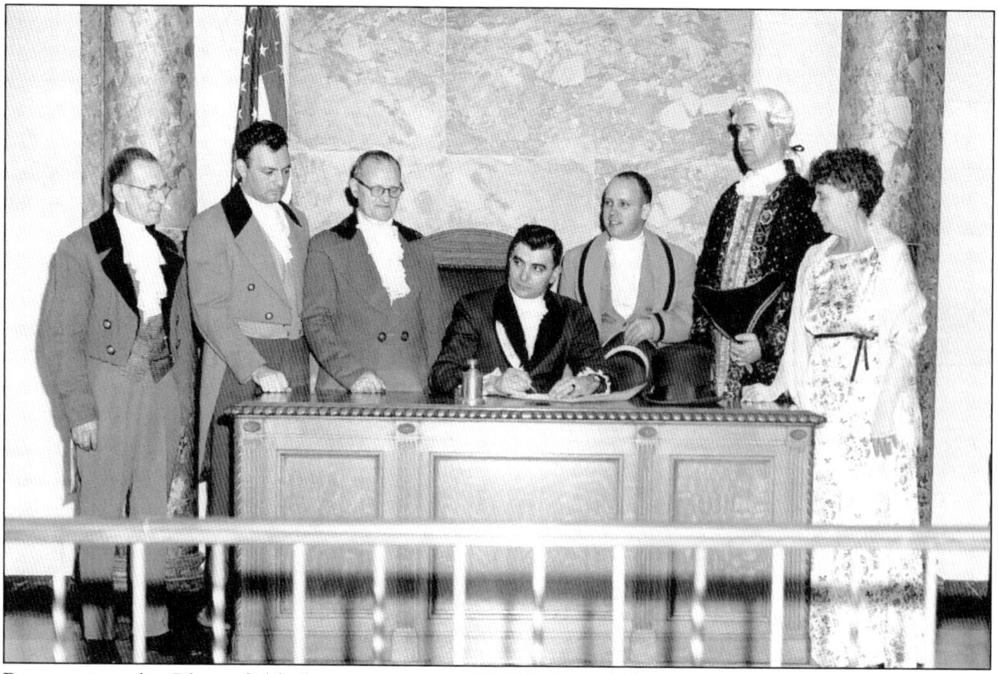

Re-creating the Bloomfield charter signing of 1812, from left to right, are councilmen Arthur Schmidt, Ralph Conte, Joseph Russomanno, and Don Cetrulo, town clerk Joseph North, councilman Raymond Schroeder, and councilwoman Dorothea Jewkes. Raymond Schroeder and Dorothea Jewkes portray Isaac Ward, a 19th-century civic leader, and Mrs. Ward. On a day that celebrated the sesquicentennial, 30 historic sites in town were named and honored.

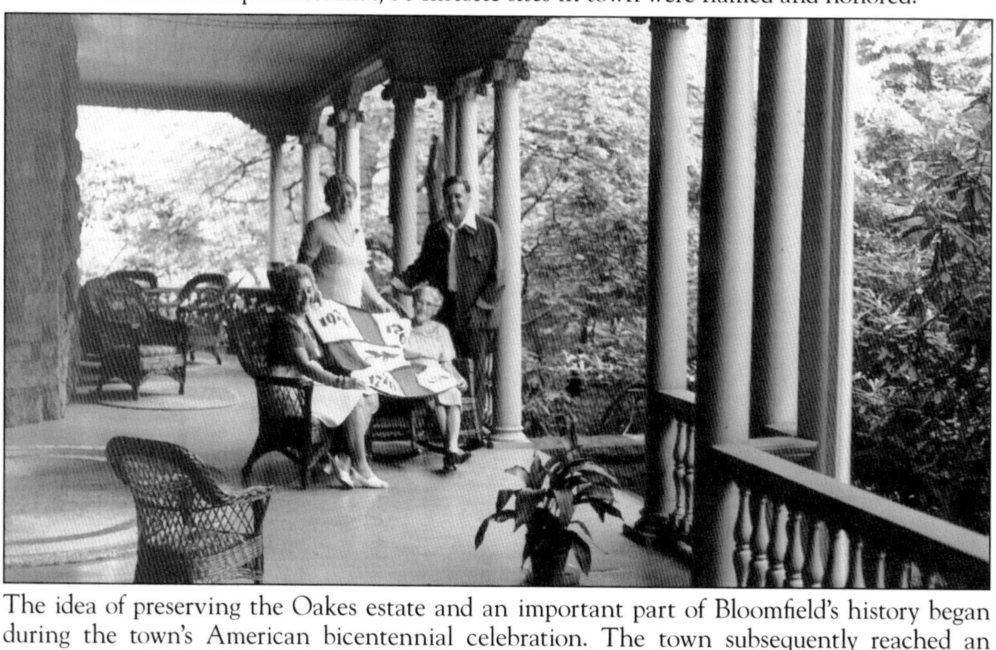

The idea of preserving the Oakes estate and an important part of Bloomfield's history began during the town's American bicentennial celebration. The town subsequently reached an agreement with the family and acquired the entire estate. The Oakes mansion became Oakeside, the town arts and cultural center, in 1980. On its sweeping veranda, in 1976, Bea Alstein, Lucy Galioto, Jean Oakes, and Bob Carter discuss the future of the Oakes mansion.

Lt. Percival H. Chance, made a tour of inspection of International Arms and Fuze Company in August 1918. He was a former employee of the plant that manufactured munitions. The brave and gallant lieutenant thrilled his company with stories of his long distance flights, one of which was 1,800 feet down while he was upside down in his plane, hanging on a wire.

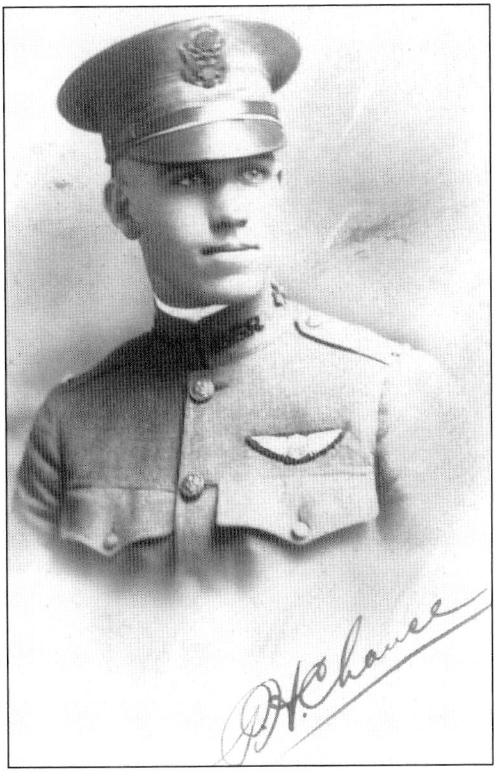

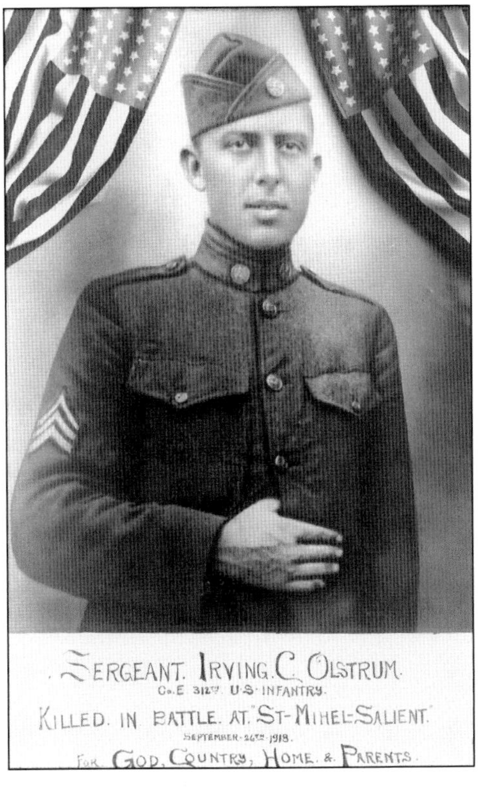

Sgt. Irving J. C. Olstrum, Company E, 312th Infantry, was killed in the Battle of the Argonne Forest, September 26, 1918, and was buried with full military honors. He rendered such distinguished service on the battlefield as to receive the mention for a commission as lieutenant, whose duties he was performing as he led his platoon into battle. Olstrum, of Lawrence Street, was 22 years old when he died.

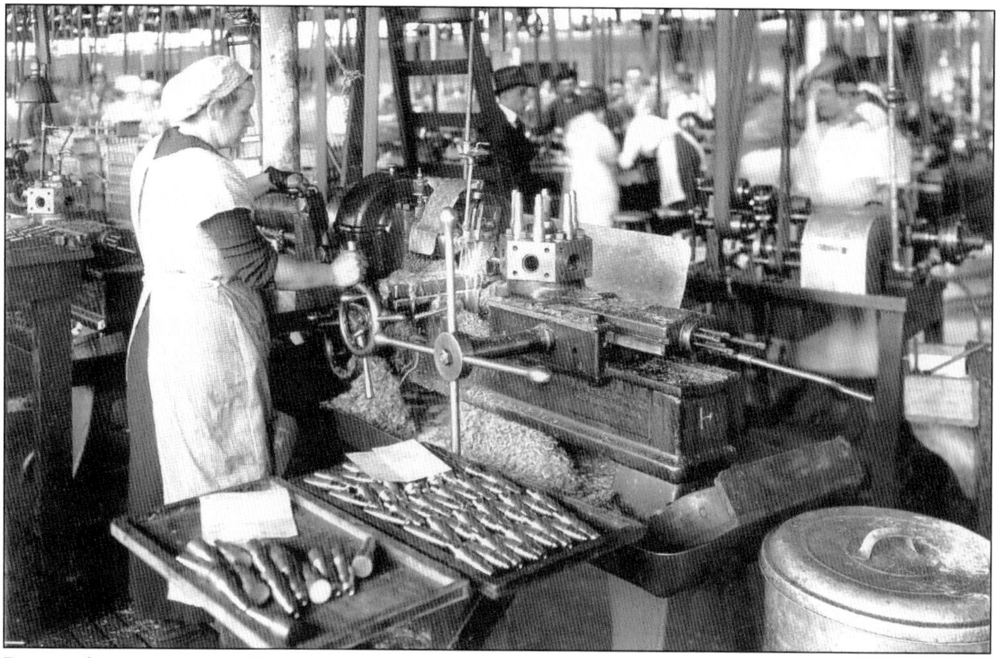

Responding to every call where they could be of service in the place of men who had gone to fight, these women met the challenges of 1918, working the machinery that produced shells and detonation fuzes for a country at war. Women wore the colors of patriots and did their best for Uncle Sam. With courage and endurance, about 4,000 women worked at the International Arms and Fuze Company.

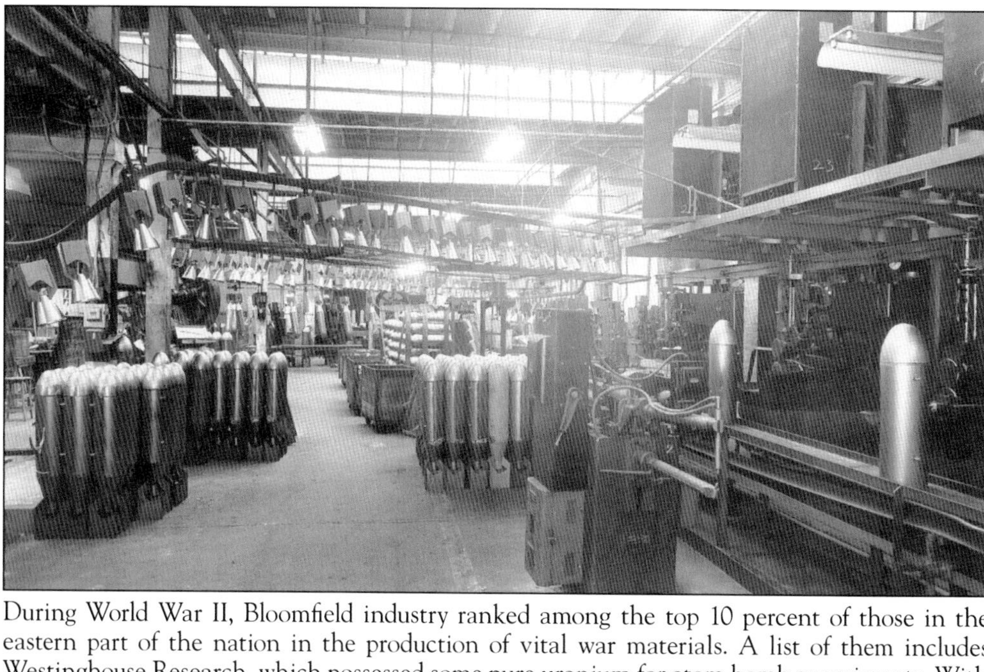

During World War II, Bloomfield industry ranked among the top 10 percent of those in the eastern part of the nation in the production of vital war materials. A list of them includes Westinghouse Research, which possessed some pure uranium for atom bomb experiments. With new fluorescent lighting illuminating the work site, the International Arms and Fuze plant, active during World War I, once more began producing munitions.

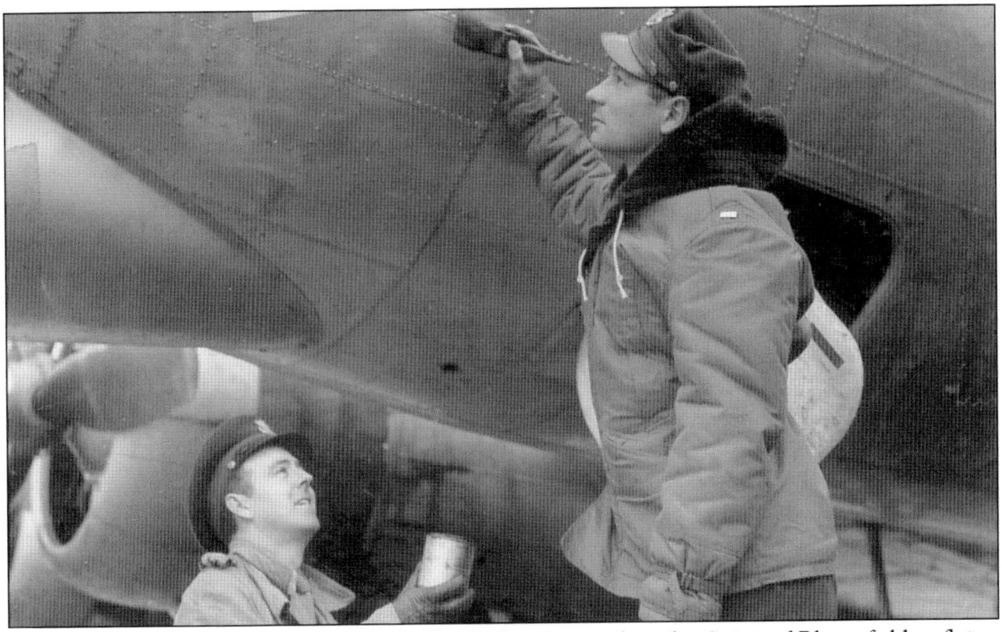

Every football fan for miles around was thrilled to know that the Spirit of Bloomfield, a flying fortress bought and paid for through the efforts of school children, was to be piloted by a home town hero, Lt. Mike Kochell. Lieutenant Kochell was captain of the high school football team and was twice named All-State Tackle. He went on to make football history as one of Fordham University's Seven Blocks of Granite.

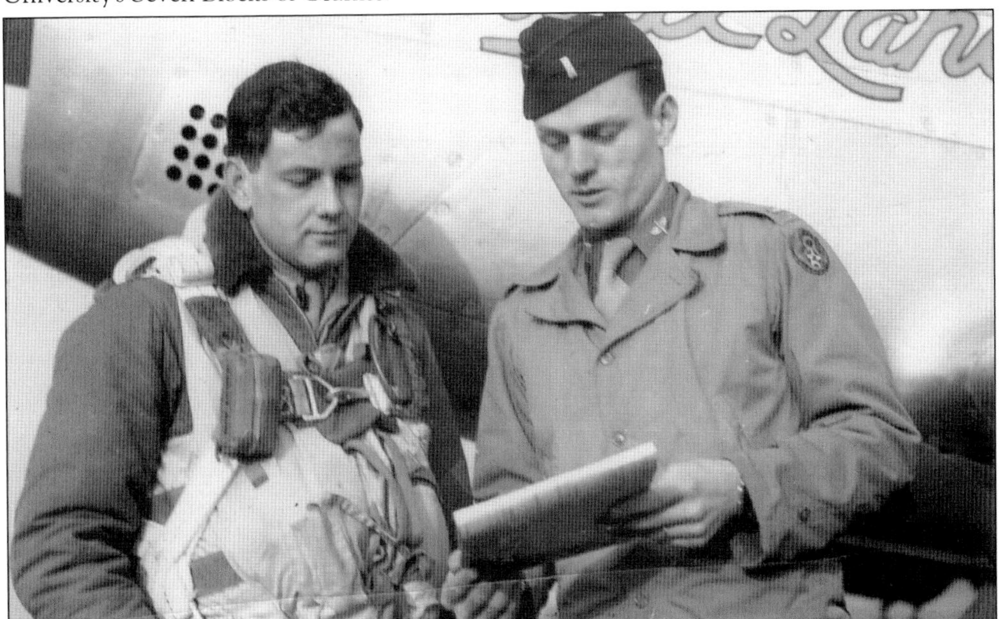

In the fifth war loan drive of World War II, schoolchildren raised $475,000 selling war bonds and stamps. Their accumulated dimes and quarters purchased six P-51 Mustang fighter planes. In honor of the high school's teams, one plane was named the *Bengal Lancer* and assigned to a New Jersey pilot, Lt. Frank M. Stillwell (left). The plane downed a Messerschmidt 109 on its first mission.

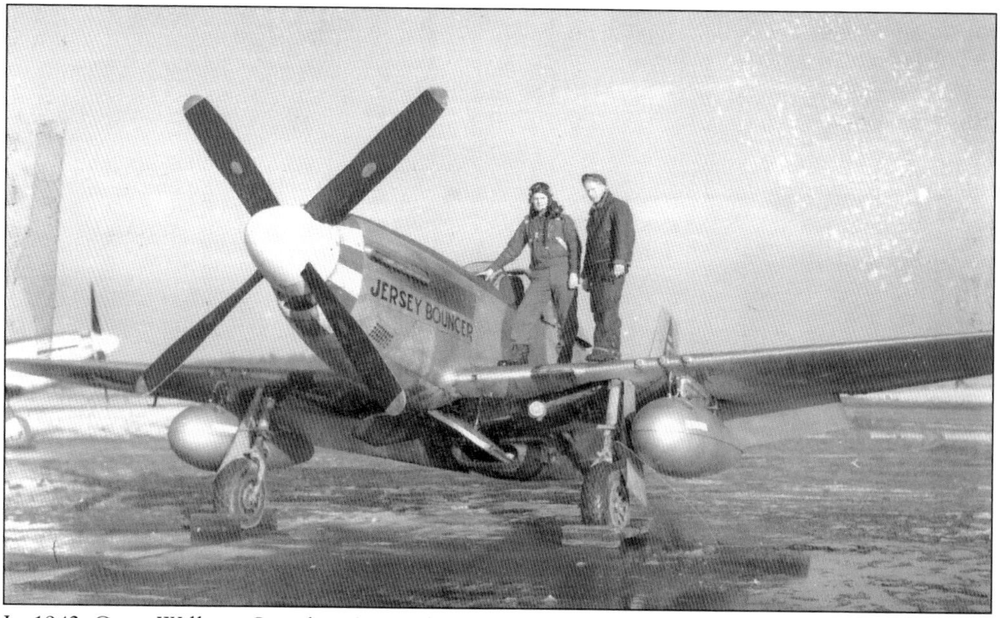

In 1943, Capt. William Crombie, 385 Fighter Squadron, wrote, "My dear Sir, Young Ladies and Young Gentlemen: Your airplane, a P-15D has been named 'Jersey Bouncer' in tribute to you who subscribed funds for its purchase." The *Jersey Bouncer* flew 33 combat missions and shot down two enemy fighters. Lt. Eugene Murphy of New York was the pilot. Sgt. Vernon Samuelson of St. Cloud, Minnesota, was the crew chief.

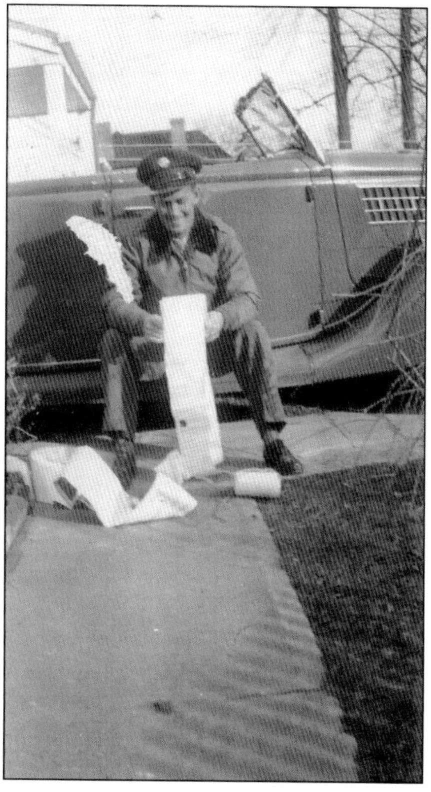

One of the proud home front accomplishments of the Bloomfield Federation of Music was creating "train letters" for its members overseas. Consisting of letters, clippings, pinup pictures, drawings, and poetry, they averaged 30 feet in length. All this was pasted on paper five inches wide, decorated, and neatly rolled on a small dowel and tied with a ribbon. A grinning Cpl. Luther Pearson seems to be enjoying his mail.

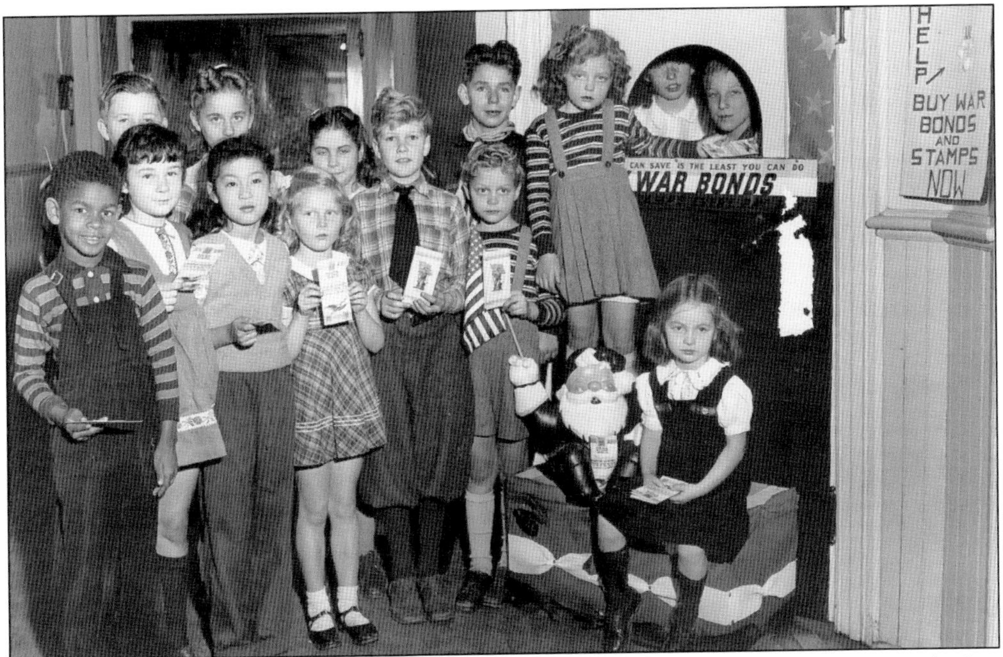

The generosity of the town in the war effort was reflected and enhanced by the record of its schools. Children were phenomenal salesmen for war stamps and bonds. In only three weeks of the Schools at War Program, their purchases totaled $26,750.60. This booth was in the entrance foyer of Berkeley School.

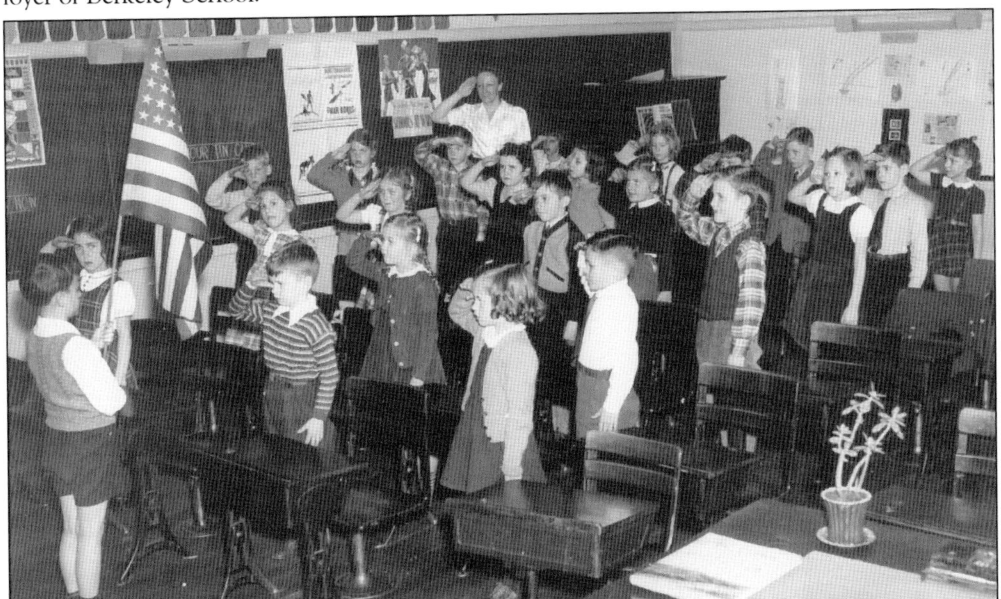

"We are going to win the war and we are going to win the peace that follows," Pres. Franklin Roosevelt told the nation. With all the efforts in the Schools at War Program, the regular school day still went on. Children, such as these Brookdale youngsters, needed something more than war if they were to preserve the peace in years to come. Parents and teachers worked hard to provide this.

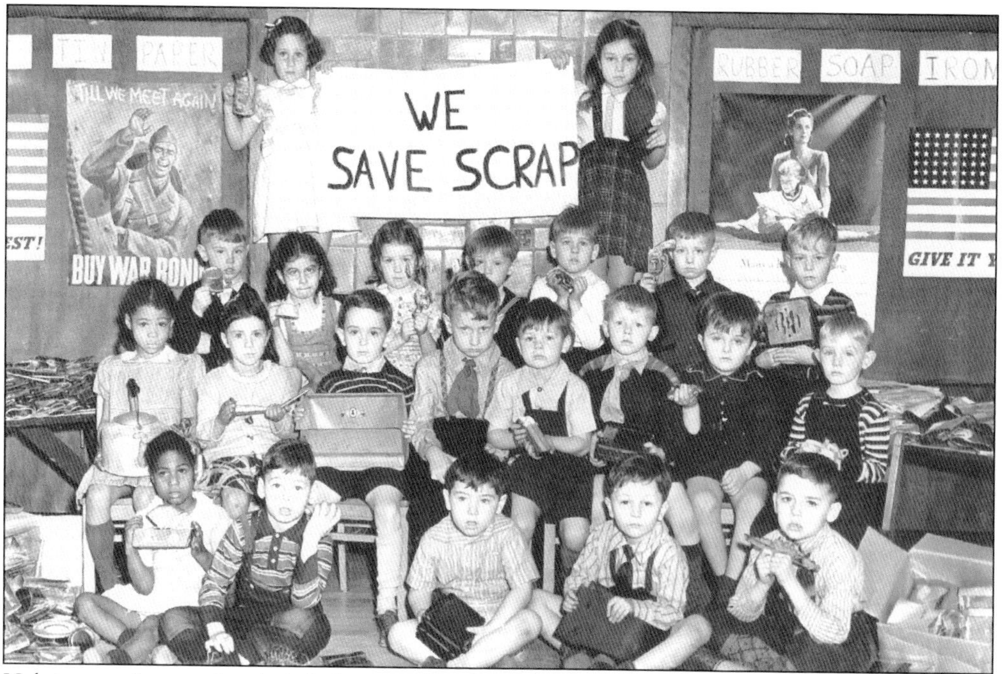

Helping to "scrap the Axis," the town's schoolchildren did their share in collecting large quantities of salvage: tin cans, rags, scrap metal, kitchen fats, and keys were among their trophies. Their success in selling war bonds and stamps bought one flying fortress, six P-53 fighter planes, 83 jeeps, and an ambulance plane. United for victory, every Bloomfield schoolchild, as these Demarest School youngsters show, did his or her patriotic best.

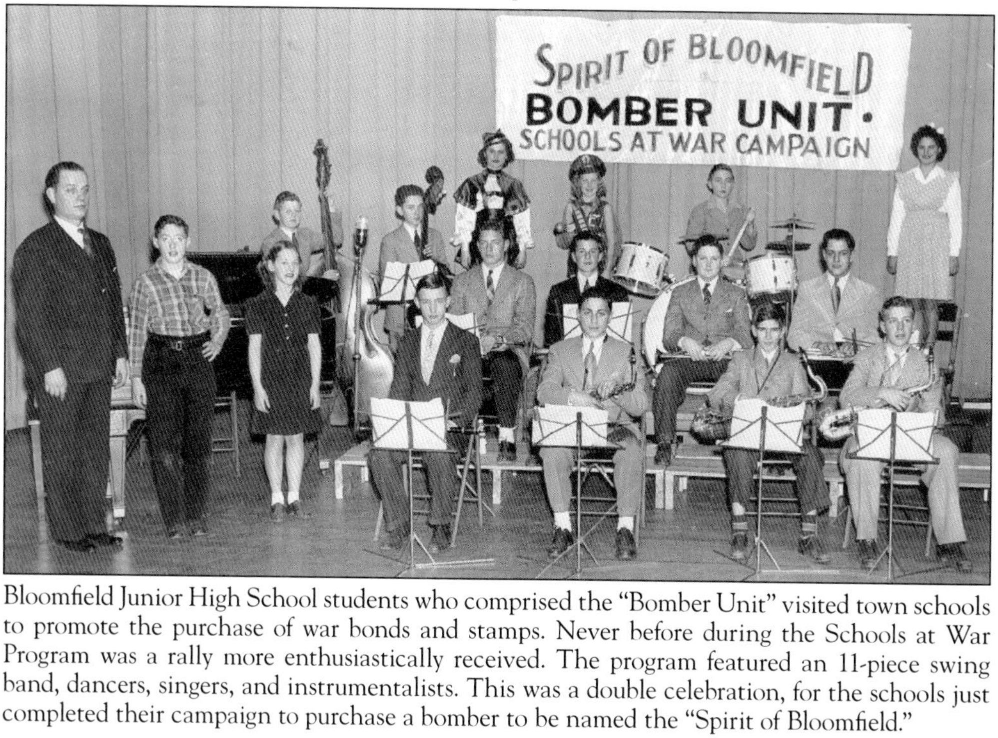

Bloomfield Junior High School students who comprised the "Bomber Unit" visited town schools to promote the purchase of war bonds and stamps. Never before during the Schools at War Program was a rally more enthusiastically received. The program featured an 11-piece swing band, dancers, singers, and instrumentalists. This was a double celebration, for the schools just completed their campaign to purchase a bomber to be named the "Spirit of Bloomfield."

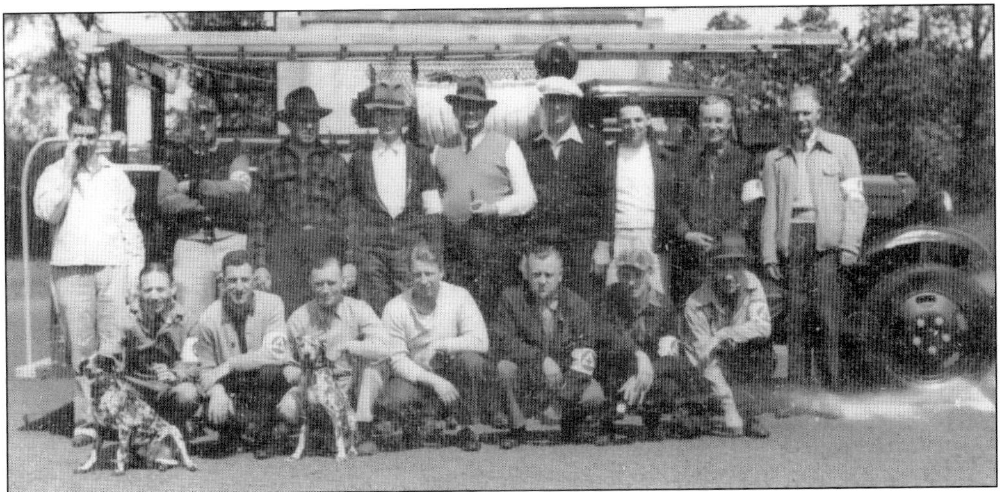

In the days and nights of World War II, the Bloomfield Civil Defense League went to work. The fire trucks were the most visible of defense activities, but there was much more: air wardens, first aid, bonds and stamps, and scrap drives. The civil defense volunteers (and dalmatians) chose to assist the fire department. The first instruction was fundamental: how to put out an incendiary bomb.

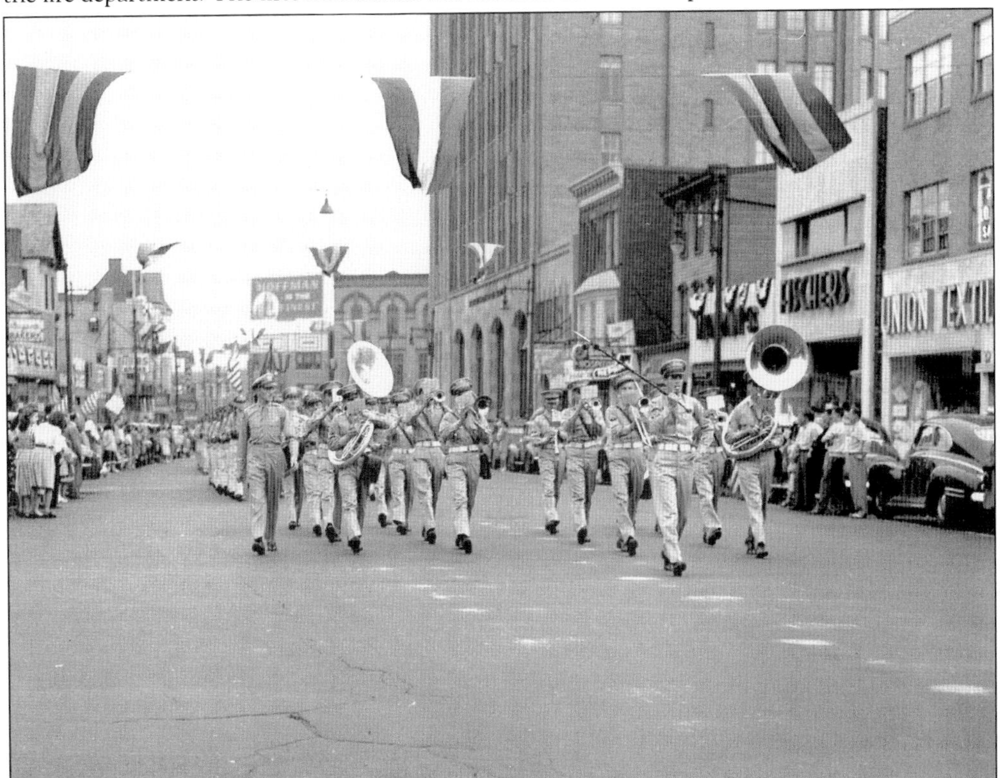

In 1949, national honors went to Bloomfield as a model town in the nation's war bond effort. For being the first town in the country to achieve 100 percent plant payroll deduction, the town received a special citation and flag. The parade on flag-draped streets for the Treasury Department's "Salute to Bloomfield" traveled from Municipal Plaza to the football stadium. It included 20 marching units, bands, and floats.

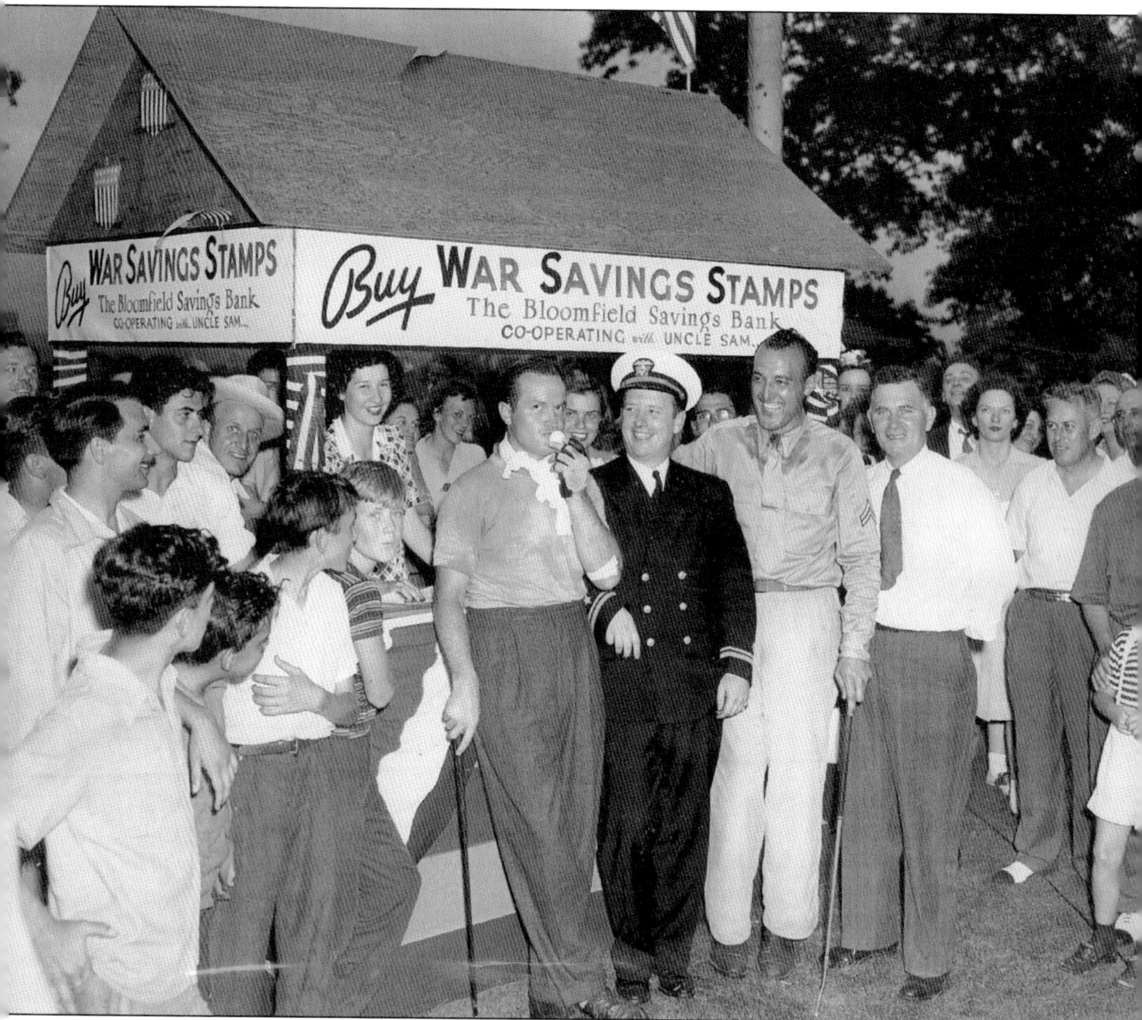

He was born in England and left as soon as he realized he could not become king. On these shores, Bob Hope fell in love with America and America fell in love with him. On battlefields from North Africa to Europe to the South Pacific, he was cheered and admired by men and women in uniform. The great Hope visited Forest Hill Field Club to pitch the war bond drive.

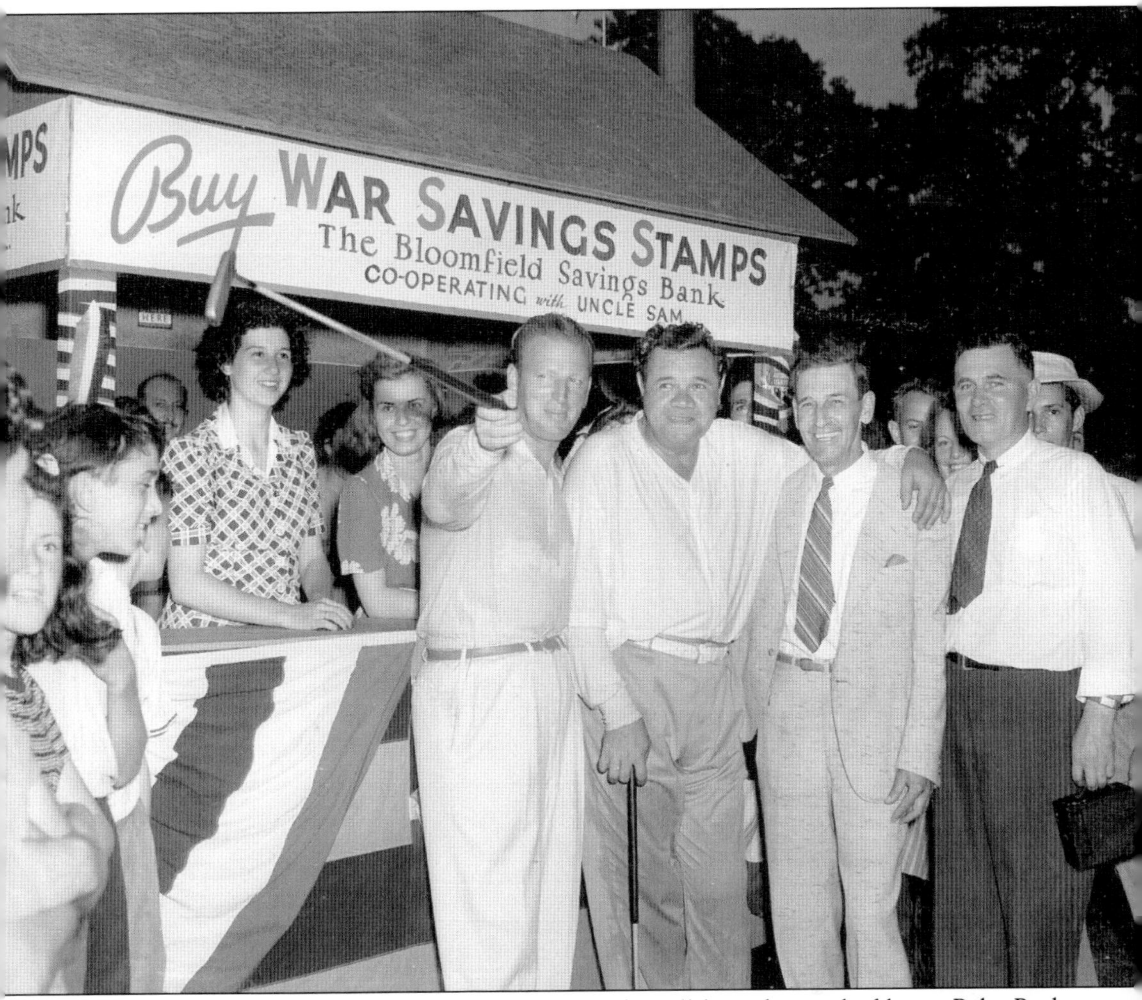

It was part of the United States' national history that all boys dreamed of being Babe Ruth before anyone else. Ruth was too old to wear the uniform in World War II, but whenever he was wanted to solicit funds or blood for the Red Cross, sell war bonds, or simply talk to soldiers, Ruth offered his strength and time with generosity and grace. America's baseball idol was welcomed to town.

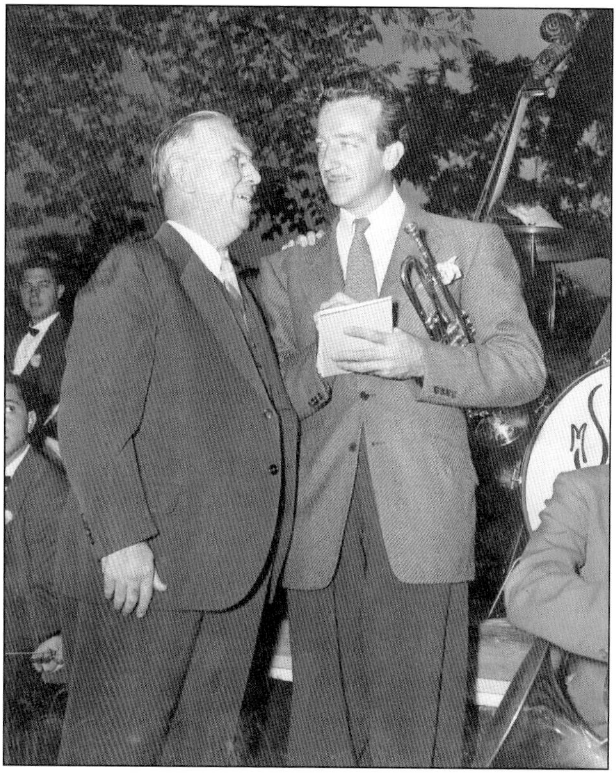

Ignited by Adolf Hitler's threat that American aid could not save Britain, the town sprang into action. The war bond drive was a crucial part of many efforts. Playing with astonishing skill and great flair, Harry James and his band were hugely popular and successful during the swing era. The famous bandleader, greeted by Mayor John Reed, was a welcome ally in promoting the sale of war bonds for freedom.

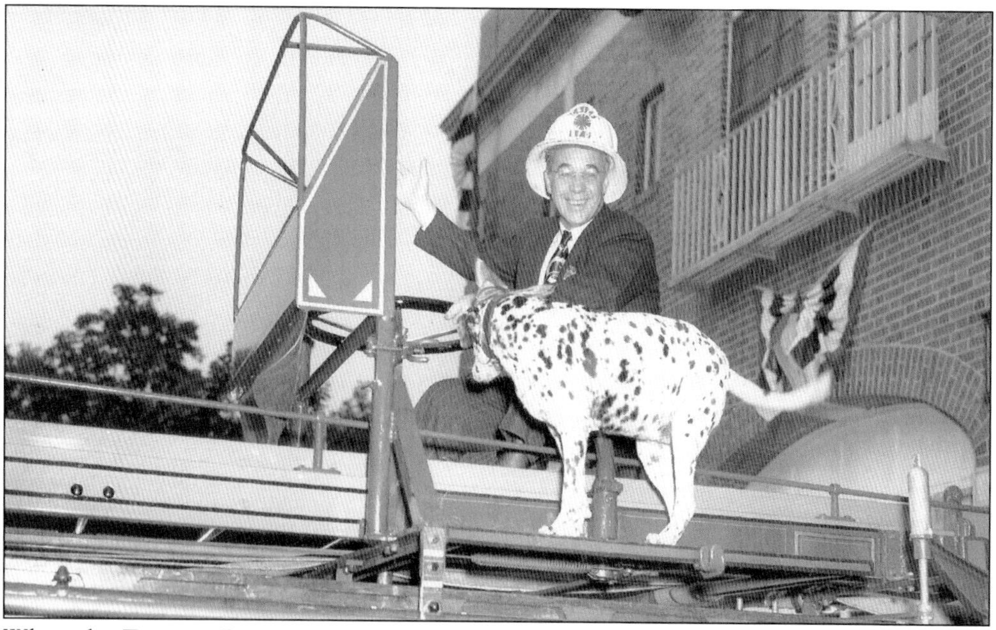

When the Treasury Department came to honor the town for war bond sales in 1948, there was a mammoth parade and 10,000 people packed Foley Field. John Gambling, a WOR radio personality, was made honorary fire chief and invited to drive the end of a hook and ladder truck. Hank Borowy, a Bloomfielder who pitched for the Chicago Cubs, and Dorothy Dalton, a town Olympic gymnast, were also guests.

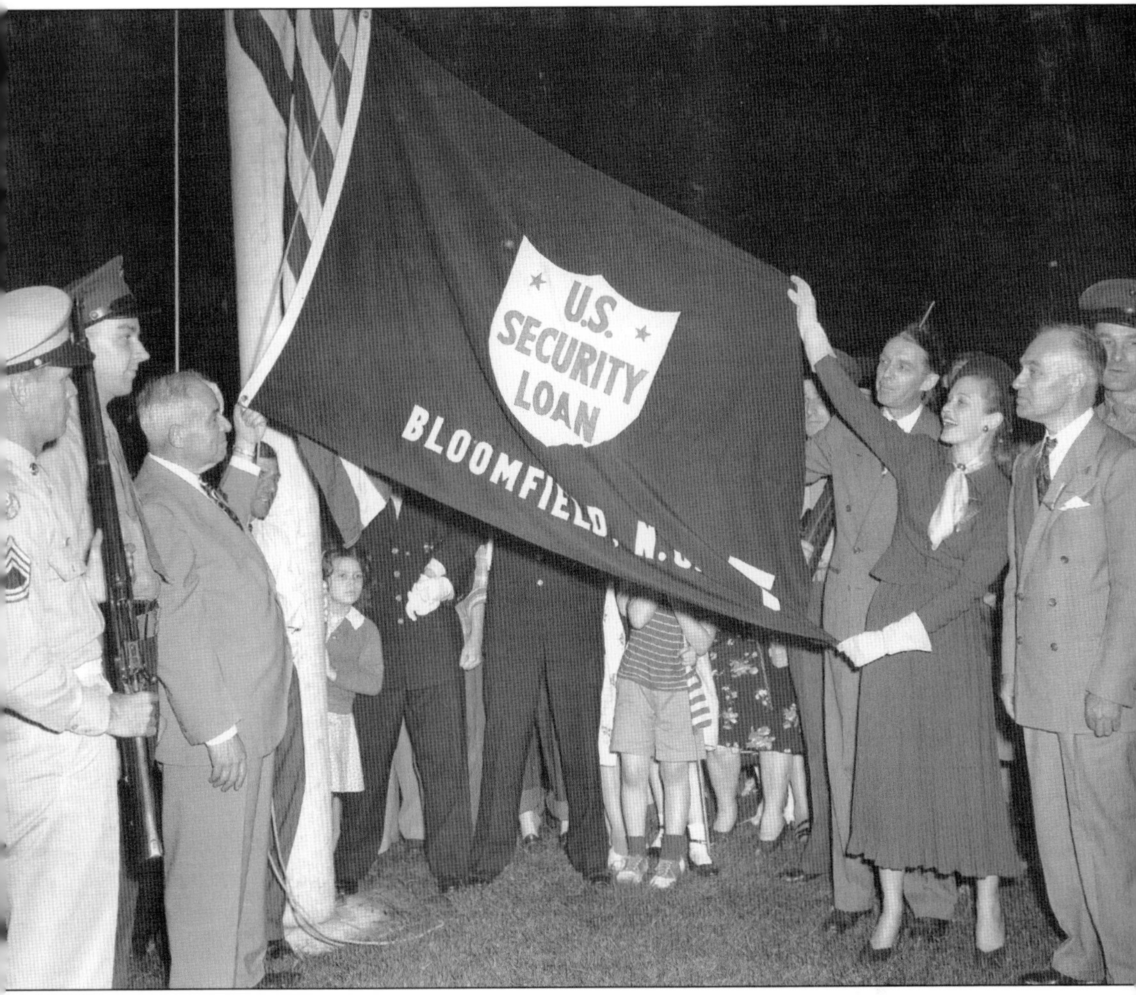

The army band played, a navy blimp hovered overhead, and police and firemen, with Boy Scouts assisting, directed traffic and crowds. Platform guests at Foley Field were treated to a thunderous ovation. Joan Caulfield, a popular Hollywood movie star, greeted folks in a neighborly fashion. The special flag she admires with Mayor William Huck was raised with the Stars and Stripes on a floodlit Municipal Plaza.